basic forces

The Moon

HOW POSTERS WORK

Ellen Lupton

COOPER
HEWITT

COOPER HEWITT

Published by Cooper Hewitt,
Smithsonian Design Museum
2 East 91st Street
New York, NY 10128
USA

cooperhewitt.org

Distributed Worldwide by ARTBOOK | D.A.P.
155 Sixth Avenue, 2nd floor
New York, NY 10013
USA

artbook.com

Library of Congress Cataloging-in-Publication Data

Lupton, Ellen, author.
How posters work / by Ellen Lupton.
    pages cm
Includes bibliographical references and index.
ISBN 978-0-910503-82-2 (flexi-bound)
1. Posters. 2. Graphic arts. 3. Visual communication.
4. Cooper-Hewitt Museum. I. Cooper-Hewitt Museum,
issuing body. II. Title.

NC1825.N49C665 2015
741.6'74--dc23

ISBN 978-0-910503-82-2 (flexi-bound)
ISBN: 978-1-942303-00-8 (epub)
ISBN 978-1-942303-01-5 (.mobi)

2015 2016 2017 2018/ 10 9 8 7 6 5 4 3 2 1

Printed in Canada

Editor	Pamela Horn
Book design	Wenjie Lu
Cover art	Felix Pfäffli
Diagrams	Wenjie Lu, Yushi Luo, Jennifer Tobias, and Chen Yu
Typography	Neutral, designed by Kai Bernau, Typotheque
Image rights	Matthew Kennedy
Copy editor	Joelle Herr
Separations	Embassy Graphics
Printing	Transcontinental

Smithsonian Design Museum

How Posters Work is made
possible by major support from
Adobe Foundation

Foreword

Caroline Baumann, Director

Cooper Hewitt, Smithsonian Design Museum

Two-dimensional design is all around us. We see it in the advertise–ments, road signs, and websites of today and in the decorative patterns and functional marks that have existed for all of human history. Designers use line, shape, color, and texture to delight the eye and challenge the mind. *How Posters Work* delves beneath the surface of two-dimensional design to show how designers use diverse design principles to engage our eyes, minds, and emotions.

On the following pages you will see posters seeking goals both lofty and low, from ending war, fascism, and poverty to selling airline tickets and office machines. Some posters argue revolutionary causes, while others promote rock concerts or Hollywood films. Some posters reduce complex messages to a few lines and shapes, while others bombard the senses with elaborate concoctions of color and line. Together, this diverse collection of works depicts the richly varied practice of graphic design, a field that has made enormous contributions to visual culture over the past century.

Cooper Hewitt's collections, exhibitions, and programs celebrate designers and their work by reaching back into the past for inspiration and looking ahead to future practices. *How Posters Work* enabled us to conduct new scholarship on historic works as well as add dozens of new pieces to the collection.

We are extremely grateful to Adobe Foundation for their major support of *How Posters Work*. I'd also like to express our thanks and appreciation to the people who've helped to build our exciting and rich poster collection, a graphic design resource of remarkable depth, over the years: Sara and Marc Benda, Merrill C. Berman, Arthur Cohen and Daryl Otte, Ken Friedman, Steven Heller, and Karrie Jacobs. Also, very special thanks to the talented designers whose poster donations were made on the occasion of this publication and exhibition: Philippe Apeloig, Theseus Chan, Experimental Jetset, Albert Exergian, Götz Gramlich, Mark Gowing, Felix Pfäffli, Shiro Shita Saori, and Sulki & Min.

Acknowledgments

Ellen Lupton

Cooper Hewitt, Smithsonian Design Museum

Since joining Cooper Hewitt, Smithsonian Design Museum in 1992, I have worked with many outstanding colleagues. Among the most inspiring has been Gail S. Davidson, Curator of Drawings, Prints, and Graphic Design, with whom I have collaborated on numerous exhibitions, including *Mixing Messages: Graphic Design in Contemporary Culture* (1996), *Elaine Lustig Cohen, Modern Graphic Designer* (1997), and *Rococo: The Continuing Curve* (2007). *How Posters Work* is the last major project Gail completed at Cooper Hewitt, before retiring at the museum in 2015. I will always be proud to have worked alongside such a distinguished scholar and such a generous, creative human being.

Caitlin Condell, Assistant Curator, Drawings, Prints, and Graphic Design, is an intellectual powerhouse whose talent, knowledge, and stamina drove this project from start to finish. Caitlin marshaled a team of scholars to assist us, including Cabelle Ahn, Andrew Gardner, Virginia McBride, Kristina Parsons, Julia Pelkofsky, Rebekah Pollock, and Carolina Valdes-Lora.

This book was edited and published by Pamela Horn, Cooper Hewitt's Head of Cross-Platform Publishing, assisted by the stalwart and savvy Matthew Kennedy. The photographs were shot with precision and care by Matthew Flynn; the images were managed with patience and aplomb by Allison Hale; and Joelle Herr brought her scrupulous editorial eye to every page.

Several writers contributed essays to this volume; thanks go to Karrie Jacobs, Rianne Petter, René Put, and Graham Twemlow, and posthumously to Edward McKnight Kauffer and Bruno Munari.

Dozens of professionals at Cooper Hewitt made this project possible, including curators, conservators, digital media producers, educators, registrars, development staff, and more. I'm grateful to Caroline Baumann, Director, and Cara McCarty, Curatorial Director, for pushing our team to think creatively. Special thanks to all our staff, including Julie Barnes, Laurie Bohlk, Sam Brenner, Elizabeth Broman, Helynsia Brown, Sherrine Brown, Susan Brown, Seb Chan, Michelle Cheng, Perry Choe, Kimberly Cisneros, Sarah Coffin, Jennifer Cohlman Bracchi, Lucy Commoner, Aaron Straup Cope, Motrja Fedorka, Deborah Fitzgerald, Kira Eng-Wilmont, Gregory Gestner, Vasso Giannopoulos, Yvonne Gomez-Durand, Paul Goss, Jocelyn Groom, Annie Hall, Kimberly Hawkins, Kevin Hervas, Brooke Hodge, Halima Johnson, Sarah Keefe, Amanda Kesner, Steve Langehough, Jessica Leaman, Matilda McQuaid, Antonia Moser, Kelly Mullaney, Jennifer Northrop, Matthew O'Connor, Caroline Payson, Kimberly Randall, James Reyes, Wendy Rogers, Sara Rubinow, Katie Shelly, Larry Silver, Ann Sunwoo, Cindy Trope, Stephen van Dyk, Micah Walter, Mathew Weaver, Paula Zamora, Justin Zhuang, and Karin Zonis.

Most of the works reproduced in this book were gifted to Cooper Hewitt by dozens of collectors and designers. I extend warm thanks to all of them, especially to Sarah and Marc Benda, whose rich poster collection appears throughout this book. I also thank Merrill C. Berman for his gifts to the museum and his contribution to graphic design as our field's preeminent collector.

My own work as a writer and educator would not be possible without the support of Maryland Institute College of Art (MICA), where I serve as Director of the Graphic Design MFA program and Director of the Center for Design Thinking. Since I joined the faculty in 1997, MICA has generously supported and encouraged my work beyond the classroom as a writer. *How Posters Work* brings together my two voices—both as a design educator and a museum curator. Many thanks to my colleague Jennifer Cole Phillips for using the design of this book as a project in her Graduate Typography course, and for bringing her wisdom and taste to the process. The final book design was conceived and implemented by Wenjie Lu, a talented young designer with a great career ahead. Yushi Luo and Chen Yu designed the graphic icons. Thanks also go to MICA's MFA Class of 2016 for creating an outstanding social media campaign for *How Posters Work*.

Finally, thanks to my husband, Abbott Miller, to my children, Jay and Ruby, and to my dear friend Jennifer Tobias, for their enduring love and patience.

Essays

Vision Is a Process

Ellen Lupton

Cooper Hewitt, Smithsonian Design Museum

"What does it mean, to see? The plain man's answer (and Aristotle's, too) would be, to know what is where by looking. In other words, vision is the process of discovering from images what is present in the world, and where it is."
—David Marr, *Vision*, 1982

This is not a book about posters. It is a book about how designers see. The works assembled here show how dozens of different designers—from prominent pioneers to little-known makers—have mobilized principles of composition, perception, and rhetoric. Each poster enacts ways of thinking and making, and each poster wants to be seen. How do we look at graphic design, and how, in turn, does graphic design look back at us?

Throughout the making of this project, we explored principles of design and perception in an open-ended way. Rather than seek out definitive laws or rules, we looked for diverse, sometimes contradictory models that reflect design's rich variety of ends and means. Some works of design focus the eye on a single message, while others confound comprehension with meandering journeys and sensory overload. Designers explore clarity and complexity, flatness and depth, static representations and unfolding stories.

How Posters Work illuminates visual communication with diagrams and figures taken from a variety of discourses—from psychology and cognitive science to mathematics, semiology, and narratology. Each diagram is itself a work of design and theory, employing shape and line to make arguments about the nature of vision, communication, and human consciousness.[1]

Why posters? As a medium of communication, the poster has a long history and a wide range of social functions. Historians have been predicting the death of the poster for over forty years, yet designers keep making them.[2] Typically, posters are created to sell a product, promote an event, or argue a point at a moment in history. As time passes, most posters lose their purpose and disappear. If a poster happens to join a museum collection, however, it ceases to be mere ephemera, entering the long, slow time of preservation and study.

Thousands of posters are housed in the collection of Cooper Hewitt, Smithsonian Design Museum. They patiently wait in the museum's climate-controlled storage facility in Newark, New Jersey. Protected from light and vermin behind locked doors, these posters entered Cooper Hewitt's collection as gifts or purchases over the course of many decades. Gail S. Davidson explains the evolution of Cooper Hewitt's remarkable collection in her essay "Collecting Posters."

There are countless ways to organize a group of posters—style, technique, chronology, subject matter. The curators' shelves at Cooper Hewitt overflow with texts about modern posters, Swiss posters, French posters, and political posters. In 1992, Karrie Jacobs and Steven Heller published *Angry Graphics*, a chronicle of oppositional images created during the presidencies of Ronald Reagan and George H. W. Bush.[3] (An excerpt from *Angry Graphics* appears in this volume.) These passionate works were born in the heat of that period's wars, epidemics, and economic upheavals. Jacobs and Heller donated many of their posters to Cooper Hewitt, where they now occupy an environment set to a temperature ranging from 68 to 72 degrees Fahrenheit, 40 to 50 percent relative humidity.

What about context? A chair, a teapot, or an ad for a typewriter was created with specific users in mind at a certain point in time. Museum curators create period vignettes and collect documentary photographs to shine light on an object's origins. Cooper Hewitt acquires drawings and prototypes that document the design process. We collect sample books and manufacturers' catalogs to learn about the conditions of making and selling. Caitlin Condell's essay in this book explores the relationship between design and printing techniques.

Graphic design lives on the street and online. We see it on TV; we wear it on our backs; and we follow it to the nearest restroom. Graphic design exhibitions are often assailed for ignoring context.[4] Yet removing artifacts from their original setting could be the point and purpose of many exhibitions. A gallery or museum is a mode of representation. A painting hanging on a museum wall ceases to be a devotional object or an element of home decor and becomes something else. You can't flip through the pages of a book when it is locked inside a gleaming display case, but the book becomes visible in a new way. You might notice its typography and layout, or its physical construction. A poster framed on a wall may no longer sell you an adding machine or a pair of shoes, but it can assault your eyes and mind with its form, its structure, and its unique way of envisioning human experience.

This book deliberately ignores context. We have pushed aside the search for an originary, Edenic habitat, where each poster once struggled for survival amid a swarm of competing stimuli. These pages offer a new context—a place to think about looking.

Research often involves isolating subjects from their natural habitats. To create their book *Poster No. 524*, Rianne Petter and René Put collected hundreds of ordinary advertising posters from the streets of Amsterdam and brought them back to their studio.[5] They dissected their quarry, slicing up the posters and analyzing their parts in order to uncover common patterns and conventions. Their research is excerpted in this book.

13

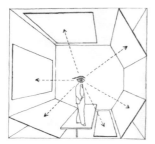

Herbert Bayer (Austrian, active Germany and USA, 1900–1985). *Diagram of 360° Field of Vision*, 1935.

Herbert Bayer (Austrian, active Germany and USA, 1900–1985). Section Allemande [*German Section*], 1930. Photolithograph. Printed by H. Chachoin (Paris, France). 158.1 × 117.2 cm (62 1/4 × 46 1/8 in.). Collection of Merrill C. Berman.

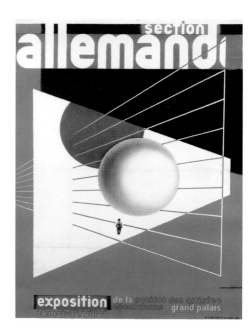

Vision is immersive. How modernist, you might say, to focus on looking. Indeed, understanding vision was a passionate quest for the artists, architects, printers, and poets who invented modern graphic design in the early twentieth century. In a diagram of an exhibition created by Herbert Bayer in 1935, a man with a giant eye for a head stands on a narrow platform. Flat planes confront him from all directions, canted from the walls, ceiling, and floor. Bayer's diagram of a 3D world built from 2D planes was a manifesto about design, vision, and the viewer.

Bayer had made the idea real a few years earlier with former Bauhaus compatriots László Moholy-Nagy and Walter Gropius. Their 1930 exhibition Section Allemande (*German Section*) celebrated the work of the Bauhaus; one room featured photographs of modern architecture installed at various angles, with chairs mounted to the walls.[6] (The exhibition catalog featured a simpler version of Bayer's *Field of Vision* diagram.) In Bayer's poster for that exhibition, a tiny human figure stands dwarfed beneath a huge white sphere. The sphere—casting a shadow on a vast white screen—symbolizes the larger-than-life optical experiences of modernity.

Optical immersion was an ongoing concern at the Bauhaus. Moholy-Nagy's 1925 Bauhaus book *Painting Photography Film* heralded modern media's "hygiene of the optical." New imaging tools—from movie cameras to X-rays—were extending the capacity of vision.[7] *Vision in Motion*, published by Moholy-Nagy in 1947, promoted the New Bauhaus in Chicago, showing how students were creating records of time and movement through drawing, sculpture, photography, and product design.[8]

"Every drawing can be understood as a motion study since it is a path of motion recorded by graphic means." László Moholy-Nagy, *Vision in Motion*, 1947.

Simplicity: We see two circles rather than three odd shapes.

Continuation: We see two long lines crossing, not four short lines.

Symmetry: We connect the lines to complete the square.

Closure: We connect the gap to make the circle whole.

Vision is active. Another classic text from the New Bauhaus, Gyorgy Kepes's *Language of Vision* (1944), applies ideas from Gestalt psychology to art and design. According to this modern theory of perception, the brain spontaneously organizes sense data into structured forms that stand out as figures against a passive ground. Human vision orders and simplifies sensory input into differentiated objects.[9]

The Gestalt psychologists called the ordered images produced by the brain *Gestalten*. Wolfgang Köhler, one of the founders of Gestalt psychology, wrote, "When *Gestalten* appear we see firm, closed structures 'standing out' in 'lively' and 'impressive' manner from the remaining field. . . . "[10] Gestalt theory employs graphic diagrams to demonstrate the laws by which ordered figures appear against an empty field. Such diagrams became icons for an aesthetic of abstraction and simplicity that was widely applied to postwar graphics.[11]

Designers use perceptual impulses as creative tools by emphasizing clear patterns and structures. While many works of design explore a blunt, diagrammatic simplicity, others challenge the viewer to fill in the blanks. Inspired by cubist collage, Edward McKnight Kauffer created images with fluid boundaries. Wolfgang Weingart turned letters into parts of bodies and parts of other letters, playing with text as both language and not-language. In a series of extraordinary experiments produced in the 1970s, Weingart's letterforms alternate between figure and ground, clustering and grouping to form larger structures.

Wolfgang Weingart (Swiss, b. 1941) for Kunstgewerbeschule (Basel, Switzerland). *NR. 4*, 1974. Letterpress. 87.4 × 61.7 cm (34 7/16 × 24 5/16 in.). Gift of Anonymous Donor, 1994-109-18.

Figure/Ground: stable

Figure/Ground: unstable

Yusaku Kamekura (Japanese, 1915–1997). *Yamagiwa International Competition for Lighting Fixtures Exhibition*, 1968. Offset lithograph. 102.7 × 72.4 cm (40 7/16 × 28 1/2 in.). Gift of Marc and Sara Benda, 2009-20-17.

Edward McKnight Kauffer (American, active England, 1890–1954). *Oak Tree Trunk, Leaf, Star*, 1936. Brush and black wash, graphite. 7.2 × 4.3 cm (2 13/16 × 1 11/16 in.). Gift of Mrs. E. McKnight Kauffer, 1963-39-873.

Input image:
reflected light

Primal sketch:
shapes

2½D sketch:
shapes layered in space

3D model:
object understood apart
from viewer's position

Vision is a process. The founders of Gestalt psychology sought universal laws that govern perception. Today, we might speak of processes instead of laws. David Marr's landmark book *Vision* (published posthumously in 1982) analyzes perception in terms of processes or constraints that could be understood both biologically and computationally. Building on the Gestalt principles of grouping (continuation, closure, simplicity, and others), Marr asked how it is that vision completes the path from receiving unfiltered visual information to creating meaningful groups. What sequences of data processing might be at work? Marr, a neuroscientist, sought to model how computers might be able to "see" the world in the intelligent, sense-making way that humans do.[12]

Perception uses two-dimensional information to model three-dimensional experience. The eyes gather flat pictures based on light reflected by objects in the environment (Marr called this the "input image"). To make sense of these detailed, data-soaked images, the brain finds edges, shapes, lines, and boundaries, piecing together stable shapes (the "primal sketch"). Human vision further interprets these basic shapes into a higher order of perception (the "2½-dimension sketch"). At this level of processing, vision uses cues such as overlapping shapes, shifts in scale, and breaks in color or tone to judge depth in relation to the viewer's location in space. Finally, the brain constructs a three-dimensional model that enables the beholder to consider the object in the round, independent of his or her own position.

Götz Gramlich (German, b. 1974) for Patrick Forgacz (Heidelberg, Germany). Herbstzeitlose [*Autumn Crocus*], 2011. Screenprint. 84 × 59.4 cm (23 3/8 × 33 1/16 in.)

Converging lines signal depth

Scale signals depth

Philippe Apeloig (French, b. 1962) for the Théâtre du Châtelet (Paris, France). *Street Scene*, 2012. Screenprint. 150 × 100 cm (59 1/16 × 39 3/8 in.). Gift of Philippe Apeloig, 2014-34-1.

Josef Müller-Brockmann (Swiss, 1914–1996). Schützt das Kind! [*Protect the Child!*], 1953. Offset lithograph. 127.5 × 90.5 cm (50 3/16 × 35 5/8 in.). Museum purchase from General Acquisitions Endowment Fund, 1999-46-1.

Diagrams based on concepts developed by David Marr in *Vision*, 1982.

The repeating curves suggest an undulating surface.

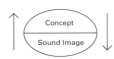

The sign is the unity of signifier (sound image) and signified (concept).

Ralph Schraivogel (Swiss, b. 1960). Cinema Afrika Filmtage [*African Film Festival*], 2006. Screenprint. Printed by Sérigraphie Uldry AG (Hinterkappelen, Switzerland). 128 × 90.3 cm (50 3/8 × 35 9/16 in.). Gift of Ralph Schraivogel, 2007-15-3.

Felix Pfäffli (Swiss, b. 1986) for Südpol (Kriens, Switzerland). Efterklang [*Echo*], 2013. Risograph. 42 × 29.4 cm (16 9/16 × 11 9/16 in.). Gift of Felix Pfäffli, 2015-3-3.

Vision is 2½ dimensions. How can Marr's influential model of vision illuminate the design process? The percepts of vision are fundamentally flat; likewise, flat planes are the graphic designer's routine workplace. Remember Bayer's diagram of the eyeball confronted by tilted planes? That diagram is not so far from how we see the world—as a multidirectional barrage of flat images.

Whether arranging ink on paper or pixels on screen, designers wring illusions of depth out of flat surfaces. Marr's idea of "2½ dimensions" is a provocation, a construct that can exist mathematically but not in the physical world. And yet this flickering state between flatness and depth is the place where graphic designers work. Every time we create an overlap between two shapes, we construct a minimal illusion of depth (one thing in front of another). Converging lines and dramatic contrasts in scale indicate deeper shifts in location. The careening car in Josef Müller-Brockmann's 1953 poster Schützt das Kind! (*Protect the Child!*) is too big to fit within the frame of the poster. It rushes toward the fleeing pedestrian, its enormous size creating a palpable sense of speed and danger. Folded sheets of cardboard form converging lines in Philippe Apeloig's poster for *Street Scene* (2012), an opera set in front of a tenement building with wide marble steps.

The physical properties of paper have provided models for communication and consciousness across the history of modern thought. Ferdinand de Saussure, inventor of semiology (the science of signs), likened the linguistic sign to a sheet of paper. On one side is the *signifier* (the material sound or mark), and on the other side is the *signified* (the concept the sign points to). The signifier and signified face off against each other back-to-back, yet they can never be cleaved apart. We can't grasp the mental concept unaided by the material signifier.[13]

Folded paper offers a way station between 2D and 3D. Critic and curator Li Edelkoort has looked at contemporary designers' fascination with cutting and folding flat materials—from paper to plywood—to construct three-dimensional objects. In her book *The Pop-Up Generation*, Edelkoort writes, ". . . our brain works like a rapid-prototyping software program which layers 2D to give the illusion of 3D . . . Will these double fictions eliminate each other, enter a duel of competing illusions or conversely will the layering reinforce the feeling of space and volume? Will the evidence pop up and unravel? Will the truth be felt that this is all but an illusion?"[14] Edelkoort heralds pop-up forms as timely expressions of design culture. Ephemeral, changeable, informal, and illusory, folded structures explore the territory between two and three dimensions.

As graphic design absorbs the language of 3D imaging and manufacturing, designers are finding new ways to simulate depth. Traditional linear perspective uses scale and converging lines to represent objects and spaces from the point of view of the beholder. In contrast, 3D representation untethers objects from a fixed vantage point so that we can understand them as independent entities. Contour lines commonly appear in maps and 3D wire frames, describing volume with series of parallel lines. The elements in such representations don't change scale from foreground to background; instead, space forms an even continuum.

Swiss designer Ralph Schraivogel creates surfaces that boil and undulate with strange energy—in *Cinema Afrika* (2006), swirling contour lines give rise to colliding texts. Felix Pfäffli's 2013 poster Efterklang (*Echo*) deploys contour lines that stack into the distance rather than sitting parallel to the picture plane (as in a topographical map); letterforms emerge from the foggy ether of this strange landscape.

Möbius strip   Möbius short

Klein bottle

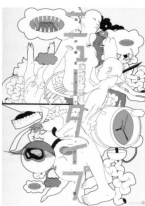

Vision is disorienting. Looping strips of paper—represented with flat blocks of color—cover the surface of Herbert Bayer's classic poster *Divisumma* (1953). This visual maze quickly disorients the wandering eye. Bayer's bands of paper, which evoke the paper in an Olivetti adding machine, resemble the geometry of the Möbius strip. Anyone can make a Möbius strip by taping a narrow piece of paper end-to-end with a simple twist in the middle. The resulting structure has an outside surface that flows to the inside without interruption, yielding an object that has, in effect, only one side. This seemingly paradoxical condition can be easily realized with everyday materials. The letterforms in Pfäffli's poster *Holy Other* (2013) channel the mind-bending energy of the Möbius strip as well as the front/back condition of Saussure's linguistic sign. The designer has mobilized both sides of his fictional planes to create letterforms that transform into different characters.

Another curious mathematical object is the Klein bottle. This self-penetrating vessel passes through itself, a condition that can't be achieved without tearing a hole in the vessel. The Klein bottle can exist mathematically with the addition of a fourth dimension, but this dimension is not accessible to us in the physical world. As Steven M. Rosen has written, ". . . space is unable to contain the bottle the way ordinary objects appear containable."[15] The French psychoanalyst Jacques Lacan referred to the Möbius strip and the Klein bottle as models of the complexity of human subjectivity.[16] Lacan asserted that consciousness is created and accessed through language and can never occupy a position outside the space of representation. The mental metropolis that unfurls across the surface of Shiro Shita Saori's poster *Solo Exhibition, New Type* (2014) recalls the free-form thought processes of doodles, graffiti, and stream-of-consciousness writing.

Herbert Bayer (Austrian, active Germany and USA, 1900–1985) for Ing. C. Olivetti and C. S.p.A., (Ivrea, Italy). *Divisumma*, 1953. Lithograph. 67.9 × 47.9 cm (26 3/4 × 18 7/8 in.). Museum purchase through gift of James A. Lapides and from General Acquisitions Endowment Fund, 2009-1-1.

Ralph Schraivogel (Swiss, b. 1960). Design Centrum Ceské Republiky [*Design Center Czech Republic*], 2002. Screenprint. 84.6 × 60 cm (33 5/16 × 23 5/8 in.). Gift of Ralph Schraivogel, 2007-15-2.

Felix Pfäffli (Swiss, b. 1986) for Südpol (Kriens, Switzerland). *Holy Other, Südpol*, 2013. Risograph. 42 × 29.4 cm (16 9/16 × 11 9/16 in.). Gift of Felix Pfäffli, 2014-30-3.

Shiro Shita Saori (Japanese, b. 1990) for the Watari Museum of Contemporary Art (Shibuya, Japan). *Solo Exhibition, New Type*, 2014. Digital print. 103 × 72.8 cm (40 9/16 × 28 11/16 in.). Gift of Shiro Shita Saori, 2014-35-2.

Roland Barthes's famous diagram shows how signs become signs for other signs. Typography is a metalanguage that represents the alphabet, which in turn represents sounds and words.

Vision isn't just visual. What is the relationship between language and perception? The Gestalt psychologists, with their tidy diagrams of "good form" and figure/ground relationships, isolated visual expression from its linguistic and cultural context. Yet human cognition is shaped by language and culture.[17] All human societies create spoken language, but only a few have produced writing systems. The Latin alphabet is a set of graphic marks representing (however imperfectly) the sounds of speech. Latin type, invented many centuries after the rise of the alphabet, is a second- or third-order sign system devised to mass-produce texts. Typography conveys the sounds coded by the alphabet along with numerous visual cues and conventions that have no analogue in speech, from roman and italic to bold and light, flush left and rag right, spacing and grids. These graphic signals alter the meaning of the text by creating emphasis, hierarchy, and multiple points of access, yet these visual signs are not linguistic.

Looking at text requires the same processes of vision used when looking at circles and squares. We group individual letters into words that stand out as objects against the neutral ground of "white space." Words gather into lines, and lines become blocks of gray matter. Yet letters are more than just shapes. Once we become literate in a particular language, we can't look at written words without also hearing them and interpreting their meaning. We can't wrestle the signifier fully free of the signified—or vice versa. Mieke Gerritzen's poster *Next Nature* (2006) depicts a body obliterated by text. This faceless, sexless automaton (with a spinning gear in place of genitalia) suggests a regime of mass communication dominated by words and information.

M/M (Paris) (Paris, France): Michael Amzalag (French, b. 1967) and Mathias Augustyniak (French, b. 1967). Crustinien des Galapagos, *a Film by François Curlet*, 2013. Screenprint. 176 × 120 cm (5 ft. 9 5/16 in. × 47 1/4 in.). Gift of M/M (Paris), 2015-4-6.

Mieke Gerritzen (Dutch, b. 1962) for The Biggest Visual Power Show (Essen, Germany). *Next Nature*, 2006. Digital print. 70 × 50 cm (27 9/16 × 19 11/16 in.). Gift of Mieke Gerritzen, 2009-39-8.

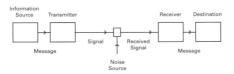

Shannon/Weaver communication model, 1949

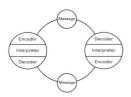

Osgood/Schramm communication model, 1954

Vision is social. Graphic design involves more than a one-way transfer from sender to receiver. In 1949 Claude Shannon and Warren Weaver published their "Mathematical Theory of Communication," widely known as the Shannon/Weaver model, depicting a straight path from transmitter to receiver.[18] Later models of communication incorporate feedback into the process. The receiver is not the end of the line but actively participates, completing the loop by encoding a response.[19] Communication takes place between two communicators.

A printed poster can't respond to receivers the way a phone call or a Twitter feed can, and yet posters and other forms of seemingly one-way media can influence thought and behavior over time. Design educator and theorist Meredith Davis has described graphic communication as a "trajectory of understanding and acceptance for ideas that result from encounters with visual messages."[20] Political posters, whether produced as top-down propaganda or underground opposition, can shape opinions and galvanize people around a shared belief or point of view.

Posters and other images can trigger emotional responses like those provoked by living beings. Images beseech us with their sorrow, wisdom, or erotic charm. The human brain is wired to recognize faces, reacting similarly to real faces and to simulated ones. An influential psychological study exposed subjects to a range of images, from human faces to doll and clock faces. The human faces triggered the strongest neural response, but the dolls and clocks still elicited a change in the brain associated with human contact. The authors of the study wrote, "Faces are visual objects that hold special significance as the icons of human minds."[21]

To connect is to communicate. Withholding connection can be as compelling as sustaining it. While many film and theater posters entice viewers with direct eye contact, others build emotional tension by denying that basic satisfaction. The giant brimmed hat featured in Waldemar Swierzy's 1973 film poster for *Midnight Cowboy* hides the character's eyes. The portrait focuses our attention on the man's full, ripe lips while suppressing feelings of intimacy or understanding. Swierzy's poster starkly translates the emotional conflict of this grim film about the life and death of a male prostitute. In a theater poster by Benker & Steiner (1996), a family is gathered around a dinner table. Flat dots of color block the faces of everyone except the beleaguered patriarch, who is leashed like a dog to a table leg. He looks at us, and we look at him. He gives the scene its point of view, its center of gravity, because he is the only one equipped to communicate—not with those around him, but with us.

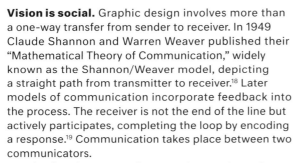

Benker & Steiner Werbeagentur AG (Switzerland) for Zürcher Theater Spektakel (Zürich, Switzerland). Zürcher Theater Spektakel [*Zürich Theater Festival*], 1996. Offset lithograph. 128 × 90.5 cm (50 3/8 × 35 5/8 in.). Gift of Sara and Marc Benda, 2010-21-91.

Waldemar Swierzy (Polish, 1931–2013). Nocny Kowboj [*Midnight Cowboy*], 1973. Offset lithograph. 82.3 × 58.5 cm (32 3/8 × 23 1/16 in.). Gift of Sara and Marc Benda, 2010-21-103.

Vision is embodied. The field of embodied cognition explores the links among eye, brain, and body, showing how physical experience shapes human thought. Words and images conjure mental representations that trigger responses in the same parts of the brain that control motor functions. People often lean slightly forward when thinking about the future, and they tilt their heads up when imagining a scene located above them. Depictions of human gesture provoke physical responses, and an athlete's perception of the size of a ball or the incline of a hill is influenced by his or her level of fatigue or readiness to perform.[22] Likewise, we see posters not only with our eyes but with our bodies. We respond physically to the taut pose of the elegant athlete in Ladislav Sutnar's 1958 poster for Addo-X. We empathize with the splayed limbs of Paul Rand's *Dancer* (1939) and with the existential laugh of Armin Hofmann's masked jester (1960).

Paul Rand (American, 1914–1996), *Dancer on Orange Ground (After Cover for* Direction *Magazine*, 1939). Offset lithograph. 96.8 × 60.8 cm (38 1/8 × 23 15/16 in.). Gift of Marion S. Rand, 2002-11-24.

Ladislav Sutnar (American and Czech, 1897–1976) for A. B. Addo (Malmö, Sweden). *addo-x*, 1958. Offset lithograph. 96.8 × 60.8 cm (38 1/8 × 23 15/16 in.). Gift of Anonymous Donor, 1994-109-7.

Armin Hofmann (Swiss, b. 1920) for Stadttheater (Basel, Switzerland). Saison *1960 / 61*, 1960. Offset lithograph. 127.8 × 90.2 cm (50 5/16 × 35 1/2 in.). Gift of Ken Friedman, 1997-19-148.

kiki   bouba

Vision is multisensory. The descriptors soft/hard, rough/smooth, and warm/cold are commonly used across the senses of sight, sound, and touch. A famous study conducted by Gestalt psychologist Wolfgang Köhler in 1929 showed a correlation between the nonsense words "kiki" and "bouba" with angular and blobby shapes. The study was repeated under modern experimental conditions by renowned psychologists Vilayanur S. Ramachandran and Edward Hubbard in 2001, confirming the "bouba-kiki effect" as a cross-cultural phenomenon with a basis in the anatomy of speech: "the sharp changes in visual direction of the lines in the right-hand figure mimic the sharp phonemic inflections of the sound kiki, as well as the sharp inflection of the tongue on the palate."[23]

We can feel an image in our bones and muscles. We can also hear it with our ears and touch it with our skin. Blinded with rage, the piercing cry in Jan Lenica's poster *Wozzeck* (1964) penetrates the psyche. The knitted wool glove in Herbert Matter's *Engelberg, Trübsee, Switzerland* (1935) is so real we can almost sense it against our skin. Designers speak of "texture" as a basic design element, and yet this quality often exists as a flat representation or abstraction rather than a physical surface characteristic.

Herbert Matter (Swiss, active USA, 1907–1984). *Engelberg, Trübsee, Switzerland*, 1935. Photogravure. Printed by A. Trüb & Cie (Aarau, Switzerland). 101.9 × 63.7 cm (40 1/8 × 25 1/16 in.). Museum purchase from General Acquisitions Endowment Fund, 2006-15-1.

Jan Lenica (Polish, 1928–2001). *Wozzeck*, 1964. Lithograph. 97.3 × 67.6 cm (38 5/16 × 26 5/8 in.). Museum purchase from Friends of Drawings & Prints Fund, 2013-30-1.

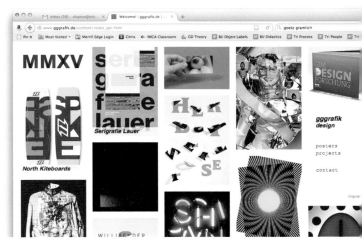

To grasp an idea is, metaphorically speaking, to hold it in our hands. Erving Goffman, the great social psychologist and theorist of body language, saw all communication as a kind of performance. The most important information one delivers isn't the words spoken ("Hello, how are you?") but a presentation of the self through nonverbal cues (manners, dress, tone of voice, and so on).[24] People have roles to play in any situation, and they play them with their whole bodies. So, too, with graphic design and visual communication. We use color and form, text and texture, icon and symbol to embody messages and take the eye and mind on a journey. Posters and other graphic media rally the senses, unleashing a process not only within each viewer, but also, potentially, within a broader culture or subculture that might find itself swayed toward new beliefs or behaviors by the messages it receives and transforms.

The idea of viewing posters as visual expression is not new. Over the last two hundred years, posters have served both as utilitarian communication and as design discourse. In the early twentieth century, posters were reproduced as advertising stamps that were commonly collected as graphic artifacts. During his career, Paul Rand turned some of his historic book covers into large-scale posters, eliminating identifying text to erase the work's former purpose. Today, posters still appear on city streets, but they are no longer a dominant form of mass media. Produced in order to expose ideas within the community of designers, many posters live more through social media than as printed artifacts. This book uses the medium of the poster as a proving ground for the means and methods of visual communication. Collected here is a set of ideas about looking that are manifested in works of two-dimensional design.

Thomas Theodor Heine, poster stamp, 1896. The design was also produced as a magazine cover and poster. / Street posters, Baltimore, Maryland, 2014. / Götz Gramlich, website, 2015.

How Posters Are Made

Caitlin Condell

Cooper Hewitt, Smithsonian Design Museum

Lithography

For the vast majority of history, posters have been printed on paper, created through an indirect transfer process, and duplicated to create multiple copies. Most of the printing methods that are represented by the posters in these pages were invented in the service of other industries, but were adopted and transformed by enterprising designers in pursuit of their graphic vision. It is often impossible in reproduction to identify the manner in which a poster was printed. But nearly every decision a designer makes is guided by or evolved from the possibilities and limitations of his or her chosen method of reproduction.

Lithography, the printing process that laid the groundwork for the modern poster, was invented to solve a problem that had nothing to do with graphic design. Working in Munich in 1798, Alois Senefelder hoped to be able to print the text of the plays that he had authored, but he lacked the necessary funds to purchase a press and type. He began experimenting with alternative printing methods, and stumbled upon the lithographic process while absentmindedly jotting down a laundry list on a piece of stone.[1]

Lithography is based on the chemical principle that oil and water do not mix. To create a lithograph, the printer draws an image on a flat matrix with a greasy medium. The matrix is wiped with a chemical solvent to bond the image to the surface. Water is then used to moisten the areas around the greasy image, after which an oil-based ink is rolled onto the matrix. The ink adheres only to the image, resisting the wet surfaces around it. A sheet of dampened paper is then laid over the matrix, and the two are run together through a printing press. The pressure of the press transfers the ink to the paper. The printed image appears on the paper in the reverse of how it was drawn. Lithography's ability to reproduce a drawn image enabled designers to work spontaneously to create entirely unique letterforms and integrate them with an image, free from the constraints of wood type and letterpress.

Although Senefelder anticipated lithography's potential to reproduce multiple colors, it was several decades before chromolithography was commonly practiced. It was chromolithography's transformative ability to reproduce colorful designs that gave rise to the modern poster. Printing lithographs in color was a laborious process that required that the designer execute the portions of his or her design in each color on a different matrix. Few designers participated in the printing of their own artwork because of this challenging and time-consuming technique. Instead, the mid-nineteenth century saw lithographic workshops spring up throughout Europe and America to service the burgeoning poster industry.

Illustrations by Yushi Luo

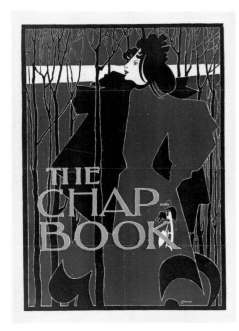

Johan Thorn-Prikker turned to the lithographic firm S. Langhout & Co. in the Netherlands to produce his 1903 poster advertising a Dutch art exhibition. *Holländische Kunstausstellung* takes its inspiration from the batik textiles of Java, Indonesia, which at the time was part of the Dutch Empire. Working in his distinctive art nouveau style, he framed the rigid letterforms in the center with thick black lines, and then surrounded the text with abstract forms to kaleidoscopic effect. Thorn-Prikker buried graphic references into the abstract design. Tulips, a classic Dutch motif, can be found to the right and left of the large orange circles, which are a nod to Holland's House of Orange-Nassau. Thorn-Prikker created a design using four colors: black, green, orange and yellow. This demanded the use of four heavy polished limestone matrices printed one after the other. The design cleverly incorporates the white space of the paper, effectively utilizing it as a fifth color. Not only did the design have to be conceived of with four different stones, but all of the text had to be drawn on the stone backward, so that when printed in the reverse it would be legible.

While lithography was initially developed using a limestone matrix, a variation on the printing method using a zinc plate, sometimes referred to as zincography, also became popular in the nineteenth century: zinc

is more affordable and less cumbersome than heavy limestone. Although at first glance William Henry Bradley's poster *Blue Lady* from 1894 appears to feature three different colors, the poster was in fact printed in only two passes. Using two contrasting inks, a sumptuous blue and a vibrant vermilion, Bradley generated a third color by overprinting the two, resulting in the rich, dark purple of the trees and the woman's coat. The thicket of vermilion-edged trees is a sophisticated by-product of the overprinting, carefully planned by Bradley. Like Thorn-Prikker, and many designers before and after him, Bradley utilized the color of the paper to particularly strong effect, representing the woman's face and the icy translucence of the frozen lake. *Blue Lady* is also remarkable for its visual references to a different printing method: woodblock printing. Bradley's design reflects a nuanced influence of Japanese woodblock prints, ingeniously translated into the medium of lithography.

Johan Thorn-Prikker (Dutch, 1868–1932). Holländische Kunstausstellung [*Dutch Art Exhibition in Krefeld*], 1903. Lithograph. 85.4 × 121.8 cm (33 5/8 × 47 15/16 in.). Museum purchase from Members' Acquisitions Fund, 2008-4-1.

William Henry Bradley (American, 1868–1962) for Stone & Kimball (Cambridge, Massachusetts, USA). *The Chap-Book (Blue Lady)*, August 1894. Zincograph. 50.8 × 35.6 cm (20 × 14 in.). Museum purchase through gift of Mrs. Gilbert W. Chapman and Ely Jacques Kahn, 2003-6-1.

Letterpress

Hendricus Theodorus Wijdeveld
(Dutch, 1885–1987). Internationale
Economisch-Historische
Tentoonstelling [*Exhibition of
International Economic History*], 1929.
Block print, letterpress. 64.6 × 50.4
cm (25 3/8 × 19 3/4 in.). Museum
purchase through gift of Eleanor and
Sarah Hewitt and Jacob H. Schiff,
and through bequest of Mrs. John
Innes Kane, 2001-7-1.

Letterpress, introduced in the fifteenth century,
employs individual elements of wood or lead cut into
letterforms, rules, and ornaments and pieced together to
form a composition. Held together in a rectangular frame
known as a chase, the elements that receive the ink are
raised above the rest of the surface. When ink is applied,
it coats only the raised surfaces, which transfer the ink
to the paper when the type is run through a press. The
aesthetic of letterpress is thus derived from the underlying
grid, into which typographic elements are assembled.
For centuries, letterpress was used almost exclusively
to reproduce text, and intaglio printing (engraving and
etching) and woodcut were used to reproduce images. A
woodcut made the same thickness as the type (called *type
high*) can be printed alongside letterpress type.

In the 1920s and 1930s, avant-garde designers
adopted this traditional method of printing, but
manipulated the qualities of letterpress to create a
radically new aesthetic. Dutch architect and graphic
designer Hendricus Wijdeveld produced the poster
Internationale Economisch-Historische Tentoonstelling in
1929. Wijdeveld created a mosaic of stylized letterforms
and opulent fields of burnt orange and gold by tightly
piecing together geometric elements drawn from a
printer's type case.

Halftone process

Although photography was invented in 1839, its impact on poster design remained relatively minor until the late nineteenth century, as lithography and letterpress are incapable of reproducing shades of gray. A sea change in poster design arrived with the advent of the halftone process, which emerged fully in the 1880s. Halftone mimics the appearance of continuous tone and shading by creating a grid of dots that vary in size and spacing. A halftone photograph was typically cheaper to produce than a drawing, and it rapidly became the primary mode of illustration for newspapers and the burgeoning magazine industry.[2] Halftone blocks could be printed alongside type in the letterpress process, allowing type and image to be printed simultaneously.

In Soviet Russia, the drive toward a utopian culture for the masses fostered an interest among artists and designers to embrace modern technology as part of their aesthetics. Gustav Klucis was among the most influential graphic designers to emerge during this period. He is particularly notable for his sophisticated use of politically charged photomontage, a technique that uses photographic elements to make a composite image. While his work in the 1920s used photomontage in a dynamic, disruptive way, his work in the early 1930s shows the pressures of Stalinism and the new visual regime of social

realism. For his 1931 poster *The Reality of Our Program . . . Six Conditions for Victory*, Klucis tried to negotiate the supreme power of the leader with the strength of the proletariat through photographic manipulation. One mockup of this poster shows Stalin much larger than the masses, who play a more subordinate role. However, in the printed poster, Klucis chose a more egalitarian portrayal, reducing Stalin to the same scale as the marching coal miners. The final poster represents Stalin in his ascendancy, accentuating his human and comradely characteristics. He strides along next to the phalanx of miners in an overcoat and cap as a man of the people. Although Klucis did not invent photomontage, his use of the technique highlights the graphic potential of halftone reproduction when combined with lithography. Klucis's limited color palette—black and red—was both a striking allusion to the political spirit and an economical approach to lithographic production.

Among Klucis's contemporaries were Georgii Augustovich Stenberg and Vladimir Augustovich Stenberg—constructivist sculptors who began producing posters in support of the burgeoning film industry in the 1920s. Although photomontage was fast becoming a preferred method of representation, the Stenberg brothers are notable for not employing the technique. Taking

Gustav Klucis (Latvian, 1895–1938). *The Reality of Our Program . . . Six Conditions for Victory*, 1931. Lithograph (one half of complete printed poster). 71.4 × 102.6 cm (28 1/8 × 40 3/8 in.). Gift of Merrill C. Berman in honor of Ellen Lupton, 2014-20-5.

technology into their own hands, the Stenberg brothers invented a projection device that could enlarge, reduce, distort, and manipulate images. "All kinds of techniques were possible," Vladimir Stenberg later noted. "But rather than being scared of them, we motivated ourselves to integrate these new technologies for our own benefits."[3] Instead of employing halftones to reproduce photographic images, the brothers chose to create hand-drawn pictures that recalled the appearance of photographs, but remained graphic illustrations. To create a poster, they would lay frames from the spool of film directly onto the projector in order to insert an image from the movie, such as an actor's face. The resulting drawing enabled the Stenbergs to control the quality, tone, and gradation of their images and blend them seamlessly with abstracted and simplified designs. In their 1929 poster *The Ghost That Isn't Returning*, the Stenberg brothers took their inspiration from a scene in which a man walks down a dirt road that is streaked by the shadow of the fence post beside him. In the Stenbergs' illustration, the shadow of the fence post suggests the steps of a staircase to an unknown destination—a clever allusion to the suspenseful pursuit that is the subject of the film.

While Klucis worked primarily with photomontage and the Stenberg brothers worked exclusively with illustration,

many designers explored the graphic possibilities of lithography by combining the two. Among those was Edward McKnight Kauffer, an American designer who moved to London just before the First World War and stayed until the advent of the second. Kauffer often combined illustration with halftone reproductions of photographic elements, and he remained committed to lithography as his means of reproduction, as he indicates in his essay included in this book.

Cooper Hewitt's collection of Kauffer's remarkable advertising art offers us a unique window into his process for mixing photography and illustration. For his poster *Spring in the Country*, Kauffer began with a sketch of a butterfly embedded with a loosely rendered stand-in for a photographic scene. Kauffer then translated the design with gouache and collage, transforming the single butterfly into two, relocating the photographic element, and adding text. Each of these elements changes in Kauffer's next rendering, which features a leaf instead of butterflies and includes a different photograph. The composition continues to evolve, as does the color palette, in yet another preparatory sketch, before Kauffer settled conclusively on a design. Kauffer would have presented his final sketch in gouache and collage to his lithographer, who would then translate the design into a print.[4]

Georgii Augustovich Stenberg (Russian, 1900–1933) and Vladimir Augustovich Stenberg (Russian, 1899–1982). *The Ghost That Isn't Returning*, 1929. Lithograph. 94.6 × 61.9 cm (37 1/4 × 24 3/8 in.). Gift of Merrill C. Berman in honor of Ellen Lupton, 2014-20-4.

Georgii Augustovich Stenberg (Russian, 1900–1933) and Vladimir Augustovich Stenberg (Russian, 1899–1982). *Adventures of an Abandoned Child*, 1926. Lithograph. 101.3 × 71.9 cm (39 7/8 × 28 5/16 in.). Gift of Merrill C. Berman in honor of Ellen Lupton, 2014-20-1.

Edward McKnight Kauffer (American, active England, 1890–1954) for Transport for London (London, England). *Spring in the Country*, 1935. Crayon, graphite. 16.5 × 11.9 cm (6 1/2 × 4 11/16 in.). Gift of Mrs. E. McKnight Kauffer, 1963-39-512.

Edward McKnight Kauffer (American, active England, 1890–1954) for Transport for London (London, England). *Spring in the Country*, 1935. Brush and gouache, photographic collage. 30.2 × 18.9 cm (11 7/8 × 7 7/16 in.). Gift of Mrs. E. McKnight Kauffer, 1963-39-513.

Edward McKnight Kauffer (American, active England, 1890–1954) for Transport for London (London, England). *Spring in the Country*, 1935. Brush and gouache, photographic collage. 30.4 × 18.7 cm (11 15/16 × 7 3/8 in.). Gift of Mrs. E. McKnight Kauffer, 1963-39-510.

Edward McKnight Kauffer (American, active England, 1890–1954) for Transport for London (London, England). *Spring in the Country*, 1935. Brush and gouache, black ink collaged illustration, graphite. 37.8 × 23.8 cm (14 7/8 × 9 3/8 in.), irregular. Gift of Mrs. E. McKnight Kauffer, 1963-39-511.

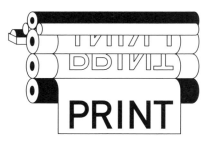

PRINT

Offset lithography

Around the turn of the twentieth century, the new process of offset lithography emerged within the commercial printing industry. "Offset" refers to the process of transferring ink from a flexible matrix to a rubber cylinder, which then transfers the image to the paper. Offset printing replaced heavy stones with light, flexible plates and automated the printing process. Since its inception, offset lithography has appealed to designers for its ability to reproduce virtually any graphic design in large quantities. This made it an ideal method for the production of propaganda posters during the tumultuous Second Republic of Spain. Vincent Canet Cabellón's poster Campesinos [Peasants] from 1936 features a laborer at work in a vibrantly colored landscape, highlighting the mismanagement of Spanish agricultural properties. The multicolor offset lithograph beautifully reproduces his hand-drawn design while offering an affordable, efficient means of distributing his message.

Swiss-born designer Erik Nitsche was hired by General Dynamics in the 1950s to design the company's exhibition for the International Conference on the Peaceful Uses of Atomic Energy, held in Geneva, Switzerland. General Dynamics was the manufacturer of the first atomic submarine and had been commissioned to produce the first atomic airplane. Since most of these projects were top secret, Nitsche was forced to find a way to express the company's mission with only the vaguest suggestion of actual products. His solution was a series of symbolist graphic presentations of peaceful uses of the atom, Atoms for Peace. Steeped in the tradition of Swiss graphic design, Nitsche suspected that his European audience would be drawn to the medium of posters, and he had his vibrant designs printed at Lithos R. Marsens in Lausanne, Switzerland.

In the 1990s, as many designers turned to digital means to produce their graphic imagery, pioneering postmodernist designer Ed Fella created hand-drawn abstract typographic systems that featured letterforms containing expressive drawings. His irregularly spaced characters were easily and inexpensively printed through single-color offset printing. Fella produced dozens of posters over several decades, including this poster for an event about Obsessive-Compulsive Design.

Offset lithography has continued to be one of the most popular forms of printing for poster designers, regardless of whether the design is produced by hand or born digital. In 2008, Fanette Mellier employed offset lithography to produce her oversize tongue-in-cheek poster Specimen, a large, graphic tapestry that features the symbols of printer's control marks.

Vincente Canet Cabellón (Spanish, 1887–1951) for Federación Provincial Campesina (València, Spain). Campesinos: Para Acabar con la Especulación Solo Hay un Medio la Cooperación [Peasants: In Order to Stop the Speculation, There is Only One Way, the Cooperation], 1936. Lithograph. 90.3 × 63.3 cm (35 9/16 × 26 7/8 in.). Gift of William P. Mangold, 1997-21-21.

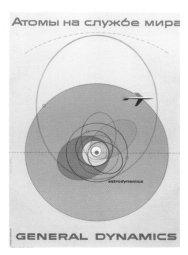

Erik Nitsche (Swiss, 1908–1998) for General Dynamic Corporation (USA). *Atoms for Peace, General Dynamics.* Offset lithograph. Printed by Lithos R. Marsens (Lausanne, Switzerland). 132.5 × 96 cm (52 3/16 × 37 13/16 in.). Gift of Arthur Cohen and Daryl Otte in memory of Bill Moggridge, 2013-42-11.

Ed Fella (American, b. 1938) for AIGA, American Institute of Graphic Arts (New York, New York, USA). *Obsessive-Compulsive Design*, 1999. Offset lithograph. Printed by Pip Printing. 43.3 × 28.1 cm (17 1/16 × 11 1/16 in.). Gift of Edward Fella, 2002-8-16.

Fanette Mellier (French, b. 1977). *Specimen*, 2008. Offset lithograph. 175 × 118.6 cm (5 ft. 8 7/8 in. × 46 11/16 in.). Gift of Fanette Mellier, 2013-18-1.

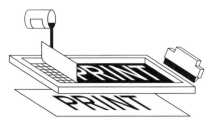

Screenprinting

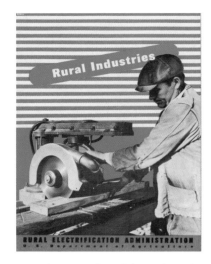

Unlike the invention of lithography, which is well documented, the birth of screenprinting went unrecorded. It emerged as a method for printing commercial materials in the early years of the twentieth century in America, and developed out of the tradition of stencil printing.[5] A screenprint is produced using a gauzy screen that has been stretched across a rectangular wooden frame. Ink is spread across the top portion of the screen by the printer, who then pulls the ink towards him or her with a rubber blade called a squeegee. The pressure forces the ink through the screen and onto the paper below. Parts of the screen are blocked with a stencil; ink passes through the open mesh to create the print. A different screen is used for each color.[6] The stencil can be applied to the screen in a variety of ways, such as affixing a cut-paper stencil directly to the screen or applying hardening glue. The most common, however, is the use of a light-sensitive gelatin, enabling the screen to reproduce photographic imagery.

The printed surface of a screenprint differs dramatically from that of a lithograph. Lithography is a planographic technique, meaning the printed surface is flat. In screenprinting, ink is deposited in a thick layer that builds up on the paper's surface. The two techniques have distinct characteristics that make them appealing for different purposes. Unlike lithography, which can hold even the most thin, delicate line, the screen does not permit a minute level of detail. Offset inks are typically transparent, whereas screenprinting inks are often opaque. Screenprinting produces a rich impasto of ink that lends the poster a velvety presence, a quality that attracts it to many designers. Because it does not require an expensive press or a large amount of equipment, screenprinting has remained popular as a hands-on medium for artists, activists, and designers, more approachable to some producers than lithography or offset lithography.

In 1935, under the umbrella of the Works Progress Administration (WPA), the United States government established the Poster Division of the Federal Art Project in New York City. Over the subsequent eight years the department produced hundreds of thousands of posters promoting the work of federal departments, most of them in screenprint.[7] Although he was young, Lester Beall was already a successful graphic designer when he was commissioned in 1937 to produce a series of posters that would increase awareness in rural areas about the benefits of electricity for the Rural Electrification Administration (REA). The initial posters were so successful that Beall designed two more. In the final series, which included *Rural Industries* from 1941, Beall created a sophisticated group of posters featuring a patriotic color scheme,

Lester Beall (American, 1903–1969) for Rural Electrification Administration (USA). *Rural Industries*, 1941. Screenprint. 101.6 × 76.2 cm (40 × 30 in.). Museum purchase through gift of Mrs. Edward C. Post and from Friends of Drawings and Prints, General Acquisition Endowment, Sarah Cooper Hewitt, and Smithsonian Institution Collections Acquisition Program Funds, 1995-106-1.

angled typography, silhouetted photographs, and strong graphic elements. Beall had to consider how each color would overlap and in what order. By examining the layered elements comprising *Rural Industries*, we learn that Beall printed first the red, then the blue, and then the black ink.

Screenprinting became popular outside the United States as well. Following the revolution in 1959 in Cuba, the Instituto Cubano del Arte e Industria Cinematográficos (Cuban Institute of Cinematographic Art and Industry) was formed. The organization has been responsible for producing over fifteen hundred posters advertising films, many of them in screenprint. Designer Antonio Pérez (Ñiko) González created a poster for La Linea Delgada (*The Thin Line*). The haunting line symbolizes the female protagonist's infidelity. The line's shift from white to red echoes her murder at the hands of her husband. Produced in only two colors, the rich matte surface underscores the film's emotional subject matter.

Andy Warhol was introduced to screenprinting in the 1950s when he was working as a commercial artist, and it became the medium through which he produced his most celebrated canvases and works on paper. Until Warhol, screenprinting remained largely the purview of commercial printing, with the mark of the designer's hand distinctly absent. An enthusiastic and experimental

printmaker, Warhol created screenprints with constantly changing variables including mutable colors and shifts in registration. For his poster *Admit One* from 1967, Warhol mimicked the appearance of a movie ticket, printed on a massive scale over off-kilter layers of neon flowers. While perfectly registered, the poster carries the impression of a quickly assembled design. Though Warhol famously said he wanted "to be a machine," he transformed the aesthetic of screenprinting into a medium that revealed and reveled in its own making.

That same spirit has carried through to our contemporary moment. In 2010, in the wake of the Deepwater Horizon oil spill, designer Anthony Burrill teamed up with Tom Galle and Cecilia Azcarate Isturiz of the communications agency Happiness Brussels to design a poster to raise money for recovery efforts. Isturiz and Galle flew to Louisiana to capture oil from the spill that had leeched into the sandy beaches of the coastline. The oil and sand was brought to the print shop Purple Monkey Design, where it was mixed with extender base, which allowed the oil-turned-ink to pass smoothly through a screen. When the oil was pushed through the screen onto the paper, it produced a shimmering, golden color that gives radiance to Burrill's straightforward slogan of protest and warning: "Oil & Water Do Not Mix."

Antonio Pérez González (Cuban, b. 1941) for the Cuban Institute of Cinematographic Art and Industry (ICAIC) (Havana, Cuba). La Linea Delgada [*The Thin Line*], 1969. Screenprint. 76.2 × 51.1 cm (30 × 20 1/8 in.). Museum purchase from Smithsonian Institution Collections Acquisition Program Fund and through gift of Anonymous Donors, 1994-65-8.

Andy Warhol (American, 1928–1987) for the Lincoln Center for the Performing Arts (New York, New York, USA). *Admit One*, 1967. Screenprint. 114.1 × 61.3 cm (44 15/16 × 24 1/8 in.). Gift of Donald Karshan, 1972-58-7.

Philippe Apeloig (French, b. 1962) for Cité du Livre (Aix-en-Provence, France). Bruits du monde [*Noises of the World*], 2012. Screenprint. 173.5 × 120.2 cm (5 ft. 8 5/16 in. × 47 5/16 in.). Gift of Philippe Apeloig, 2014-34-2.

Anthony Burrill (British, b. 1966) with Cecilia Azcarate Isturiz and Tom Galle for Happiness Brussels (Brussels, Belgium). *Oil and Water Do Not Mix*, 2010. Screenprint with oil culled from the Gulf of Mexico, sand, and extender base. Printed by Purple Monkey Design (New Orleans, Louisiana, USA). 76.2 × 50.8 cm (30 × 20 in.). Gift of Anthony Burrill, 2012-13-1.

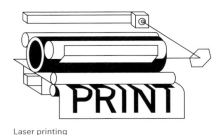

Laser printing

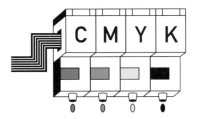

Inkjet printing

While some designers choose to produce their work in screenprint because of the mutability of the print process, other designers remain committed to the medium for its potential to enhance a design through its perfect execution. Philippe Apeloig produces limited editions of nearly all of his poster designs in screenprint—his preferred printing method. Apeloig is scrupulous about the execution of his posters, and he often goes to the print shop to supervise the process. The lush presence of the ink on the paper creates a sense of vibrancy and tactility that is essential to Apeloig's designs. In Bruits du monde (*Noises of the World*) from 2012, the contrast of the smudged black letterforms against the concentrated blue is enhanced by the substantiality of the ink on the paper's surface.

As the variety of printing methods has grown, designers have become empowered to select and manipulate the medium that allows them to convey their message most effectively. Like many activist designers, the feminist poster collective SisterSerpents turned to xerography, more commonly known as photocopying. Invented in 1938, photocopiers became commonplace tools in offices in the late 1950s and early 1960s, replacing earlier duplication technologies such as mimeograph and Photostat. Photocopies are produced by shining light through a piece of graphic matter onto an electrically charged drum. The drum acts as a conductor, charging a resinous powder or toner, which is fused to a sheet of paper with heat and set with pressure rollers. SisterSerpents used the color photocopy process to cheaply produce hundreds of small-scale posters. In *Julia's Simple Method for Stopping a Rapist* from 1993, the harsh tones of color and the graphic "noise" created by a faulty drum and toner combination become part of the aesthetic of this humorous but penetrating poster.

Risography was invented in the 1980s in Japan as a cheaper alternative to xerography for small businesses. The machine is similar in appearance to a photocopier, but as a form of stencil duplication, it is akin as a printing method to screenprint. An image, designed to print one color at a time, is cut into a master stencil, which acts as a screen and is wrapped around the ink drum. The paper is run through the machine and pressed directly against the stencil-wrapped drum. The master sheet is replaced along with the ink drum for each additional color. More affordable and less messy than screenprint, risography has become a popular alternative for many young designers in the early twenty-first century. Felix Pfäffli has used the process to print his ongoing series of posters advertising the events at Südpol, a cultural center

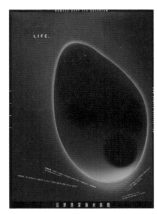

in Switzerland. In *Monotales*, Pfäffli used two colors, green and black, to create a print that gives the illusion of depth. Far from generating a sleek surface, the risograph prints convey a raw, flat effect. Risograph printing is widely used in independent book publishing.

The rise of digital printing has transformed the ability of graphic designers to produce and publish their work. Inkjet printing is a technique that propels tiny droplets of ink onto the paper. Laser printing— the updated method of photocopying—uses a laser beam to train back and forth across an electron-charged drum to define the image. The drum then transfers the image to the paper, and it is sealed with heat. Neither process requires the creation of printing plates or screens, allowing designers to quickly transform their designs in prints. Both processes offer designers the opportunity to execute their work using a myriad of CMYK color builds. And digital prints have also empowered designers to print posters in any quantity desired, not bound by minimum and maximum runs common to other printing methods. For her poster *Solo Exhibition, New Type* from 2014, Shiro Shita Saori was able to send her digital files to a printer and order the number of posters that she wanted to advertise her monographic exhibition. When Cooper Hewitt decided to acquire the poster, she was able to order yet another print.

The flexibility and spontaneity enabled by digital printing joined with online distribution have spurred the popularity of print-on-demand posters. Albert Exergian has become widely known for his series of minimalist posters that celebrate popular television shows such as *Game of Thrones*. Exergian, working completely independently of the shows he features—in some cases shows that have not aired for decades—has tapped into the appetite of television fans as well as admirers of the Swiss modernist style, which his aesthetic humorously celebrates. Consumers can purchase the posters online in a variety of sizes. Because Exergian can print posters as they are ordered, he is able to create a growing series of designs without a significant financial risk.

As printing has expanded into three dimensions, designers have also turned to forms of "printing" that play with the physicality of paper. For one of their earliest commissions, the design collective Experimental Jetset created a screenprinted poster that featured die-cut capsule-shaped holes. Die-cutting is the process of using a shaped metal blade (a die) to cut through sheets of paper. Since the Paradiso posters were advertising the schedule for a rock concert venue, they were typically hung over other posters on walls in bars and music stores. The die-cut holes allowed the layers of previously hung posters

SisterSerpents (Chicago, Illinois, USA). *Julia's Simple Method for Stopping a Rapist*, 1993. Photocopy, rubber-stamped ink, photographic reproduction. 34.1 × 21.7 cm (13 7/16 × 8 9/16 in.). Gift of SisterSerpents, 1995-114-2.

Felix Pfäffli (Swiss, b. 1986) for Südpol (Kriens, Switzerland). *Monotales*, 2012. Risograph. 42 × 29.4 cm (16 9/16 × 11 9/16 in.). Gift of Felix Pfäffli, 2015-3-2.

Shiro Shita Saori (Japanese, b. 1990) for Numazu Deep Sea Aquarium (Numazu, Shizuoka, Japan). *Life*, 2014. Digital print. 102.9 × 73 cm (40 1/2 × 28 3/4 in.). Gift of Shiro Shita Saori, 2014-35-1.

Albert Exergian (Austrian, b. 1973). *Game of Thrones, Iconic TV*, 2011. Digital print. 118.9 × 84.1 cm (46 13/16 × 33 1/8 in.). Courtesy of the designer.

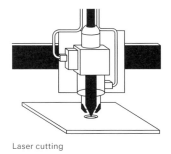

Laser cutting

beneath them to show through, making each individually hung poster its own unique entity.

Sean Donahue turned to the centuries-old technique of **embossing** for his poster *Touching Graphic Design: A Tactile Reading*. In embossing, paper is run through a press over engraved dies or plates, yielding depressions or elevations on the surface of the paper. Donahue used the method to reproduce raised type and braille, a method that made his poster accessible to a low-vision and no-vision audience.

Marian Bantjes sought out the unusual technique of **laser cutting** to produce her poster *Design Ignites Change*. A high-powered laser directed by CNC (computer numerical control) is trained on the paper, melting or burning it in the form of the designer's pattern. "Aside from the fact that it is just plain bitchin'," she has said, laser cutting allowed for a design that played on the title phrase.[8] Departing from normal laser-cutting procedure, Bantjes chose to cut the text from the front of the sheet so that the burn marks around the letters show in the final work, literally igniting the phrase featured on the poster.

As digital screens become increasingly prevalent, the printed poster has taken on new roles. For his commemoration of the transition from summer to fall in his poster Herbstzeitlose (*Autumn Crocus*), Götz Gramlich

created both a digital animation and a screenprinted poster around the same design concept. In the animation, the letters peel away one by one from the surface to which they have been affixed, revealing their black undersides. Tucked into these corners are bits of information about the event. In the screenprinted version, the static image features each letter partially turned down, with faint black dots forming shadows behind the full letterforms.

It is tempting to look back at the history of the poster through the lens of production and see a steady march forward, with technological innovations triggering new aesthetic ideas. As the function of posters has evolved, designers have sought out methods of production that serve their aesthetic criteria within the constraints of time, budgets, and access to technology. Designers have explored the limits of each printing technique to craft a range of visual languages. Today, designers are showing a resurgent interest in the seemingly outmoded domain of print. At the same time, new technologies have enabled an emerging generation of designers to produce, market, and distribute posters across the globe. Even as the act of "posting" has been transmuted by the rise of Internet and social media, printed posters continue to proliferate. With so many methods of production at designers' fingertips, there has never been a more exciting moment for posters.

Erwin Brinkers (Dutch, b. 1973), Marieke Stolk (Dutch, b. 1967), and Danny van den Dungen (Dutch, b. 1971) of Experimental Jetset (Amsterdam, Netherlands) for Paradiso (Amsterdam, Netherlands). *Paradiso 1996*, 1996. Die-cut screenprint. Printed by Zeefdrukkerij Kees Maas (Amsterdam, Netherlands). 59.4 × 42 cm (23 3/8 × 16 9/16 in.). Gift of Experimental Jetset, 2014-40-1.

Götz Gramlich (German, b. 1974), for Patrick Forgacz (Heidelberg, Germany). Herbstzeitlose [*Autumn Crocus*], 2014. Digital animation. Courtesy of the designer.

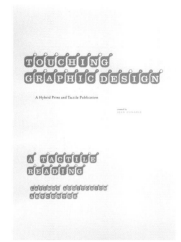

Marian Bantjes (Canadian, b. 1963)
for the Academy for Educational
Development (Washington, D.C.,
USA). *Design Ignites Change*, 2008.
Laser cut. Laser cut by Arkwell
Industries (Vancouver, British
Columbia, Canada). 71.3 × 51 cm
(28 1/16 × 20 1/16 in.). Gift of Marian
Bantjes, 2013-23-1.

Sean Donahue (American, b. 1973).
*Touching Graphic Design: A Tactile
Reading*, 2008. Digital print with
embossing. 91.4 × 61 cm (36 × 24 in.).
Gift of Sean Donahue, 2011-45-3.

Kauffer's Technique

Graham Twemlow

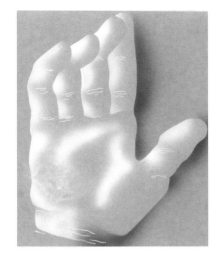

For the catalog that accompanied a major exhibition of his posters held at the Museum of Modern Art (MoMA) in 1937, Edward McKnight Kauffer provided a "brief biography" and a section titled "A Note on Technique." In the text he alluded to the fact that many of his posters were still reproduced using direct printing via the lithographic stone process, rather than the more commercially efficient method of offset printing using zinc plates. One of Kauffer's key strengths was his innate feel for, and understanding of, the lithographic printing process, and it is possible that working on stone allowed the artisans—who translated his designs into printed artifacts—more scope to apply richer textural effects. In the catalog's foreword, English writer and philosopher Aldous Huxley expanded upon Kauffer's hazy references to his working methods by explaining how he simplified and formalized his reference sources, resulting in a " . . . more expressive symbol of the things being represented." Although Kauffer's notes are somewhat vague, they act as one of the few sources that offer insight into his working methods. However, from a telegram Kauffer sent to MoMA two months after the February 10 opening, it appears that Kauffer was shocked and embarrassed to see them printed in the note form in which he sent them. The telegram, dated April 2, 1937, coldly demanded:

> Announcement Of Publication In England Of Catalogue
> To My Exhibition In Literary Supplement STOP Under No
> Circumstances Whatsoever Can I Permit This STOP My
> Biographical Notes Were Sent To Be Edited And Not Printed
> As Published In New York

The original telegram is preserved in the archives of Cooper Hewitt, Smithsonian Design Museum.

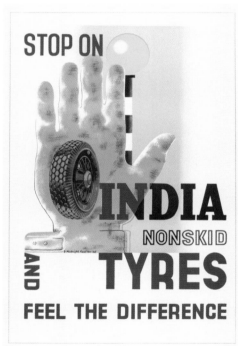

Edward McKnight Kauffer (American, active England, 1890–1954). *Hand*, 1935–38. Airbrush and white gouache. 22.9 × 19.1 cm (9 × 7 1/2 in.). Gift of Mrs. E. McKnight Kauffer, 1963-39-960.

Edward McKnight Kauffer (American, active England, 1890–1954) for India Tyre and Rubber Co. (Inchinnan, Scotland). *Stop on the India Nonskid Tyres and Feel the Difference*, 1935. Lithograph. 71.5 × 47.7 cm (28 1/8 × 18 3/4 in.). Gift of Mrs. E. McKnight Kauffer, 1963-39-79.

A Note on Technique

Edward McKnight Kauffer, 1937

The American-born designer Edward McKnight Kauffer (1890–1954) studied art in Germany and then went to work in London. There, he designed numerous posters for the London Underground and other clients. Although Kauffer was not as well-known in the U.S. during his lifetime, the Museum of Modern Art exhibited his work in 1937. The note is reprinted here as it appeared in in the catalog for that exhibition, *Posters by E. McKnight Kauffer.*

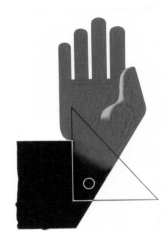

I have used all kinds of instruments common to most contemporary painters, such as tooth brushes, cheese cloth, wire netting, etc.—in fact anything that suggests interesting textures. The air-brush I seldom use now, but when I did use it a few years ago I realized that it was a tricky instrument and that its use required an exceedingly disciplined technique. At the moment I prefer methods less exacting and with more direct contact between my idea and the medium.

Lithography still tends to be commercially practical for reproduction, and most of my posters are done by an old firm still using in many cases actual lithograph stones.

When I began advertising design in England in 1916, the outstanding work then was of the Munich realistic school, more pictorial than poster. My enthusiasm, to counteract that influence, was at first by violent methods, but such designs as I did were confined to exhibition posters for the then modern group of painters known as the London group, of which I was secretary.

In 1919 I produced the first and only Cubist poster design in England—a flight of birds, which was sold to an advertising agent for fifty dollars. It eventually appeared without my layout or lettering and for the Labour paper, the Daily Herald. This design was so much noticed that Mr. Winston Churchill, then at the War Office, asked to

see me with the idea of designing a new flag for the Royal Air Force. Mr. Churchill's appreciation of this "modernistic" design was flattering, but nothing further happened. I think at this moment a new direction in poster designing was created, but I realized that more persuasive methods would have to be employed. Rightly or wrongly, the progress of poster designing as done by myself has been slowly won, mostly by discussion, argument and a good deal of fighting. But English clients, once they are convinced, are prepared to go full steam ahead.

The cover design for the catalog is the most recent experiment I have made, and it is an endeavour to dramatize shapes in space, to give an excitement to the mind with the use of non-naturalistic symbols and to suggest to the person who sees it a conflict of which he is a solitary witness. I am working more on these experiments, about which I shall write you later.

Edward McKnight Kauffer (American, active England, 1890–1954).
Abstraction with a Hand, 1935–38.
Brush and gouache, graphite. 31.1 × 21.6 cm (12 1/4 × 8 1/2 in.). Gift of Mrs. E. McKnight Kauffer, 1963-39-963.

Poster with a Central Image

Bruno Munari, 1966

The Italian designer and artist
Bruno Munari (1907–1998) wrote
extensively about art and design.
During the 1920s, he joined the
futurist movement, led by F. T.
Marinetti. Well-known as a children's
book author, Munari also contributed
to the discourse of design theory
and education. This essay, reprinted
here as it appeared in Munari's
book *Design as Art,* describes the
optical effects of different geometric
structures and makes fun of
recurring ideas in poster design.

Basic pattern of a poster in the form
of the Japanese flag. The eye is
attracted by the dark disc and has no
way of escaping. It has to tear itself
away. The space around the disc
isolates the image from any other
nearby forms.

The old idea in advertising was that a poster should
hit you in the eye, and even today many people would
agree. It is a way of getting information across to the
average passer-by, who might well be thinking about the
transformation of a caterpillar into a butterfly: a violent
transformation, and everyone knows that violence has to
be opposed with equal violence.

But joking apart, what did these old-fashioned
advertising men mean by "hitting you in the eye"? They
probably meant that a poster must stand out a mile
from the other posters displayed around it in the street.
It must jump out at you, surprise you, capture your
attention by an act of banditry. The same thing goes for
all the other posters nearby.

A poster for soap, for example, or for some
detergent, must be quite different from any other poster
for soap. We already know that a certain detergent
washes white, that another washes whiter, that a third
washes whiter still, that a fourth washes whiter than the
first and second put together, that a fifth washes easily
twice as white, and that a sixth (which is in fact the same
powder as the one which started the whole idea) washes
so white that it makes things look black.

It usually happens that when someone cannot keep

his end up in an argument he begins to shout. In this
way he does not add anything new to his argument, but
at least he makes himself heard. Many posters want to
make themselves heard at all costs, and so they shout
with their colours, yell at you with strident shapes. And
the worst thing of all is that there are thousands of
them all bellowing at you in satanic discord. Not having
studied the exact techniques of visual communication,
advertisers fall back on commonplace images that they
multiply ad nauseam and without thinking whether the
forms and colours they are using could not equally well
be applied to tyres, soap or aperitifs. But the designer's
experiments have taught us that it would be enough
to employ an unusual colour, a different form, and to
give the passer-by exact and immediate information
instead of assaulting him time and time again until he is
battered senseless.

On the other hand one sometimes sees posters so
jaded they seem to have been deliberately camouflaged,
and it is incredible that they could have been accepted
and printed. It probably happens like this. The painter
(not a graphic designer) makes a rough sketch of the
poster and takes it along to the advertising manager's
office. This sketch is full size, say three feet by five, and

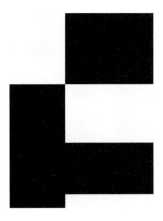

Basic pattern of a poster cut up into separate sections. The eye wanders over the surface and is continually forced to follow the dividing lines between the light and dark sections. These lead it out and away from the poster. Besides this, the sections themselves may easily seem to belong to the posters next door.

done on canvas or stiff paper. It is propped up opposite the advertising manager's desk for his approval. Now his office is furnished with exquisite taste, as befits the head of a department: for one must not only be the head of a department, but must be seen to be such. The colours are muted, the furniture of a classical restraint. There is nothing in the least gaudy about it. In these surroundings the poster, even if it is ugly, has an explosive force. The picture hanging on the wall beside it looks like a washed-out photograph. The poster is accepted and printed, and only then is it realized that surrounded by a mass of other posters it is barely noticeable. But what's done is done, and all we can hope is to do better next time.

There is one basic kind of poster that graphic designers often use, because it is so visually compelling. This is the Japanese flag, a red disc on a white background. Why is such a simple design so effective? Because the white background isolates the disc from everything around it, from the other posters, and because the disc itself is a form that the eye finds it hard to escape from. The eye is in fact accustomed to making its escape at the points or corners of things, at the head of an arrow for example. A triangle offers three escape routes; a square offers four. A circle has no corners, and the eye is forced to go round and round in it until it tears itself away with an effort.

How is this basic pattern used in a poster? The disc may represent or become a tomato, a plate of soup, a clock, a football, a shell, a steering-wheel, a cooking pot, a round cheese, a button, a champagne cork, a gramophone record, a flower, a road sign, a wheel, a tire, a target, a ball-bearing, a Gothic rose-window, an open umbrella, a cogwheel . . . and last but not least the globe. A photo of a globe, the globe painted with bold strokes of the brush, a globe made of strips of paper or torn paper scraps, in black and white, in colour. . . .

Even today you will find this basic design used for countless posters. On the other hand it is a mistake to divide the surface of a poster into different blocks of colour or print. Such a poster fades too easily into its surroundings, and each part of the composition flows off into the poster next door, confusing the public and absolutely nullifying the effect of the message.

Bruno Munari (Italian, 1907–1998). *Shell*, 1936. Photocollage and mixed media. 18.3 × 16.6 cm (7 1/5 × 6 1/2 in.). Collection of Merrill C. Berman.

Although Bruno Munari critiqued the formulaic use of circles as a compositional device, he certainly explored the possibilities of the circle in his own work. In these advertising designs created early in his career, Munari attempted to treat the circle as an open form rather than a static trap for the eye. The segmented circle in this design for an advertisement becomes a semi-transparent lens connecting air, land, and sea.

Bruno Munari (Italian, 1907–1998).
Olimpiadi [Berlin Olympics], 1936.
Lithograph. 70 × 50 cm (27 7/16 ×
19 3/4 in.). Collection of Merrill C.
Berman.

Bands of white cut through the
red-orange circle, fragmenting this
symbol of totality into an open,
permeable form.

Poster N° 524: Focal Point

Rianne Petter and René Put, 2012

Poster N° 524 presents graphic designers René Put and Rianne Petter's visual research on the medium of the poster. For three months, Petter and Put collected posters from all over the city of Amsterdam, a total of 523 different posters. They carefully studied and deconstructed this collection, researched certain elements, isolated and then reconstructed them. Presented here in its original format is Petter and Put's research on Focal Point, in which they isolate and map the principle point of interest in each poster. The complete project includes studies of Graphic Forms, Reading Direction, Language, Afterimage, Templates, Female/Male, Foreground/Background, Composition and Form, and Color.

Cutting Straight Through 523 Posters

By taking a collection of posters from the public space to the studio, we were able to consider the work in a completely different way. We left aside the context in which each poster had been separately developed and had functioned so that we could isolate the material. That gave us scope to work on a visual inquiry alongside our professional practice in which we literally cut straight through the posters in order to dissect them. In doing so, we focused on the elementary components of the poster: text, image, color, and composition. Detached from the original design, isolated and combined in new arrangements, these components became the leitmotiv of an image. This makes it possible to compare them and to shift the focus to the form in which they are manifested. The resulting images are visual data that do not offer any direct, new solutions that can be applied to the poster of the future. Moreover, their value for us lies not in the outcome, but just as much in the development of the different working methods. Both give rise to a renewed awareness, stimulate reflection, and invite a reappraisal of the potential of this fantastic medium.

Poster No. 524 was produced under the auspices of the Lectoraat Art and Public Space, the Gerrit Rietveld Academie, Amsterdam. The complete research project is published in the book *Poster No. 524: Exploring the Contemporary Poster* (Amsterdam: Valiz, 2012), with contributions by Jouke Kleerebezem and Jeroen Boomgaard.

FOCAL
POINT

FOCAL POINT

Format
A0 posters
Number
220 posters
Working method
From each poster we cut out the focal point the size of a circle with a diameter of 10 cm. These separate circles are pinned to a wall within an empty space the size of a sheet of A0 and placed in exactly their original position.

Ultimate focal point
If we look at a poster, what do we focus on first and how is this focal point determined? Does the composition determine it, or does your own interest determine where you start to view/read a poster?

Identifying, discussing, defining and cutting out the focal point of each poster resulted in a variegated collection of circles. Comparing them with one another and rearranging them brought certain recurrent motifs into sight such as eyes, colour contrasts and faces.

Placing the cut out focal points in the empty space resulted in a large concentration of circles that added up to a thickness of 12 mm at one point in the poster, roughly one-third from the top left corner. This point is the ultimate focal point of the poster where reading and viewing starts in many cases.

Composition theory
The result of this image coincides perfectly with the classical views of composition, such as that of the golden section.

The highest concentration of focal points is almost exactly in the heart of the spiral within the golden section distribution.

Almost all of the focal points are situated around the two intersections within this golden section distribution.

See also: animation Focal Point
www.poster524.com/focalpoint

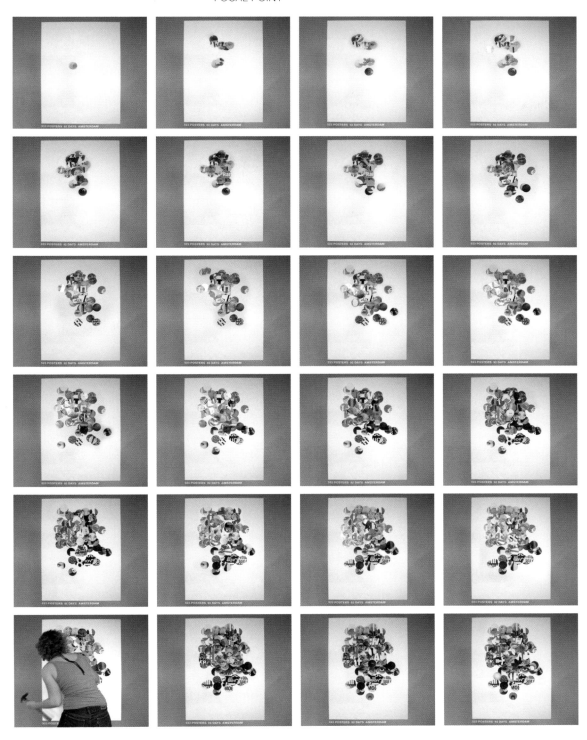

Focal points: work in progress

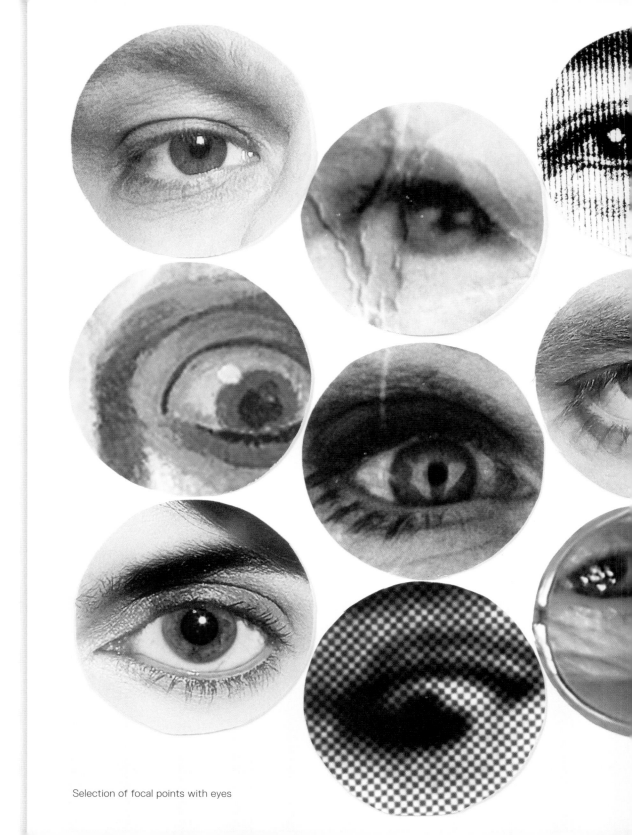

How Posters Work

Selection of focal points with eyes

Selection of focal points with form and color

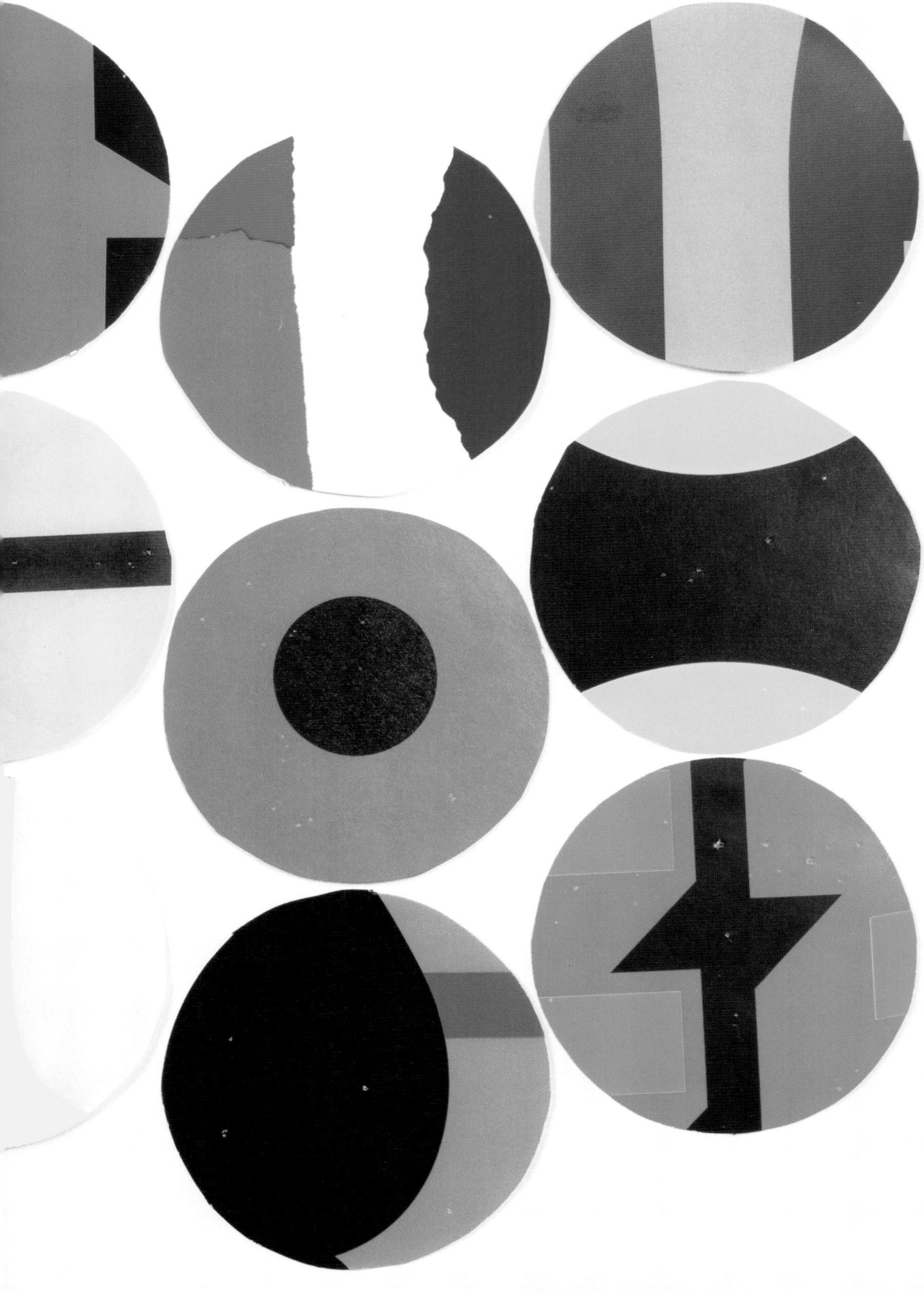

Poster N° 524: Focal Point

Selection of focal points with typography

Night Discourse

Karrie Jacobs, 1992

In 1992, Karrie Jacobs and Steven Heller published their book *Angry Graphics: Protest Posters of the Reagan/Bush Era*. In the process of researching their book, Jacobs and Heller collected dozens of posters reflecting the conflicts of the period. The authors donated this vital record of design activity to Cooper-Hewitt, Smithsonian Design Museum. Jacobs's essay from the book is reprinted here courtesy of the author.

In New York City, at the point where the logically numbered grid that covers two-thirds of Manhattan abruptly ends, where Zero Street ought to be, there is a broad, raucous, smelly boulevard called Houston Street. And at the comer of Broadway and Houston, an intersection that can be thought of as the gateway to Soho, New York's art district, there is a pair of billboards mounted on the side of a building. These billboards have unofficially been, for a number of years, the art billboards. One of them is usually an ad for Keith Haring's Pop Shop, while the other one is frequently a project or political statement by an individual artist.

Early in 1991, during the Gulf War, there appeared here a billboard that said, in crude orange letters: "The New World Order." Beneath the type was a reproduction of *Guernica*, Picasso's outcry against Fascist bombing during the Spanish Civil War. The other billboard carried an antiwar message by a prolific conceptualist from Jersey City, New Jersey, who goes by the name of "Artfux." Several days after these protests appeared, I looked up and both billboards had been covered over with identical maps of the Persian Gulf, decorated with stars and stripes, bearing the message: "Support our troops in the Middle East."

I couldn't figure out how this switch had happened. The pro-war sentiment seemed so un-New York, so un-Manhattan. I started making phone calls. Eventually I reached the billboards' leasing agent to ask what was going on and discovered that neither set of billboard images had actually been put up legally. This was not surprising. This was very New York.

The lessor said, "I don't know anything about it. Sounds like who's doing it is President Bush and the other guy. What's that guy's name? The one who's causing all this trouble?"

"Saddam Hussein?" I ventured.

"Yeah. Sounds like they're doing it."

Whoever did it, however it happened, this exchange of opinions occurred during the night: surreptitiously, illegally, mysteriously. This political debate about the Gulf War transpired while the rest of us were sleeping. I think of this phenomenon as "night discourse."

Night discourse is a much more blunt, more argumentative form of communication than its daytime counterparts, the editorial pages of newspapers and the Sunday-morning public-affairs television shows. Think of it as 3:00 a.m. talk radio made visible. The most biting political statements are pasted up all over the city at night: on walls, over existing billboards, and especially on plywood construction fences. Then in the daytime we see them as we walk the streets: on our way to work, to get some scrambled eggs, to have our teeth cleaned. Sometimes we

David Virgien and Julie Fox. *Buyer Beware*, ca. 1980. Screenprint. 62.4 × 43.7 cm (24 9/16 × 17 3/16 in.). Gift of Steven Heller and Karrie Jacobs, 1993-53-5.

Post No Bills (New York, New York, USA): John Gall (American, b. 1964) with Steven Brower, Leah Lococo, Morris Taub, James Victore, Susan Walsh. *hmmm . . . Bush / Quayle '92*, 1992. Lithograph. 73.5 × 51 cm (28 15/16 × 20 1/16 in.). Gift of Steven Heller and Karrie Jacobs, 1993-53-46.

pay attention, and sometimes we don't.

This form of public display is called "sniping" by its practitioners. Sniping is the repeated and methodical postering of a given location. The posters placed by the most skilled and persistent snipers will survive the longest. The rest will be swiftly torn down or pasted over. The poster walls that result from sniping offer a highly visible, continuous graphics exhibition, one that's neither judged nor curated. It's a show that's hung and rehung nightly, mostly by professional posterers, the pirates of the outdoor advertising world. These walls, called "hoardings," have been used in this matter, more or less illegally, for at least a century.

Magazines and newspapers have standards that govern the appearance and content of the advertising they accept. Companies that lease outdoor and transit advertising space have rules about what is and isn't appropriate. But the city's walls and fences operate beyond the forces of law and propriety. As a result, some of the strongest and most innovative graphics can be found only in this setting.

Postering as a means of advertising for pop bands and concerts, art events, movies, and even television shows appears, in my unscientific estimation (based on what I see when I walk down the street), to be on

the rise. It is used even by those who also employ more conventional means of advertising—who generally pay for space on billboards and airtime on television as a way of generating word of mouth, of getting the man on the street—literally—to talk about their product or event. So the fences and walls are crowded with posters advertising a new Sean Connery movie called *Highlander 2: The Quickening,* or a festival of movies by the director Henry Jaglom, or a poster for an exhibition by photographer Matthew Rolston. The hoardings have cachet. Things advertised on them seem hip, whether or not they really are. Because they are advertised through a pirate medium, these events possess an air of obscurity, as if they're emanating from the underground.

If we think of the fences as a kind of outdoor magazine, the commercial posters are the advertising and the political posters comprise the editorial content. The political posters are missives from people with a message, snipers with a chip on their shoulders. For instance there is currently an anonymous sniper, angry about the state of the art market, who has been pasting detailed editorial cartoons on the fences of Soho. "Art is buisiness [sic] and buisiness [sic] is art," says the headline of one such cartoon. On the left is a drawing of a poor, worn-out-looking man sitting on an apple crate, his shabby walls

Peter Kuper (American, b. 1958) and Seth Tobocman (American, b. 1958). *Crack House White House,* 1991. Airbrush on tracing paper. 61 × 48.4 cm (24 × 19 1/16 in.). Gift of Steven Heller and Karrie Jacobs, 1993-53-83.

Terry Forman (American, b. 1950) of Fireworks Graphics Collective (San Francisco, California, USA) for Prairie Fire Organizing Committee (Chicago, Illinois, USA) and the John Brown AntiKlan Committee (USA). *Build a Wall of Resistance,* 1984. Screenprint. 61 × 45.9 cm (24 × 18 1/16 in.). Gift of Steven Heller and Karrie Jacobs, 1993-53-32.

Terry Forman (American, b. 1950) of Fireworks Graphics Collective (San Francisco, California, USA). *U.S. Out of Central America!,* ca. 1980. Screenprint. 61 × 46 cm (24 × 18 1/8 in.). Gift of Steven Heller and Karrie Jacobs, 1993-53-20.

Lucy Lippard (American, b. 1937) and Mike Glier (American, b. 1953). *RED PERIL: The Return of the Anti-Commies*, 1982. Lithograph. 56 × 43.3 cm (22 1/16 × 17 1/16 in.). Gift of Steven Heller and Karrie Jacobs, 1993-53-71.

Terry Forman (American, b. 1950) of Fireworks Graphics Collective (San Francisco, California, USA) for Prairie Fire Organizing Committee (Chicago, Illinois, USA). *Build a Wall of Resistance*, 1983. Lithograph. 56 × 40.7 cm (22 1/16 × 16 in.). Gift of Steven Heller and Karrie Jacobs, 1993-53-107.

hung with paintings by the great masters. The caption says, "I sold art." On the right is a fat man sucking on a cigar; a computer on his desk is spewing a printout of his clients: the Museum of Modern Art, the Guggenheim Museum, the National Endowment for the Arts. On his walls are collages made from broken record albums and objects like a Quaker Oats container. The caption says, "I sold 'fadism' as art."

Further down the fence is a more professionally made poster. Its headline says, "Unnatural Histories: Pea Brains." Below there is a blowup of a *Newsweek* cover: "The New Politics of Race." Running on top of the cover reproduction, there's the text of an article that pretends to be from that issue of *Newsweek*. It's about White House officials trying to formulate an appropriate response to a nineteenth-century study in which the cranial capacity of different races was measured by filling skull cavities with peas. The supposed study demonstrated that the skulls of black men could hold fewer peas.

The article says: "A senior White House official added, 'At first we thought we were in a no-win situation. If we denounce the study, we'll be accused of trashing Western culture and tradition, and if we support its findings, we'll be accused of being insensitive to blacks.'"

For a paragraph or two, the article seems stupid but plausible. Then as it progresses, its satirical message becomes more evident. White House officials also deny that "a pubic hair for every Coke" is George Bush's new campaign slogan. It becomes clear that this poster is a commentary on the inability of Congress or the media to effectively cope with the Clarence Thomas Supreme Court nomination. What isn't clear is the exact political viewpoint of the person who made the poster.

Political posters these days are rarely as predictable as they once were. Today it's difficult to distill one's political views down to an effective poster. Nothing is simple and clear. The posters of the sixties and seventies relied on a set of symbols—the peace sign, the dove, the clenched fist, the sign for female paired with the clenched fist, the altered flag—that made their messages blatant. There was little ambiguity in those graphics, just as there was little ambiguity in the politics of that period. The battle lines were clearly drawn.

Today's movement politics are very different. There is no one issue such as the Vietnam War to neatly identify the side. Posters still address the standard themes: peace, the environment, and social justice. But there are new themes as well. AIDS and the questions it raises about health care, sexuality, and the government's priorities in funding research have inspired a whole new category of angry graphics. And today's political posters seem less likely to be the recognizable output of a coherent movement and more likely to be an individual expression of outrage, the work of one angry person, or one angry person along with a few angry friends. It is as if the Reagan era's idealization of private enterprise has even affected the way people protest.

The one symbol that has emerged in the last decade, as powerful and recognizable as the icon of earlier decades, is the pink triangle paired with the equation SILENCE = DEATH. First pasted onto New York City's walls by a group of six gay men who called themselves the SILENCE = DEATH Project, the symbol was, in 1987, adopted and popularized by the AIDS Coalition to Unleash Power, ACT UP. It's directly inspired by the upside-down pink triangle that the Nazis required homosexuals to wear,

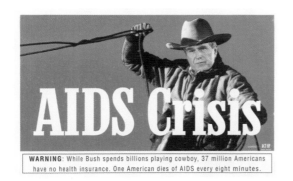

but in the way it assigns meaning to an abstract form, it's reminiscent of El Lissitzky's great constructivist political poster, "Beat the Whites with the Red Wedge." In that 1920 poster the artist used a red triangle to stand for the Bolsheviks and their cause.

In the book *AIDS DemoGraphics*, the authors, art critic Douglas Crimp and architect/artist Adam Rolston, document the graphics used by ACT UP and related organizations through a chronological account of AIDS protests. Of the SILENCE = DEATH logo, the authors write: "It is not merely what SILENCE = DEATH says, but also how it looks that gives it its particular force. The power of the equation under a triangle is the compression of its connotation into a logo, a logo so striking that you ultimately have to ask—if you don't already know—"What does that mean?"

Rolston, in an interview, has commented: "SILENCE = DEATH, it looked like a corporate logo, like some institution was speaking to me. It's the appropriation of the voice of authority. Like a trick."

Of all the political posterers, of all the participants in night discourse, the anti-AIDS activists are the most forceful and unambiguous. While others tend to obscure their meaning with awkward delivery, ACT UP and its spin-off collectives, Gran Fury (named for the Plymouth car model favored by undercover police in New York) and Gang, exploit the knowledge they've accumulated from daily exposure to advertising. They are in the business of generating anger as efficiently as possible. Notes Gran Fury member Loring McAlpin, "We are trying to fight for attention as hard as Coca-Cola fights for attention."

The best political graphics today exist on the cusp

of art and graphic design. The people responsible often see themselves as both artists and designers. The posters don't look like they were done to express the views of a client, but rather to express the viewpoint of the creator. The work doesn't exhibit the sort of cool professionalism typical of pro bono projects done by design firms. Because the designer and client are one and the same, the designer works without any emotional distance or imposed limitations.

It takes a small, young, committed group like Gran Fury to produce posters like "Sexism rears its unprotected head. Men use condoms or beat it. AIDS kills women." The poster features a color photograph of an erect penis. "We're not answerable to a government agency that would commission a public-service announcement and then say, 'Tone it down,'" explains McAlpin of Gran Fury.

On the other hand, organizations that lobby for left-of-center political causes have, since many of them started out as radical movements in the 1960s and early 1970s, grown large, mainstream, and cautious. Their approaches are safe, corporate, and designed to reach as wide an audience as possible. They have left the anger behind.

Barbara Kruger, one of the best-known American political artists, works in a style inspired by her years in magazine design. Her pieces appear on billboards and bus shelters funded by the Public Art Fund or other organizations in this country and abroad. In 1989 a poster she made for a major pro-choice march in Washington, D.C., was pasted onto the city's walls and fences. It shows a woman's face, divided in two lengthwise, one side a positive photographic image, the other side a negative

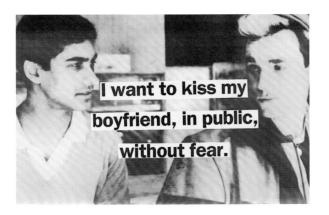

cheap art. *I want to kiss my boyfriend, in public, without fear*, ca. 1980. Photocopy. 28 × 43.3 cm (11 × 17 1/16 in.). Gift of Steven Heller and Karrie Jacobs, 1993-53-101.

Sabrina Jones (American, b. 1960). *Our Bodies / Our Choice*, 1990. Airbrush. 61 × 46 cm (24 × 18 1/8 in.). Gift of Steven Heller and Karrie Jacobs, 1993-53-105.

one. The type, white Futura on a red background, says, "Your body is a battleground. Support Legal Abortion, Birth Control and Women's Rights."

Kruger recalls, "When I first found out that there was going to be a march to Washington, I called NOW [National Organization of Women]. I said: 'Can I volunteer my services?' They never called me back. And then I called NARAL [National Abortion Rights Action League]. And they were nicer, a little hipper. But forget it. They just said: 'Well, we have someone that we use pro bono.' You know, ads with pictures of the Statue of Liberty . . . And finally I just got frustrated and I did it myself, and I and my students at the Whitney were out till five o'clock in the morning for about a week, putting those posters up."

Later that year a public-relations firm that operates in the art world approached NARAL. The firm offered to raise money for NARAL with an auction. They asked Kruger to create a poster for that auction. "I did another 'Your Body Is a Battleground' poster for them. The PR firm brought NARAL my image, and the people at NARAL said: 'It's too strong. We don't want to use it.' So I said: 'Could you please tell them that the Right is using pictures of fetuses? What is so strong?' It was a picture of a woman's face. What were they thinking? And finally they got through to Kate Michaelman [the president of NARAL] and she said, 'It's wonderful. Let's do it.'"

Kruger's poster was subsequently run in the Op-Ed section of the *New York Times*. However, the word "body" was deemed too strong for that newspaper's readers—too confrontational for day discourse—and the image was run with the words "You are a battleground."

Another battleground is New York City's East Village,

where Anton van Dalen, Eric Drooker and others have, like the WPA artists of the 1930s, developed a powerful, expressive style of graphic—their own version of social realism—in print and stencils that protest the injustices they see outside their doors. Their works deal with homelessness, police brutality, drugs and gentrification. The East Village, for a few years, was New York's up-and-coming fashionable neighborhood. Hip art galleries, coupled with real-estate development, attracted affluent, young residents to a poor, tough, troubled neighborhood. The East Village became a focal point for a great deal of grass-roots political activity. *World War 3*, a collectively edited, political comic book, is one product of East Village politics. In issue number fifteen, Seth Tobocman used a high-contrast, hard-edged drawing style to tell the story of a riot in Tompkins Square Park, a shabby urban park that became the stage for a long conflict between the homeless who camped in the park, the young anarchists who allied themselves with the homeless, and the New York City Police Department, which ultimately shut the park down. Often graphics done for *World War 3* become street posters, and street poster artists, in turn, publish their work in *World War 3*.

Another East Village collective called Bullet took over a vacant, city-owned building in the East Village and turned it into a home. When not struggling to connect sewage lines so they could have an indoor toilet, they set up a performance and exhibition space and once covered a whole wall on the street with bright, forceful posters on topics like AIDS and homelessness.

The last decade has produced some masters of political graphics, such as Kruger and Gran Fury. Another

Lady Pink (Ecuadorian, b. 1964) for
Bullet (New York, New York, USA). *This
Side Up*, 1991. Screenprint. Printed by
Lower East Side Print Shop, Inc. (New
York, New York, USA). 58.4 × 50.8 cm
(23 × 20 in.). Gift of Steven Heller and
Karrie Jacobs, 1993-53-118.

Anton van Dalen (Dutch and American,
b. 1938). *Concrete Crisis*, 1986.
Screenprint. Printed by Lower East
Side Print Shop, Inc. (New York, New
York, USA). 56 × 66 cm (22 1/16 × 26
in.). Gift of Steven Heller and Karrie
Jacobs, 1993-53-121.

Anton van Dalen (Dutch and American,
b. 1938). *Two-Headed Monster Destroys
Community*, 1983. Screenprint. Printed
by Lower East Side Print Shop, Inc.
(New York, New York, USA). 61.1 × 48.4
cm (24 1/16 × 19 1/16 in.). Gift of Steven
Heller and Karrie Jacobs, 1993-53-117.

leader is Robbie Conal, a Venice, California–based artist whose posters feature vicious caricatures of Bush, Quayle, Jessie Helms and other political figures. They are pasted up late at night in cities around the United States by dedicated volunteer brigades. The Guerrilla Girls, a New York–based collective of anonymous artists, have been protesting sexual and racial discrimination among museum and gallery curators for years. They have recently branched out to address issues of war and censorship.

In San Francisco screen printer Jos Sances adjusts his style to match the issue. His works range from the crudely expressionistic "Piss Helms," to a colorful, cartoonish account of Colonel Sanders's audience with the pope, to a tense realism on a poster supporting improved benefits for schoolteachers. "Screen printing was a medium that could give me a voice," Sances wrote in the catalog for a retrospective of his work.

The roster above could go on and on, listing the skilled artists who are making political posters to vent their outrage and give them a sense that they are, in some way, effectively addressing the problems that anger them. And then there are those who have anger but fewer skills. The city's walls and utility poles are covered with the homemade posters that look the way such tracts have looked for decades. It's as if there is a style dictated by the use of the photocopier that is as coherent as any aesthetic from the world's famous design academies. Much of it is so raw and so ephemeral that it's hard to think about it as design. Xeroxed posters are often so gray that they almost seem as if they are a part of the poles to which they're affixed.

Design isn't the right word to categorize these flyers. They are more primitive than that, more a product of reflex. Posters are supposed to shout. But these little posters whisper. They are like the drug dealers who quietly list the names of their wares as you walk by; sometimes they speak so softly you can't be sure you heard anything at all. "Worship the yuppie god," murmurs one distributed by a person or organization called Mutant. As daytime discourse gets thinner and more banal, year by year, as fewer genuine sentiments or opinions are voiced by politicians, and bold political statements vanish from mainstream media, street posters are becoming the one medium in which controversial opinions can find a general audience. In China political posters are a way around official censorship. Here they sidestep a less official set of restrictions: those having to do with commercial expedience.

Political posters can be read as an expression of frustration from artists, designers and regular people trying to transform a political system that seems thoroughly insulated from individual action, a system that seems moribund. The posters that appear on the walls of our city in the night can spark real political debate. Maybe night discourse is the last form of political debate.

"You need to seize authority," says Gran Fury member McAlpin. "The way we started was with Xerox machines. If you're angry enough and have a Xerox machine and five or six friends who feel the same way, you'd be surprised how far you can go with that."

Collecting Posters

Gail S. Davidson

Cooper Hewitt, Smithsonian Design Museum

A museum collection changes over time, reflecting the shifting currents of taste and the priorities of the institution and its staff. In 2002, the name of Cooper Hewitt's department of Drawings and Prints was formally changed to Drawings, Prints, and Graphic Design (DPGD) in recognition of the growing number of posters and other printed ephemera in its collection and the museum's commitment to the acquisition and exhibition of these holdings. Told here is the story of how Cooper Hewitt's view of graphic design evolved from a marginal concern to an important focus. While not exhaustive, this survey of the poster collection singles out the larger or more important acquisitions over more than sixty-six years.

Posters are a relatively recent area of collecting for Cooper Hewitt, appearing to have begun in the main only in 1949.[1] As far as we know, the Hewitt sisters, founders of the Cooper Union Museum for the Arts of Decoration (today's Cooper Hewitt), never collected posters. There was no explicit plan for building the collection, and it seems from the early correspondence that the museum was somewhat ambivalent about graphic design.[2] The collection grew haphazardly, occasionally through the receipt of large unsolicited donations but more often through smaller unsolicited gifts or with individually targeted purchases. The current poster collection can be grouped in a few general categories: unsolicited works; designers' posters donated as part of larger, industrial design archives; objects that came via other museums; and objects solicited for exhibition.

The earliest significant acquisitions came as unsolicited gifts from Louise Clémencon, who contributed thirteen World War I and World War II posters in 1949, and Teresa Kilham, who donated circus posters ten years later.[3] Unfortunately, there are no records in the museum about how or why these two women acquired their posters, or why they chose Cooper Hewitt to be the recipient of their objects. Among the Clémencon gifts is a series of World War II recruitment posters enlisting young men to sign up for military service. Commissioned by the War Production Board and printed by the U.S. Government Printing Office, these were rather basic, straightforward compositions with a single figure appealing to future servicemen and their spouses or girlfriends, such as John Fazter's *You Knock 'Em Out, We'll Knock 'Em Down.* Note the seductive girl in a bathing suit drawn on the side of the plane.

With the 1963 acquisition of Edward McKnight Kauffer's archive, given by his wife Marion Dorn, the museum decidedly stepped into the arena of graphic design.[4] The collection of Edward McKnight Kauffer, among the most gifted of America's early-twentieth-century

John Falter (American, 1910–1982). Published by the War Production Board (Washington, D.C., USA). *You Knock 'Em Out . . .* , 1942. Lithograph. Printed by U.S. Government Printing Office (Washington D.C., USA). 102 × 72.4 cm (40 3/16 × 28 1/2 in.). Gift of Louise Clémencon, 1949-108-12.

graphic designers, covers his work in London (from 1915 until 1939) and New York (from 1940 until his death in 1954). Kauffer is known for having integrated aspects of cubism and modern typography into his graphic work. In London, he became known initially for his London Underground posters. His early posters advertised travel destinations like the striking 1915 *Oxhey Woods*, which reflects his admiration for Ludwig Hohlwein, as well as Cézanne, van Gogh, Gauguin, and the Fauves. But his 1937 poster for the *New Architectural Exhibition of the Elements of Modern Architecture*, with its cubist-inspired forms and overlapping diagonal text, is more typical of his designs in the 1930s.[5] The extensive Kauffer archive also includes posters that the designer made in America for his chief client, American Airlines. The over thirty posters date between 1946 and 1953, and are more formulaic when compared with his English graphics, presenting one iconic motif or figure to represent a city or country. *American Airlines, All Europe* from ca. 1948, is one of the most compact and compelling of this series. A collection like this tells the story of a graphic designer's entire career.

In 1976, the museum acquired an archive of the Czech graphic designer Ladislav Sutnar, which included posters, but remained under the care of the Smithsonian Design Library. The next significant acquisition came in 1979 with

Edward McKnight Kauffer (American, active England, 1890–1954) for Underground Electric Railways Company (London, England). *Oxhey Woods*, 1915. Lithograph. 75.9 × 50.5 cm (29 7/8 × 19 7/8 in.). Gift of Mrs. E. McKnight Kauffer, 1963-39-13.

Edward McKnight Kauffer (American, active England, 1890–1954) for the MARS Group (England). *The Elements of Modern Architecture*, 1937. Lithograph, red-ink stamped. 76.2 × 50.6 cm (30 × 19 15/16 in.). Gift of Mrs. E. McKnight Kauffer, 1963-39-97.

Edward McKnight Kauffer (American, active England, 1890–1954) for American Airlines (USA). *American Airlines, All Europe*, ca. 1948. Lithograph. 24.1 × 17.7 cm (9 1/2 × 6 15/16 in.). Gift of Mrs. E. McKnight Kauffer, 1963-39-164-f.

the donation of forty psychedelic posters gifted by Mr. and Mrs. Leslie J. Schreyer. These comprise a stunning group of objects: thirty-two posters for the Fillmore Auditorium in San Francisco by Lee Conklin, Bonnie MacLean, and Wes Wilson, and eight works for the Avalon Ballroom, also in San Francisco, including three by Victor Moscoso and all dating between 1966 and 1971. A horizontal poster by David Singer, *Fillmore West/Closing Week* (1971), is distinguished from the more well-known vertical compositions by Wilson and Moscoso, and recalls the Jugendstil/Secessionist graphics that proved significant inspiration for graphic designers during this period. Mr. Schreyer donated 125 additional Fillmore posters in 1981. In a collaborative gesture, Cooper Hewitt donated the majority of the gift to the Victoria and Albert Museum.[6] Nowadays, the museum is very proud of its psychedelic graphics, which are considered landmarks in American design and culture.

While the first Schreyer gift was being processed, the museum began a campaign to acquire more recent posters for the collection, kicking off with an exhibition called *Ephemeral Images: Recent American Posters* (January 29–March 29, 1981). This project was undertaken by the museum's in-house graphic designer at the time, Heidi Humphrey, with Stephen Doyle, before he joined with

David Singer (American, b. 1941) for Bill Graham (American, 1931–1991). *Fillmore West / Closing Week*, 1971. Offset lithograph. 55.8 × 70.7 cm (21 15/16 × 27 13/16 in.). Gift of Mr. and Mrs. Leslie J. Schreyer, 1979-34-20.

Dan Friedman (American, 1945–1995) of Anspach Grossman Portugal (New York, New York, USA) for Citibank (USA). *Citicorp Center*, ca. 1980. Lithograph. 121.8 × 81.8 cm (47 15/16 × 32 3/16 in.). Gift of Various Donors, 1981-29-19.

Armin Hofmann (Swiss, b. 1920) for Stadttheater (Basel, Switzerland). *1965 / 66 Season Poster*, 1965. Offset lithograph. 128 × 90 cm (50 3/8 × 35 7/16 in.). Gift of Ken Friedman, 1997-19-144.

William Drenttel to form Drenttel Doyle Partners. The aim was to solicit posters from the graphic design community and choose between fifty and seventy-five of these works to exhibit in the museum's ground-floor gallery. Of the one thousand posters that were submitted to the museum, about half were officially acquired. Major designers whose names were known to the design public—such Milton Glaser, Ivan Chermayeff, Seymour Chwast, and Saul Bass—were represented as well as the younger generation of graphic designers, including Dan Friedman. Friedman was working at Anspach, Grossman, Portugal, Inc., when the firm secured the account for the new Citicorp identity. He designed Citicorp's logo and other key elements of the brand campaign. His poster *Citicorp Center,* advertising Citicorp as a venue for cultural entertainment, owes much to his teacher Armin Hofmann, whose poster *Stadttheater Basel 1965–66* seems to have served as a model. Friedman's own copy of Hofmann's poster turned up in the Dan Friedman Collection donation in 1997.[7]

Also included among the 500-odd posters selected for acquisition before and following the 1981 poster exhibition was a series of posters by the designer Ken White (1935–1985), who served as art director for IBM in the 1970s. Using typography and illustration, White promoted values that IBM projected both inside and

outside the firm: an emphasis on bold thinking; imagination; individual creativity; and conservation of resources, as in *IBM/Suggest!* Reducing the visual content to a single image and contracting the message to one word or a provocative statement, White's work reflects the powerful influence of Paul Rand on the design culture of IBM.

In an effort to document poster achievements beyond North America and Western Europe, Cooper Hewitt curators acquired eight Soviet posters, including a poster by Valentina Kulagina (11902–1987), in 1992, followed by thirteen Cuban posters in 1994. One of the most eye-catching of the Cuban works is a poster by Luis Vega de Castro, who designed film posters for the Cuban Institute of Cinematographic Art and Industry. *El dominio del fuego* (*The Domain of Fire*) advertises the 1972 Cuban showing of the award-winning Soviet film of that title. The poster's colorful palette belies the rather ordinary propagandistic storyline based on the career of the Soviet engineer Sergei Korolev (name changed to Bashkirtsev in the film), who created the rocket that launched *Sputnik* into orbit in 1957 and that sent the first man in space. The poster presents on a blue ground, an orange and blue hand cupping clouds of yellow and orange smoke from which a blue, white, green, and orange rocket triumphantly blasts upward. A conceptual illustration such as this is characteristic of Cuban posters of this time.

Ken White (American, 1935–1985) for IBM (USA). *IBM / Suggest!*, ca. 1980. Screenprint. 53 × 38.2 cm (20 7/8 × 15 1/16 in.). Gift of Various Donors, 1981-29-440.

Valentina N. Kulagina (Russian, 1902–1987) for Main Administration for Literary and Publishing Affairs (Russia). *International Women Workers Day*, 1930. Lithograph. Printed by Gosudarstvennoye Izdatelstvo [State Publishing House] (Russia). 108.3 × 71.6 cm (42 5/8 × 28 3/16 in.). Museum purchase through gift of George A. Hearn, 1992-164-1.

Luis Vega De Castro (Cuban, b. 1944). El Dominio del Fuego [*The Taming of Fire*], 1972. Screenprint. 75.9 × 50.8 cm (29 7/8 × 20 in.). Museum purchase from Smithsonian Institution Collections Acquisition Program Fund and through gift of Anonymous Donors, 1994-65-13.

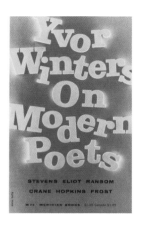

Sometimes new acquisitions come our way from other museums. In 1996, colleagues at the Museum of Modern Art recommended to a donor that Cooper Hewitt be offered an opportunity to review a collection of rare Spanish Civil War posters. These had been gathered by journalist William Mangold, who worked for the *New Republic* in Spain during the war. Thirty posters representing campaigns of the Popular Front were selected depicting a range of messages—calling people to work, showing solidarity with the soldiers and their families, and denouncing fascism. ¡Esto es el Fascismo! *(This is Fascism!)* . . . , by Antonio López Padial, commissioned by the International Red Aid, displays an imposing black swastika enclosing four war photographs labeled "misery," "destruction," "persecution," and "death." Blood spews from corpses and pools at the feet of the viewer, making the brutality even more horrific.

When the museum hired writer and graphic designer Ellen Lupton as a curator in 1992, it set the course for future graphic design acquisitions. Between 1996 and 2014, Lupton curated several graphic design exhibitions for Cooper Hewitt, including *Mixing Messages: Graphic Design in Contemporary Culture* (1996), *Graphic Design in the Mechanical Age: Selections from the Merrill C. Berman Collection* (1999), *Graphic Design: Now in Production*

(2012), and now *How Posters Work*, all of which have led to poster acquisitions by gift or purchase. (Her participation in Cooper Hewitt's *Triennial* exhibitions from 2000 to the present has also led to acquisitions of graphic design material.) With Lupton's guidance, the Drawings and Prints Department collected and documented over a ten-year period from 1992 to 2002 hundreds of examples of graphic design. Posters and graphics by Michael Bierut, Paula Scher, Willi Kunz, and others entered the collection for the first time. These included antiwar and AIDS/HIV activism posters donated by Stephen Heller and Karrie Jacobs in 1993. A small monographic exhibition of work by Elaine Lustig Cohen in 1996 resulted in the acquisition of an important group of book covers and other modernist graphics from the 1960s.

A fortunate phone call came from Marion S. Rand, Paul Rand's widow, in 2002. She was moving from her modernist New Canaan house designed by her late husband and offered Cooper Hewitt the rare opportunity of selecting graphic design pieces from her collection of Paul Rand graphics. Excited about the prospect of this visit, DPGD curators drove up to Connecticut and returned with sixty-six objects, including thirty-two posters, one of which advertised a 1993 Richard Sapper exhibition at the Museum für Kunst und Gewerbe, Hamburg. This iconic

Antonio López Padial (Spanish, 1926–2011) for Socorro Rojo Internacional [International Red Aid]. ¡Esto es el fascismo! miseria . . . destrucción. . . persecución . . . y muerte [*This is Fascism! misery . . . destruction . . . persecution . . . and death*], ca. 1935. Lithograph. 100.3 × 70.7 cm (39 1/2 × 27 13/16 in.). Gift of William P. Mangold, 1997-21-10.

Elaine Lustig Cohen (American, b. 1927). Book Cover for *On Modern Poets*, by Yvor Winters, ca. 1959. Lithograph. 18.3 × 11.1 cm (7 3/16 × 4 3/8 in.). Gift of Tamar Cohen and Dave Slatoff, 1993-31-22.

Paul Rand (American, 1914–1996). *Richard Sapper Design*, 1993. Offset lithograph. 83.8 × 59.1 cm (33 × 23 1/4 in.). Gift of Marion S. Rand, 2002-11-25.

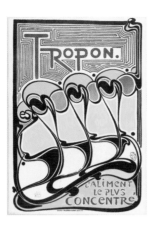

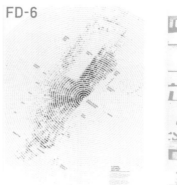

poster is an exception in Rand's work as it makes a pattern out of a design object, in this case Sapper's celebrated Tizio lamp, rather than geometric shapes, type, or logos.

A few isolated purchases in between 1997 and 2008 beefed up the collection in major areas. Two posters by Dagobert Peche supported Cooper Hewitt's collection of Wiener Werkstätte designs for textiles and wallpapers: Wiener Werkstätte Mode Stoffe Kunstgewerbe Messaustellungen (*Wiener Werkstätte Fashion, Textiles, and Decorative Arts Exhibition*), 1921; and his poster Spitzen der Wiener Werkstätte (*Lace of the Wiener Werkstätte*), ca. 1919. Herbert Matter's *Engelberg, Trübsee, Switzerland*, 1935, added a quintessential example of photomontage graphics to the collection. These posters are considered masterworks in the history of design.

Preparations for the museum's 2008 *Rococo: The Continuing Curve, 1730 to 2008,* exhibition coincided with Christie's sale of objects owned by New York dealer Historical Design. This auction included the large-size example of the celebrated Henry van de Velde poster for Tropon that the DPGD curators had been coveting for some time. Fortunately, the poster appeared early in the sale, and the museum was able to acquire it for much less than the dealer's former asking price. This icon of art nouveau design was displayed in the Rococo exhibition

and is one of the most recognizable and influential objects in the museum's poster collection. In 2008, the museum was able to acquire a film poster by the Stenberg Brothers, *Symphony of a Big City*, which was on the market at a New York dealer. Fortunately, by combining funds from different sources, the museum was able to make the purchase.

Between 2009 and 2010, Cooper Hewitt solicited graphic design examples from China, which had become a major hub of contemporary graphic design. The designer Bi Xue Feng responded with an offer of two works for the collection, one of which is *Bridges on the Seine*. The department also acquired examples of infographics with a series of six posters called *Flocking Diplomats,* by Catalogtree (Joris Maltha and Daniel Gross). In each poster, data is translated into a graphic that maps the parking violations of diplomats in New York City during a week of United Nations meetings. The sixth poster in this group shows the illegal parking locations, which span concentrically from the UN headquarters to the outer reaches of Brooklyn and the upper Bronx.

Among the largest of the museum's poster gifts— numbering 158 film and exhibition posters—is the 2009–2010 donation coming from Sara and Marc Benda of the Friedman Benda Gallery. In an interview about his poster collecting rationale, Marc Benda said that he began

Henry van de Velde (Belgian, 1863–1957) for Tropon Werke Company (Mülheim am Rhein, Germany). Tropon est l'aliment le plus concentré [*Tropon, the Most Concentrated Food Supplement],* 1898. Lithograph. Printed by Hollerbaum & Schmidt (Berlin, Germany). 111.8 × 77.5 cm (44 × 30 1/2 in.), Museum purchase through gift of Mr. and Mrs. Lee S. Ainslie III, Marilyn Friedman, and Nancy Marks; General Acquisitions Fund; Drawings & Prints Council Fund, 2007-2-1.

Catalogtree (Arnhem, Netherlands): Joris Maltha (Dutch, b. 1974) and Daniel Gross (German, b. 1973). Geocoding and programming by Lutz Issler (German). *FD6: Flocking Diplomats New York: Locations, 1998–2005,* 2008. Offset lithograph. Printed by PlaatsMaken (Arnhem, Netherlands). 100.2 × 68.9 cm (39 7/16 × 27 1/8 in.). Gift of Joris Maltha and Daniel Gross, 2009-30-6.

Bi Xuefeng (Chinese, b. 1963). *The Bridges on the Seine*, 2005. Offset lithograph. 101.3 × 70 cm (39 7/8 × 27 9/16 in.). Gift of Bi Xuefeng, 2010-30-2.

collecting posters as a teenager, buying what appealed to him. He did not have a plan and had limited funds, but one purchase would invariably lead to the next. As he started acquiring objects, he noticed how a poster for the same film would be designed so differently from one country to the next. It is fascinating to compare the visual concept behind Hans Hillmann's poster Panzerkreuzer Potemkin *(Battleship Potemkin)* for the 1966 German rerelease of Sergei Eisenstein's 1925 film with that of Stanislaw Zamecznik's for the same film dating a year later in Poland. It is hard to imagine a more minimalist design than Hans Hillmann's striking composition. One white rectangle floats on a black ground. Only two black tubular shapes dangle down from the upper right to the lower left above a rectangular gray and white text box in the lower center. This stark image is threatening even if you have no knowledge of the film's plot, but once knowing the story of the mutiny on the *Potemkin* and the slaughter of sailors and their revolutionary supporters on shore, one recognizes the black forms as canons shooting overboard from the battleship at the Russian authorities called to suppress the rebellion in Odessa on June 14, 1905. Stanizlaw Zamecznik's poster for the Polish release is disturbing in a different way. It actually shows the conflict taking place against the background of stairs, with police

on horseback and the revolutionaries running down the wide stairway. The solarized image makes the figures seem already obliterated in the conflict. The red vertical bar at the upper left is echoed by the blood spilled below.

Andrew Blauvelt and Ellen Lupton's 2012–2014 exhibition *Graphic Design: Now in Production,* organized by Walker Art Center and Cooper Hewitt, introduced many new designers to the public and to the Drawings, Prints, and Graphic Design curator. Philippe Apeloig, whose work was included in this show, has become a major interest of the department. The museum acquired five posters, including Le Havre, Patrimoine mondial de l'humanité (*Le Havre, World Heritage*), designed in 2006 to commemorate UNESCO's designation of the city as a World Heritage Site. It was of particular interest to DPGD, whose curator had earmarked for acquisition posters integrating architecture and typography.

In the same year the museum went back to Paula Scher to update her representation in the collection. In addition to posters collected for the 1996 exhibition *Mixing Messages*, a targeted goal was a drawing for one of her key projects. Scher's assistants went through boxes and boxes of her archive material before they found a revealing sketch laying out a poster/flyer for the Public Theater that the museum had acquired earlier. This lucky donation is a

Hans Hillmann (German, 1925–2014) for Neue Filmkunst (Germany). Panzerkreuzer Potemkin [*Battleship Potemkin*], 1966. Screenprint. Printed by Druckerei Wittig (Berlin, Germany). 83.8 × 59.3 cm (33 × 23 3/8 in.). Gift of Sara and Marc Benda, 2010-21-76.

Stanislaw Zamecznik (Polish, 1909–1971). Pancernik Potiomkin [*Battleship Potemkin*], 1967. Offset lithograph. 78.2 × 56.4 cm (30 13/16 × 22 3/16 in.). Gift of Sara and Marc Benda, 2010-21-27.

Paula Scher (American, b. 1948) for the Public Theater (New York, New York, USA). *Sketch for Public Theater Flyer*, 1994. Colored pencil and graphite. 27.8 × 21.6 cm (10 15/16 × 8 1/2 in.). Gift of Paula Scher.

Paula Scher (American, b. 1948) for the Public Theater (New York, New York, USA). *Simpatico*, 1994. Offset lithograph. 115.7 × 75.4 cm (45 9/16 × 29 11/16 in.) Gift of Paula Scher, 1996-88-13.

good example of how the museum has been focusing on the design process by acquiring objects that illustrate the evolution of a designer's thinking when creating an object.

During the past several years the museum has also gained the support of the legendary graphic design collector Merrill C. Berman, who has assembled perhaps the largest collection of avant-garde and contemporary posters and graphic design materials in the United States. Berman has worked with Cooper Hewitt on the acquisition of Piet Zwart's iconic poster ITF: Internationale Tentoonstelling op Filmgebied (International Film Exhibition) from his collection and has recently donated six Soviet posters, some of which are included in the present book and exhibition, and one magazine cover by the painter/textile designer Liubov Popova, *Musical New Land, N. 10,* to supplement the Soviet material already in the museum's collection. *How Posters Work* has added dozens of new posters to the collection representing work by emerging graphic designers from around the world to display along with its pre-twenty-first–century posters.

The Drawings, Prints, and Graphic Design department continues to reach out to young graphic designers internationally for donations of their posters and other ephemera, just as it encourages collectors to donate historical and contemporary objects and works with graphic design dealers to make affordable purchases. The relatively new field of digital design has presented different opportunities for collecting. Thus far, the museum has acquired digital corporate identity projects by Stefan Sagmeister and animations by Philippe Apeloig. We will have to see what happens to the field of poster design: will digital design wipe out the need for posters in hard copy, or will they become totally digital design objects? In any case, the department, reenergized by the museum's reopening in December 2014, is moving into the future with its search of the most innovative, up-to-the-minute graphic design.

All posters are from the collection
of Cooper Hewitt, Smithsonian
Design Museum, except as noted.
Commentary by Ellen Lupton,
except as noted.

Posters

Focus the Eye

In the early twentieth century, the German Plakatstil or "poster style" movement created arresting advertisements that highlighted single objects. Designers employed heavy lines and flat colors to focus the eye on the commercial goods of the day—from hats, shoes, and pens to matches and cigarettes. In Lucian Bernhard's poster *Adler* (1909–1910), sturdy letterforms match the heft of the illustration.

Bernhard's poster is not as simple as it might seem, however. He has created a sense of depth by making the typewriter overlap the product name. A black and red frame directs our attention to the text, and the outline around the letters gives them dimension and focus. The main lettering and the sheet of paper in the typewriter are the composition's brightest elements, providing a clear and uncontested anchor.

Bernhard's design techniques remain commonly used today. Book covers, advertisements, websites, and packages often establish a clear point of focus. Designers use line, color, contrast, and placement to show viewers where to look first. A basic way to make someone notice an image is to make it big and put it in the middle of a space. Symmetry is one of design's oldest and most reliable conventions. The human body is symmetrical from side to side (bilateral symmetry), while flowers are symmetrical around multiple axes (radial symmetry).

Although symmetrical arrangements are inherently balanced, strict symmetry can yield dull results. A centered picture or a centered line of text can feel as dead and static as letters carved on a tombstone. Bernhard chose to push his typewriter off to one side, creating diagonal movement, but he centered the product name at the top. Many Plakatstil posters employ a similar mix of centered and off-centered elements to create compositions that have a clear focus while also conveying a sense of movement.

In José Bardasano's Spanish Civil War poster, a glass of water looms above the tiny fighters on the ground, acquiring monumental stature from the exaggerated shift in scale. Light and shadow intensify the drama, while the angle of the glass breaks the poster's dominant symmetry. The hand-drawn text conveys movement through both its form and placement.

The U.S. Office of War Information's poster *Food is a Weapon* (1942) centers our gaze on a still life depicting the aftermath of an ordinary meal. A story unfolds as we read the poster from top to bottom. A meal has been eaten, and no scrap has been wasted. Dramatic lighting heightens attention on everyday objects. The napkin and water glass interrupt the symmetry, throwing a diagonal movement across the surface. Without that break, the poster would feel cold and stagnant.

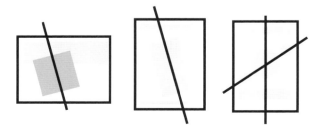

Lucian Bernhard (German, 1883–1972) for Adler (Germany). *Adler*, 1909–10. Lithograph. Printed by Hollerbaum & Schmidt (Berlin, Germany). 45.9 × 58.7 cm (18 1/16 × 23 1/8 in.). Gift of the Eric Kellenberger Collection, Switzerland, and museum purchase from General Acquisitions Endowment, 2005-12-2.

When Lucian Bernhard produced this poster in 1909, typewriters were an advanced technology. Bernhard saw the image of the typewriter itself—with its potential for speed and efficiency—as an effective way to advertise the product. His poster embodies the simplicity of the Plakatstil ("poster style"), with its bold, flat planes of color and outlined letters.—*Caitlin Condell*

José Bardasano Baos (Spanish, 1910–1979) for Army Health Service (Spain). El agua en malas condiciones produce mas bajas que la metralla [*Poisoned Water Causes More Casualties than the Shrapnel*], 1937. Lithograph. 54.2 × 40.8 cm (21 5/16 × 16 1/16 in.). Gift of William P. Mangold, 1997-21-15.

During the Spanish Civil War (1936–1939), defenders of the democratically elected Spanish Republic promoted the importance of health and hygiene. The canted water glass defies gravity and creates dynamism.

Unknown designer for the Office of War Information (Washington, D.C., USA). *Food is a Weapon*, 1943. Lithograph. 57.8 × 41.6 cm (22 3/4 × 16 3/8 in.). Gift of Unknown Donor, 1987-24-23.

This poster shines a spotlight on a plate of chicken bones, pulling drama from mundane circumstances. The arresting headline heightens the emotional intensity.

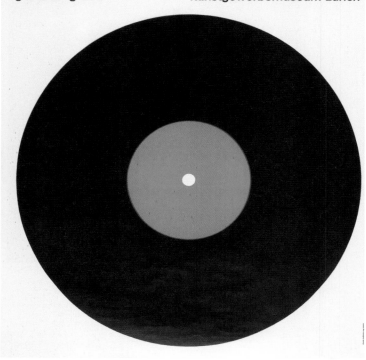

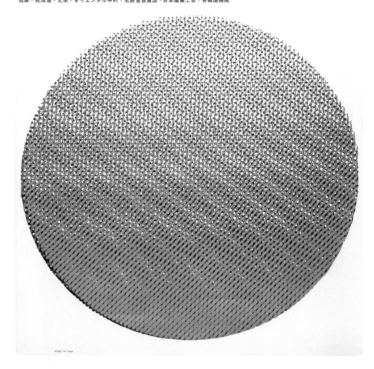

Gottlieb Soland (Swiss, 1928–2011) for Kunstgewerbemuseum (Zürich, Switzerland). Grammo-Grafik [*Recorded Music Graphics*], 1957. Lithograph. 100.2 × 70.3 cm (39 7/16 × 27 11/16 in.). Gift of Sara and Marc Benda, 2009-12-19.

Swiss designers in the 1950s and 1960s used gridded layouts, sans serif typefaces, and stark images. Italian designer Bruno Munari may have had this famous poster in mind when he mentioned "phonograph records" in his essay "Posters with a Central Image" (1966).

Tai Tsuge (Japanese). *Nippon Good Design Show*, 1963. Lithograph. 102.5 × 68.8 cm (40 3/8 × 27 1/16 in.). Gift of Sara and Marc Benda, 2009-12-20.

The large ball shape is centered toward the bottom of the poster, but the typography is set flush left. This is a common—even prototypical— layout for modern posters.

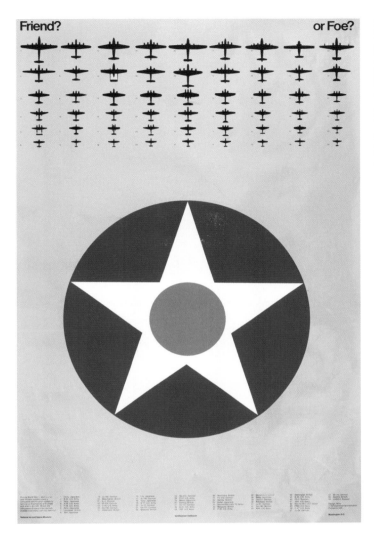

James Miho (American, b. 1933) and Tomoko Miho (American, 1931–2012) for Smithsonian National Air and Space Museum (Washington, D.C., USA). *Friend? Or Foe?*, 1976. Screenprint. 91.7 × 61.2 cm (36 1/8 × 24 1/8 in.). Gift of Various Donors, 1981-29-153.

During World War II, civilian and military spotters learned to distinguish enemy aircraft from allied planes. This poster shows the alphabet of silhouettes that spotters learned to recognize. A military emblem dominates the center.

Dan Friedman (American, 1945–1995). *Moon*, ca. 1988. Offset lithograph. 63.5 × 48.4 cm (25 × 19 1/16 in.). Gift of Ken Friedman, 1997-19-198.

This poster emphasizes the moon and makes the sun a small and distant object.

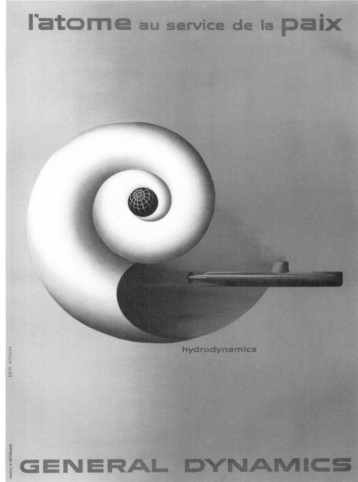

Erik Nitsche (Swiss, 1908–1998) for
General Dynamics Corporation (USA).
Atoms for Peace, General Dynamics,
1955–6. Offset lithographs. Printed
by Lithos R. Marsens (Lausanne,
Switzerland). Approx. 133 × 96.5
cm (52 3/8 in. × 38 in.) (each). Gift
of Arthur Cohen and Daryl Otte in
memory of Bill Moggridge, 2013-42-
8, -9, -11, -12.

Erik Nitsche had an unusual design
challenge at General Dynamics: to
convince a fearful public that atomic
energy could be used for the benefit
of society through research and
technological advancement, without
revealing the details of their top
secret projects. His poster campaign
Atoms for Peace melds influences
from modernist art with scientific
imagery to evoke a dynamic,
innovative, and peaceful future.
—*Caitlin Condell*

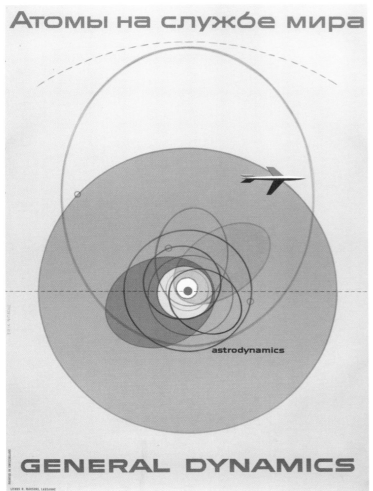

Equal Opportunity | Color Blind

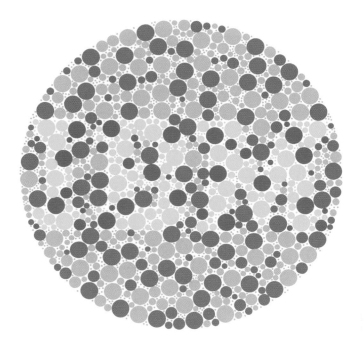

Yusaku Kamekura (Japanese, 1915–1997). *Soul and Material Things, ICSID 1973*, Kyoto, 1973. Offset lithograph. Printed by Toppan Printing Co., Ltd. (Japan). 103.2 × 72.7 cm (40 5/8 × 28 5/8 in.). Gift of Unknown Donor, 1980-32-1237.

Graphic designer Yusaku Kamekura was a chief organizer of the 1973 World Industrial Design Conference (ICSID) in Kyoto, on the topic of "Soul and Material Things." In his poster for the event, a tiny cube—defined by the conference initials—occupies a vast, optically activated sphere.

Ken White (American, 1935–1985) for IBM (New York, New York, USA). *Equal Opportunity / Color Blind*, 1974. Screenprint. 53.5 × 38.1 cm (21 1/16 × 15 in.). Gift of Various Donors, 1981-29-455.

The characters "IBM" are hiding in a swarm of colored dots. Created by in-house designer Ken White for an internal campaign devoted to IBM's equal opportunity policy, the poster features colors that people with color blindness have difficulty distinguishing.—*Rebekah Pollock*

Shiro Shita Saori (Japanese, b. 1990). *The Core*, 2014. Digital print. 103 × 72.8 cm (40 9/16 × 28 11/16 in.). Gift of Shiro Shita Saori, 2014-35-4.

Japanese posters with a big circle in the center are often nodding to the country's flag, with its red circle on a white ground. As Bruno Munari wrote, "the disc itself is a form that the eye finds it hard to escape from." Commenting on this tradition, Shiro Shita Saori's poster repeats the word "JAPAN" six times against a black ground. The central black circle that crowds the text is filled with thin, white concentric circles, further drawing the eye to the center—or, as Munari would say, "hitting you in the eye."—*Caitlin Condell*

Felix Pfäffli (Swiss, b. 1986) for Südpol (Kriens, Switzerland). *Future Islands*, 2014. Risograph. 42 × 29.4 cm (16 9/16 × 11 9/16 in.). Gift of Felix Pfäffli, 2015-3-4.

A circular void dominates this poster for a concert by Future Islands. The blurred edges of the poster's empty center turn the white of the paper into a ravenous, almost destructive source of light and focus.

Overwhelm the Eye

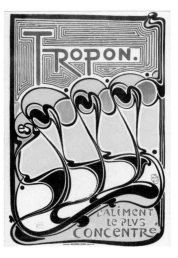

Henry van de Velde (Belgian, 1863–1957) for Tropon Werke Company (Mülheim am Rhein, Germany). Tropon est l'aliment le plus concentré [*Tropon, the Most Concentrated Food Supplement*], 1898. Lithograph. Printed by Hollerbaum & Schmidt (Berlin, Germany). 111.8 × 77.5 cm (44 × 30 1/2 in.), Museum purchase through gift of Mr. and Mrs. Lee S. Ainslie III, Marilyn Friedman, and Nancy Marks; General Acquisitions Fund; Drawings & Prints Council Fund, 2007-2-1.

In Henry van de Velde's 1898 advertisement for Tropon, extravagant curves overwhelm the poster's surface, and an intricate maze surrounds the product name. The poster advertises a food made from processed egg whites; perhaps such an abstract product warrants this abstract presentation. Van de Velde, a proponent of the international Jugendstil or art nouveau movement, has left no space untouched by line, shape, and ornament. The poster engages the viewer in an optical experience rather than depicting a product or telling a story. Van de Velde and other designers of the era sought to lead the eye on restless journeys across the surfaces of posters, products, textiles, and architecture.

The psychedelic posters of the 1960s revived the organicism of Jugendstil and art nouveau. Bonnie MacLean, Victor Moscoso, Wes Wilson, and other designers of the era employed swirling lines and repeating forms to keep the viewer's eye in motion. Their hand-lettered text flouted traditional typographic values of legibility and uniformity.

Inspired by modern color theory, especially the work of former Bauhaus master Josef Albers, the designers of psychedelia often juxtaposed colors that compete for attention, challenging the urge to focus the eye. Colors that have different hues (such as red and green) yet are close in value (having a similar level of lightness or darkness) are said to "vibrate."[1] A shimmering effect occurs where the edges of these competing colors meet. Intensely colored inks amplify the effect, distracting the eye with visual noise. The line and color in these posters tend to fill and flatten the surface rather than shaping and articulating it. Here, modernist ideals of flush-left type, open "white space," rational grids, and intellectual concepts give way to the rush of immediate sensation. Psychedelic posters, produced as souvenirs for concerts and events, were graphic analogues for the experience of music, sex, and drugs.

Designers in the twenty-first century have used new tools and reference points to address the thirst for visual sensation. Inspired by doodles, graffiti, and randomized and automated drawing processes, designers have created warped and layered spaces where lines and forms overlap and interconnect, confounding a viewer's attempt to pin down a stable structure or compact message. Fluid, interpenetrating surfaces appear in the works of Ralph Schraivogel, Michiel Schuurman, Felix Pfäffli, and Sulki & Min. Reaching beyond the visual "high" of psychedelia, these designs generate graphic worlds whose edgeless planes and fractal-like depth operate across multiple scales, from macro to micro.

Vibrating colors create visual noise where the two edges meet. The colors have sharply different hues but are similar in value (light and dark).

Victor Moscoso (Spanish and American, b. 1936). *Junior Wells*, 1966. Offset lithograph. 51 × 36.2 cm (20 1/16 × 14 1/4 in.). Gift of Mr. and Mrs. Leslie J. Schreyer, 1979-34-37.

Victor Moscoso (Spanish and American, b. 1936) for Neon Rose (San Francisco, California, USA). *Chambers Brothers Band, Neon Rose #12*, 1967. Offset ithograph. Printed by Graphic Arts of Marin (California, USA) and Cal Litho (California, USA). 51 × 36 cm (20 1/16 × 14 3/16 in.). Gift of Sara and Marc Benda, 2009-12-23.

From 1957 to 1959, Victor Moscoso attended Yale School of Art, where he studied color theory (including vibrating colors) with former Bauhaus master Josef Albers. Working in California in the 1960s, Moscoso produced *Chambers Brothers Band, Neon Rose #12* for his own poster company, Neon Rose. To design the poster, he selected a photograph of a model wearing sunglasses from a magazine. He hand-sketched intricate lettering inside the frames of the glasses and then used a color palette of pink, orange, and blue to produce a vibrating effect. He employed a theory from modern art to transform the experience of poster design.
—Caitlin Condell

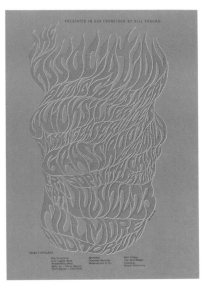

Bonnie MacLean (American, b. 1939) for Bill Graham (American, 1931–1991). *Jim Kweskin / Jug Band*, 1967. Offset lithograph. 58.2 × 36 cm (22 15/16 × 14 3/16 in.). Gift of Mr. and Mrs. Leslie J. Schreyer, 1979-34-9.

Wes Wilson (American, b. 1937) for Bill Graham (American, 1931–1991). *The Association*, 1966. Offset lithograph. 51 × 33.8 cm (20 1/16 × 13 5/16 in.). Gift of Mr. and Mrs. Leslie J. Schreyer, 1979-34-25.

Milton Glaser (American, b. 1929) for Columbia Records (New York, New York, USA). *Dylan*, 1966. Offset lithograph. 84 × 55.9 cm (33 1/16 × 22 in.). Gift of Richard Kusack, 2007-24-1.

Inspired in part by psychedelic posters, Milton Glaser used swirling colors to depict the creative mind of Bob Dylan. Glaser's poster became an enduring icon of the era.

Keith Allen Haring (American, 1958–1990) for Fun Gallery (New York, New York, USA). *Keith Haring at Fun Gallery*, 1983. Offset lithograph. 74.3 × 58.4 cm (29 1/4 × 23 in.). Gift of Ken Friedman, 1997-19-260.

In the early 1980s, Keith Haring became famous for a series of chalk drawings found on empty subway station advertising placards throughout the city. This and other work, which included brightly colored tarp paintings and sculptures, was influenced heavily by New York's burgeoning graffiti culture. In 1983, Haring was invited to exhibit his work at Fun Gallery, a favored hangout among the East Village art scene. His poster design for the show reveals the artist's unique ability to turn simple two-color line drawings into complex, visually cacophonous illustrations that communicated powerful messages. Interconnected human figures compete with zig-zags and spirals for the viewer's attention. The poster captivates the eye in its maze of lines.—*Andrew Gardner*

In 1975 Swiss graphic designer Niklaus Troxler founded the Willisau Jazz Festival, which he directed until 2009. His series of posters for the festival represents an ongoing study in design process, as Troxler explored diverse means to create letterforms outside the norms of typography and typefaces. As variations on a theme, the posters reflect on the process of jazz itself.

Niklaus Troxler (Swiss, b. 1947) for Jazz Festival Willisau (Willisau, Switzerland). *Jazz Willisau*. Offset lithographs. 128.1 × 90.6 cm (50 7/16 × 35 11/16 in.) (each). Gift of Niklaus Troxler, 2009-3-1, -15, -14, -8, -10, -6, -5.

Clockwise from top: *Charles Gayle Solo*, 2009; *Eskelin, Han Bennink*, 2009; *Carlos Actis Dato Quartet*, 2000; *The Ellery Eskelin Trio*, 2007; *Max Nagl, Otto Lechner, Bradley Jones*, 2007. Opposite page: *Marty Erlich Quartet*, 2006; Der Rote Bereich [*The Red Range*], 2008.

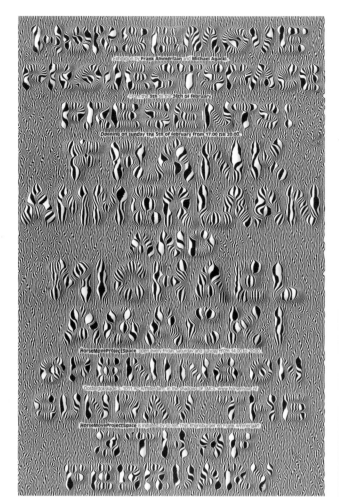

Michiel Schuurman (Dutch, b. 1974). *HorseMoveProjectSpace Presents: Frank Ammerlaan and Michael Agacki,* 2008. Offset lithograph. 118 × 73 cm (46 7/16 × 28 3/4 in.). Gift of Michiel Schuurman, 2008-22-4.

Michiel Schuurman (Dutch, b. 1974). *HorseMoveProjectSpace and Deveemvloer Present: Paraat 3,* 2007. Offset lithograph. 117.3 × 73 cm (46 3/16 × 28 3/4 in.). Gift of Michiel Schuurman, 2008-22-2.

In this series of posters, waves of linear distress engulf core typographic forms. The designer has used software tools in an unexpected way to produce an optical overload. The letterforms have no clear center point, dissolving both inward and outward to congest the field of vision.

Ralph Schraivogel (Swiss, b. 1960).
Cinema Afrika Filmtage [*African
Film Festival*], 2006. Screenprint.
Printed by Sérigraphie Uldry AG
(Hinterkappelen, Switzerland). 128 ×
90.3 cm (50 3/8 × 35 9/16 in.). Gift of
Ralph Schraivogel, 2007-15-3.

Swiss graphic designer Ralph
Schraivogel is known for his
astonishing posters for cultural
institutions, each one resulting
from intensive visual exploration.
The linear patterns that radiate
from the words "Cinema Afrika"
resemble topographic lines on a
map. Concentric lines engulf this
edgeless, borderless landscape,
leaving planes and boundaries
uncertain.

Ralph Schraivogel (Swiss, b. 1960). Schule für Gestaltung Bern [*School of Design Bern*], 1998. Screenprint. Printed by Sérigraphie Uldry AG (Hinterkappelen, Switzerland). 100 × 70.6 cm (39 3/8 × 27 13/16 in.). Gift of Ralph Schraivogel, 2007-15-1.

Flat patterns of ribbons and dots become a boiling landscape whose deformed surfaces suggest both motion and depth.

Ralph Schraivogel (Swiss, b. 1960). Design Centrum Ceské Republiky [*Design Center Czech Republic*], 2002. Screenprint. 84.6 × 60 cm (33 5/16 × 23 5/8 in.). Gift of Ralph Schraivogel, 2007-15-2.

Warped typography creates the illusion of three dimensions as the text winds its way through a strange tangle of tubular forms. With just three colors, Ralph Schraivogel has achieved a remarkable range of material effects, from weightlessness to dense, solid opacity.

Christoph Niemann (German, active USA, b. 1970). *Sustainability*, 2007. Offset lithograph. Printed by Stora Enso (Helsinki, Finland). 28.4 × 86.7 cm (11 3/16 × 34 1/8 in.). Gift of William Drenttel and Jessica Helfand, 2008-7-3.

A pattern of squares and planes creates an illusion of impossibly stacked cubes. Christoph Niemann has built letterforms from this underlying matrix of building blocks. The viewer's eye must work through the optical illusion in order to make sense of the text.

Marian Bantjes (Canadian, b. 1963). *Sustainability*, 2007. Offset lithograph. Printed by Stora Enso (Helsinki, Finland). 27.9 × 86.4 cm (11 × 34 in.). Gift of William Drenttel and Jessica Helfand, 2008-7-1.

Pattern designers create traditional arabesque patterns by mirroring and repeating curved lines, yielding a gracefully interwoven surface. Here, Marian Bantjes has extracted letterforms from a densely layered arabesque pattern in order to represent the interconnectedness of living things.

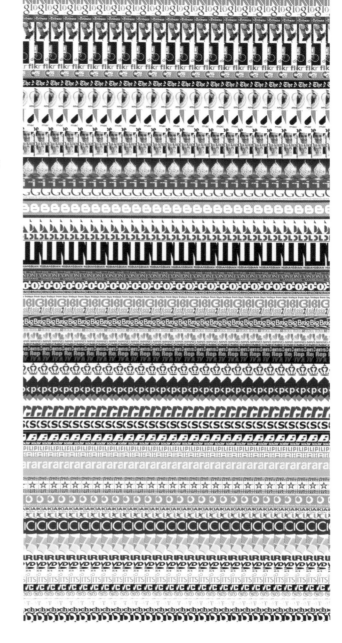

Mieke Gerritzen (Dutch, b. 1962). *Design for Logo Wallpaper*, 2006. Digital print. 104.1 × 70.1 cm (41 × 27 5/8 in.). Gift of Mieke Gerritzen, 2009-39-9.

Repetition is a core principle of pattern design. Pattern designers often strive to create an overall texture with no single focal point. To produce this pattern, Mieke Gerritzen repeated dozens of corporate logos in order to create a frantic surface buzzing with visual noise.

Mieke Gerritzen (Dutch, b. 1962) for The Biggest Visual Power Show (Essen, Germany). *Next Nature*, 2006. Digital print. 70 × 50 cm (27 9/16 × 19 11/16 in.). Gift of Mieke Gerritzen, 2009-39-8.

The posters and products of Mieke Gerritzen comment on the glut of information in digital society. Here, messages crowd into every available space, recalling the hectic rhythm of a supermarket ad or a televised news feed.

Sulki & Min (Seoul, South Korea):
Sulki Choi (South Korean, b. 1977)
and Min Choi (South Korean, b. 1971)
for Gwangju National University of
Education (Gwangju, South Korea).
Three Questions on Death, 2014.
Offset lithograph. 59.4 × 84 cm (23
3/8 × 33 1/16 in.). Gift of Sulki & Min,
2014-21-4.

For their poster publicizing dancer
Eunme Ahn's performance of *Three
Questions on Death*, Sulki & Min
designed text in a style that recalls
stenciled letters, their nod to the
impermanence of the performance
held before the opening of the Asian
Arts Theatre, Asian Culture Complex
in Gwangju. Cloudlike bubbles, culled
from poster designs advertising
earlier events, are layered beneath
the text, recalling traces of past
performances.—*Caitlin Condell*

Shiro Shita Saori (Japanese, b. 1990) for The Watari Museum of Contemporary Art (Shibuya, Japan). *Solo Exhibition, New Type*, 2014. Digital print. 103 × 72.8 cm (40 9/16 × 28 11/16 in.). Gift of Shiro Shita Saori, 2014-35-2.

Shiro Shita Saori is a Japanese designer working in Berlin. Her designs range from refined, geometric compositions to exuberant studies of Japanese pop culture. In this poster for an exhibition of the designer's work, bodies and objects melt into the landscape in this graffiti-like exploration of figure and ground. The imagery suggests impossible topologies and a dreamlike stream of consciousness. The disembodied eyeball recalls surrealism and psychedelia.—*Caitlin Condell*

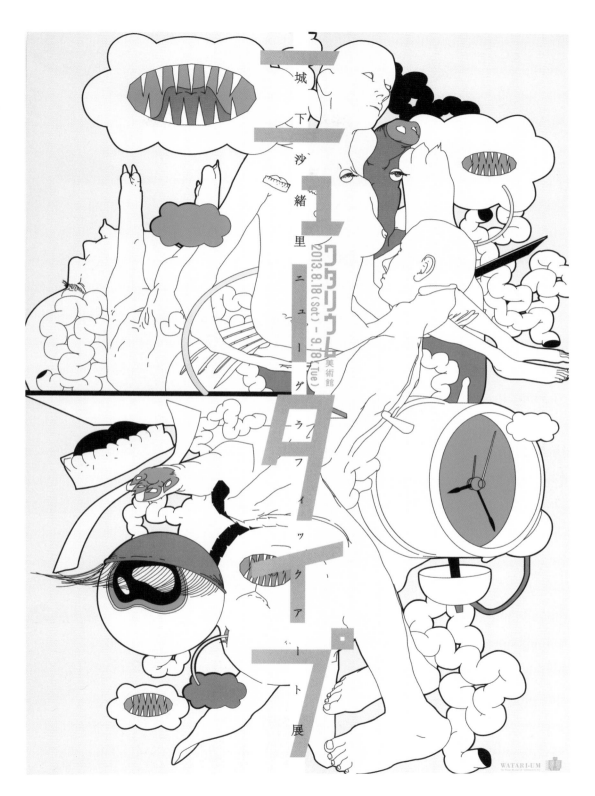

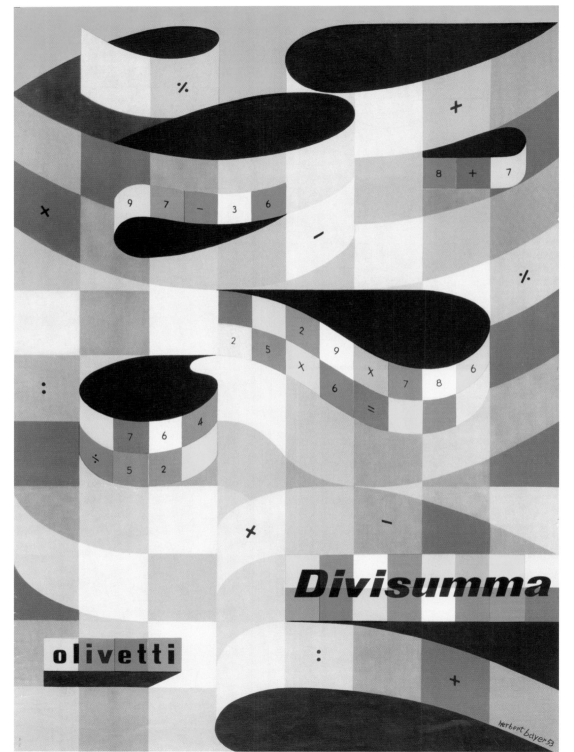

Herbert Bayer (Austrian, active Germany and USA, 1900–1985) for Ing. C. Olivetti & C. S.p.A., (Ivrea, Italy). *Divisumma*, 1953. Lithograph. 67.9 × 47.9 cm (26 3/4 × 18 7/8 in.). Museum purchase through gift of James A. Lapides and from General Acquisitions Endowment Fund, 2009-1-1.

Herbert Bayer, who studied and then taught at the Bauhaus during the 1920s, worked as a corporate designer in the United States after World War II. This stunning poster explores the space between two and three dimensions. The curved planes reference rolls of paper unfurling from an adding machine. The eye must struggle to follow the logic of these warped surfaces.

Felix Pfäffli (Swiss, b. 1986) for Südpol (Kriens, Switzerland). *Monotales*, 2012. Risograph. 42 × 29.4 cm (16 9/16 × 11 9/16 in.). Gift of Felix Pfäffli, 2015-3-3.

Felix Pfäffli (Swiss, b. 1986) for Südpol (Kriens, Switzerland). *Holy Other*, 2013. Risograph. 42 × 29.4 cm (16 9/16 × 11 9/16 in.). Gift of Felix Pfäffli, 2014-30-3.

Felix Pfäffli is a young Swiss designer based in Lucerne, whose posters are an arresting amalgam of precision and pop. As a designer, he enjoys the limitations of the poster format, explaining that its size restrictions engender discipline and economy of design. Pfäffli's largest project to date is an ongoing series of posters for Südpol, a Swiss cultural center and arts space. These small, inexpensively produced posters include letterforms created out of warped, folded, and tilted planes. Flatness and illusion strike an uneasy truce.—*Caitlin Condell*

Simplify

Designers often simplify an image in order to focus attention on a message or product. Stark silhouettes of objects became a hallmark of modern poster design in the 1950s and '60s. John Massey's 1970 poster for the Herman Miller furniture company offered a mid-century update on the German Plakatstil tradition, presenting an abstracted, high-contrast interpretation of Charles and Ray Eames's famous Soft Pad chair.

Swiss designer and educator Armin Hofmann called such images "graphic translations."[1] Although these images appear simple and direct, creating them requires painstaking hand skills as well as close observation and analysis. Learning to create such graphic translations of physical things became a rite of passage within modernist design training, and variations of this exercise are still used in many design curricula today.

Schematic icons long predate the modern poster. The tangram is a traditional Chinese puzzle made of seven shapes cut from a single square. The shapes fit together in countless ways to build angular pictures. Japanese designer Ikko Tanaka divided the surface of his poster *Nihon Buyo* (1981) into tangram-like shapes to construct an elegant yet minimal portrait of a geisha.

Storytelling and abstraction converge in the remarkable film posters produced in Poland in the 1960s and '70s. These posters advertise popular American films, yet they perform outside the conventional language of Hollywood film promotion, exemplifying the creative sensibility of Polish poster art.[2] Designers working behind the Iron Curtain often didn't have access to photographs or illustrations sharp enough to reproduce at large scale. Working with available materials, Polish designers drew on personal experience to tell the story of the films and their characters in their own way.

Poignant details bring these minimal illustrations to life. When the creature in *King Kong* makes eye contact with the viewer, his gaze is both ominous and endearing. The red lips of the *Midnight Cowboy* capture the sensuality of the film's title character, a male prostitute living at the raw edges of society. The poster designer for *Point Blank* probably enlarged a small photograph or photocopy to create a high-contrast image; by changing the scale of the picture and flattening out its interior details, the designer created an anonymous, universal everyman. In such posters, the purity of reductive abstraction gives way to the pop fascination with an empire of signs.

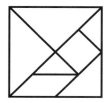
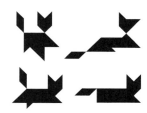

The tangram is a geometric puzzle invented in China. Children use the pieces to create simple drawings.

Waldemar Swierzy (Polish, 1931–2013). Nocny Kowboj [*Midnight Cowboy*], 1973. Offset lithograph. 82.3 × 58.5 cm (32 3/8 × 23 1/16 in.). Gift of Sara and Marc Benda, 2010-21-103.

Bronislaw Zelek (Polish, b. 1935). Zbieg z Alcatraz [*Point Blank*], 1970. Offset lithograph. 83.4 × 59.4 cm (32 13/16 × 23 3/8 in.). Gift of Sara and Marc Benda, 2010-21-101.

Marek Mosinski (Polish, 1936–1998). Ucieczka King Konga [*King Kong Escapes*], 1968. Offset lithograph. 83.7 × 57.1 cm (32 15/16 × 22 1/2 in.). Gift of Sara and Marc Benda, 2010-21-104.

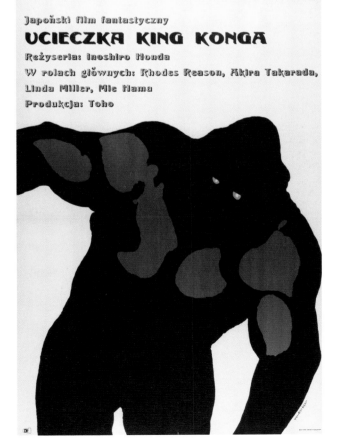

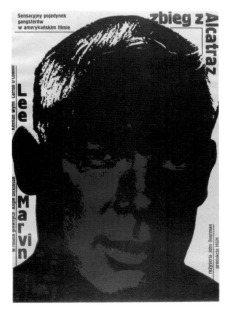

eames soft pad group herman miller inc

John Massey (American, b. 1931) and Tom Waon for Herman Miller Furniture Company (Zeeland, Michigan, USA). *Eames Soft Pad Group*, 1970. Screenprint. 122.8 × 81.2 cm (48 3/8 × 31 15/16 in.). Gift of Various Donors, 1981-29-124.

American designer John Massey met the Swiss masters Armin Hofmann and Josef Müller-Brockmann at the International Design Conference in Aspen in 1953, an event that transformed Massey's outlook on graphic design. Based in Chicago, Massey went on to become a leading practitioner of modernism for corporate applications as well as an influential educator. This poster for Herman Miller Furniture Company applies Hofmann's concept of "graphic translation" to interpret a piece of modernist furniture as an abstracted icon. The poster provides no concrete information about the product.

Malcolm Grear (American, b. 1931) for Solomon R. Guggenheim Museum (New York, New York, USA). *The Guggenheim Museum*, 1969. Lithograph. 83.8 × 55.7 cm (33 × 21 15/16 in.). Gift of Malcolm Grear, 1991-69-105.

Malcolm Grear, a leading American designer and influential educator at Rhode Island School of Design, developed a methodology grounded in Gestalt principles. Figure flows into ground in Grear's classic depiction of the Guggenheim Museum, printed in a single color of ink. The poster was designed to be overprinted with information about specific events.

The Guggenheim Museum

Mendell & Oberer (Germany): Pierre
Mendell (German, b. 1929) and Klaus
Oberer (Swiss, b. 1937) for Die Neue
Sammlung (Munich, Germany).
Plastics + Design, 1998. Screenprint.
118.9 × 84 cm (46 13/16 × 33 1/16
in.). Gift of Sara and Marc Benda,
2009-20-38.

Pierre Mendell and Klaus Oberer
met as students at the Basel School
of Design in the late 1950s, where
they studied with Emil Ruder and
Armin Hofmann. Their Munich-
based studio creates works of purity,
simplicity, and wit. This poster for an
exhibition about plastics uses bright,
flat colors and rounded forms to
complement the subject matter.

Jean Widmer (Swiss, active France, b. 1929) for Centre de création industrielle [Industrial design center] (Paris, France). Préparation du Repas [*Meal Preparation*], 1972. Screenprint. 64.8 × 50.2 cm (25 1/2 × 19 3/4 in.). Gift of Sara and Marc Benda, 2009-12-22.

Swiss-born designer Jean Widmer trained at the Kunstgewerbeschule in Zürich and launched his career in France in 1953. He founded Visuel Design in 1970 with his wife, Nicole Widmer. His exhibition posters for the Centre de création industrielle pair typography in Helvetica with abstracted graphic forms depicting industrial design objects. Gradients and soft edges bring warmth and humor to these modernist masterworks.

Alexander Gelman (Russian, active USA, b. 1967) for Biblio's. *Poetry Readings*, 1996. Screenprint. 77.8 × 52.1 cm (30 5/8 × 20 1/2 in.). Gift of Design Machine, 1998-32-15.

Russian-born designer Alexander Gelman worked in the United States during the 1990s and early 2000s. His simple icons strive not so much to capture the essence of a subject, but rather to offer an off-kilter view of it. Here, a table lamp represents a poetry reading. The illustration is, one might say, beside the point.

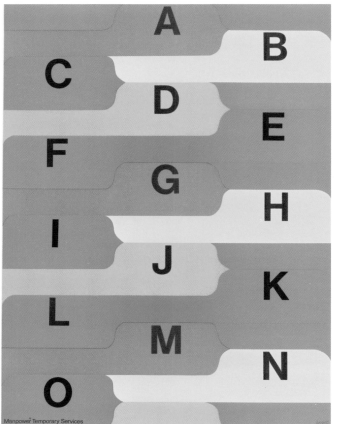

Lois Ehlert (American, b. 1934) for Manpower International (Milwaukee, Wisconsin, USA). Offset lithographs. Approx. 61.1 × 45.7 cm (24 1/16 × 18 in.) (each). Gift of Lois Ehlert, 1991-69-34, -35, -32, -38; 1981-29-96.

Clockwise from top left: *Now is the time for all good women to come to the aid of their country*, 1979; *ABCDEFGHIJKLMNO*, 1979; *Shorthand*, 1979; *Manpower Temporary Service - Office Sweet Office*, 1979. Opposite: *Manpower Temporary Services*, 1979.

Lois Ehlert is a children's book illustrator who also worked as a graphic designer in Milwaukee, Wisconsin. In the late 1970s, she created this remarkable series of posters for Manpower Temporary Services, a Milwaukee-based agency that connects temporary office workers with companies. Ehlert derived her bright, playfully simplified images from everyday office culture.—*Rebekah Pollock*

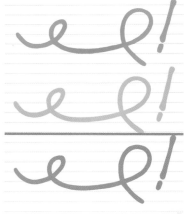

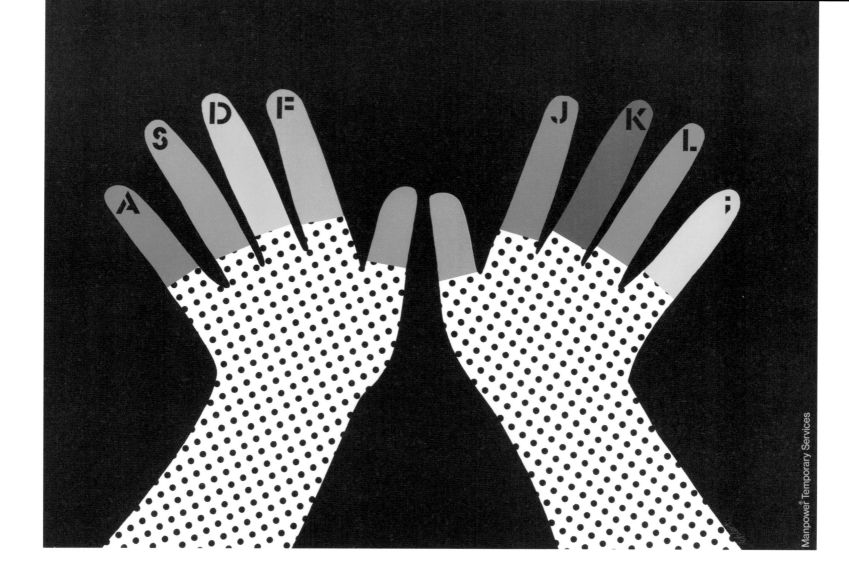

GAME OF THRONES

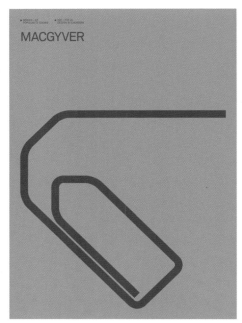

MACGYVER

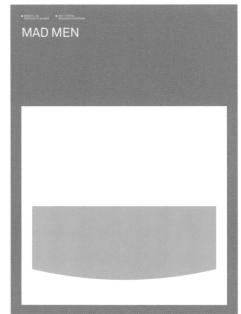

MAD MEN

THE SIMPSONS

TRUE BLOOD

Albert Exergian (Austrian, b. 1973). *Iconic TV*, 2009–2014. Digital prints. 118.9 × 84.1 cm (46 13/16 × 33 1/8 in.) (each). Courtesy of the designer.

Albert Exergian's *Iconic TV* posters represent a new generation's response to the legacy of Swiss modernism. Exergian plays with the idea of using reductive imagery to unlock the essence of a complex subject. His posters merge the international language of American television shows with modernism's high-minded "international style." The results are both comic and sincere. The posters are digitally printed on demand and sold to fans and collectors worldwide.

THE WIRE

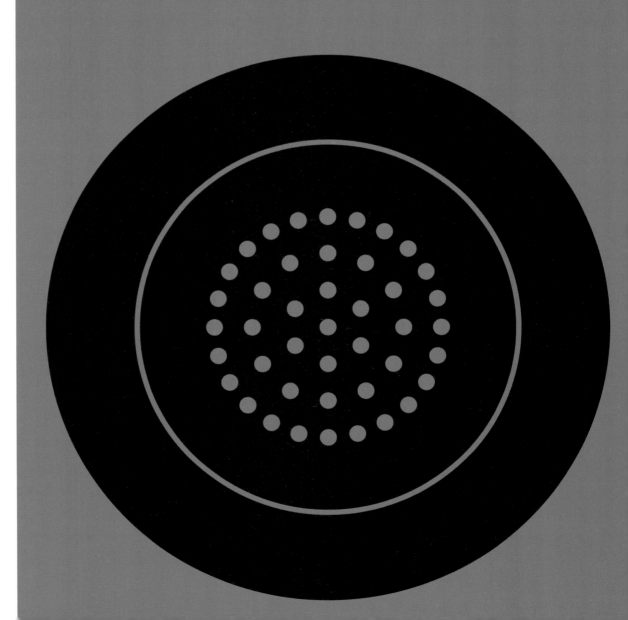

Cut and Paste

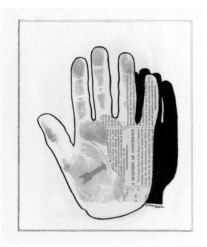

Edward McKnight Kauffer (American, active England, 1890–1954). Hand, 1935–38. Brush and gouache, graphite, newsprint collage. 31.3 × 26.8 cm (12 5/16 × 10 9/16 in.). Gift of Mrs. E. McKnight Kauffer, 1963-39-962.

Edward McKnight Kauffer actively explored the implications of cubist collage for modern design. Inspired by the physical process of cut and paste, he developed a rich and flexible visual language of fluid, interconnecting forms. An extraordinary drawing from the 1930s deploys drawing, painting, and cut paper to question the nature of graphic signs. A direct print of Kauffer's hand forms the basis of the composition. A handprint is an *index*, a sign that is a direct trace of its referent rather than a pictorial *icon* or an abstract *symbol*. Kauffer reinforced his handprint by tracing around it with a solid line, but he broke that stable frame by adding a cut-paper hand whose outline flows into the flat black shadow behind it. A bright red arrow provides a shot of color and diagonal motion. What does the arrow point to? The printed hand? The newsprint hand? The image as a whole?

While cubist collage introduced bits of real material onto the surface of paintings and drawings, Dada photomontage (beginning around 1918) mixed bits and pieces of photographs.[1] Montage plunged the cerebral realm of cubist collage into the harsher world of mass media. The constructivist El Lissitzky came to view montage as intrinsic to the process of mechanical reproduction. For Lissitzky, montage involved combining halftone images with texts to create new works.[2]

Soviet filmmaker Sergei Eisenstein called montage the "nerve of cinema," its essential, defining method.[3] The film editor juxtaposes shots that have conflicting planes, volumes, lighting, or tempo to maximize the dialectical impact of a montage sequence. A montage unit, wrote Eisenstein, means more than the sum of its parts. Graphic designers in the 1920s were inspired by cinema to juxtapose images at different scales and angles and to create new images out of fragments. With the worldwide rise of social realism in the 1930s, the idea of affirming the objective truth of photographs (their indexical link to reality) became more politically acceptable than experiments with jarring and disjunctive combinations. The Stenbergs' *Berlin: Symphony of a Big City* (1928) suggests an avant-garde assembly of parts, while Gustav Klucis's *Reality of Our Program* (1931) reflects the Stalinist turn toward social realism.

Combining bits and pieces remains central to the design process. Before the digital era, designers glued diverse elements (halftone photographs, high-contrast photostats, strips of typeset text) onto boards called "paste-ups." Digital software turned this production method into key commands, allowing designers to endlessly recompose blocks of image and text. The cut-and-paste process can be an active element of the work or it can build the illusion of a seamless and unified whole.

An icon is a recognizable image of its referent.

An index points to its referent or is a direct trace of its referent.

A symbol is abstract, relying on cultural convention.

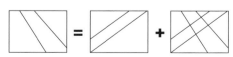

Sergei Eisenstein called for numerous modes of conflict within a shot and between two shots (montage). Shown here: graphic conflict.

Georgii Augustovich Stenberg (Russian, 1900–1933) and Vladimir Augustovich Stenberg (Russian, 1899–1982). *Berlin: Symphony of a Big City*, 1928. Lithograph. 106.7 × 70.5 cm (42 × 27 3/4 in.). Museum purchase from Drawings and Prints Council and General Acquisitions Endowment Funds, 2008-1-1.

Brothers Georgii Augustovich Stenberg and Vladimir Augustovich Stenberg were pioneers of the avant-garde film poster. Their posters captured not only a film's narrative elements, but also the spirit and cinematic experience. The Stenbergs invented a projection device that could enlarge, reduce, distort, and manipulate images, allowing them to seamlessly blend abstracted designs with those sourced from photographic material. By drawing images that recalled the appearance of photographs, they were able to control the quality, tone, and gradation of their images into a cohesive aesthetic. The part-man, part-machine figure at the heart of this poster replicates not a character in the film, but a photomontage by the Bauhaus-trained photographer Umbo (Otto Umbehr), who had worked with Walter Ruttmann as a camera assistant on *Berlin: Symphony of a Big City.—Caitlin Condell*

Gustav Klucis (Latvian, 1895–1938). *Spartakiada, Moscow 1928*, 1928. Letterpress (14.8 × 10.3 cm (5 3/4 × 4 in.) (each). Various dimensions. Collection of Merrill C. Berman.

Merrill C. Berman's vast collection of graphic design materials includes essential landmarks of modern design. The works of Gustav Klucis show how the Soviet Constructivists' revolutionary approach to photomontage shifted as Stalin rose to power. In 1928, Klucis created this series of postcards to commemorate the Moscow Spartakiada athletic competition; each one assembles cutout photographs in abruptly shifting scales to represent motion and depth. The postcards were later singled out for official rebuke as overly intellectual, unsuitable for the proletariat. Klucis's work shifted in the 1930s to accommodate the rise of social realism, which favored heroic depictions of individuals and types, and avoided the idioms of abstract art.

Opposite (clockwise from upper left)

Gustav Klucis (Latvian, 1895–1938). Real'nost' nashei programmy. Eto zhivye liudu, eto my s vami [*The Reality of Our Program Is Living People, It Is You and I*] [Reality group], 1931. Photo collage with vintage gelatin silver prints, ink, gouache, intaglio and letterpress cuttings. 2.54cm × 35.56 cm (10 × 14 in.). Collection of Merrill C. Berman.

Gustav Klucis (Latvian, 1895–1938). Real'nost' nashei programmy. Eto zhivye liudu, eto my s vami [*The Reality of Our Program Is Living People, It Is You and I*] [Reality group], 1931. Photo collage with vintage gelatin silver prints, ink, gouache, intaglio and letterpress cuttings. 24.1 × 16.5 cm (9 1/2 × 6 1/2 in.). Collection of Merrill C. Berman.

Gustav Klucis (Latvian, 1895–1938). *The Reality of Our Program . . . Six Conditions for Victory*, 1931. Lithograph (one half of complete printed poster). 72.2 × 102.9 cm (28 7/16 × 40 1/2 in.). Gift of Merrill C. Berman in honor of Ellen Lupton, 2014-20-5.

Gustav Klucis (Latvian, 1895–1938). Real'nost' nashei programmy. Eto – zhivye liudu, eto my s vami [*The Reality of Our Program is Living People, It Is You and I*] [Reality group], 1931. Vintage gelatin silver print with gouache. 22.5 × 17 cm (8 7/8 × 6 11/16 in.). Collection of Merrill C. Berman.

In this series of photomechanical mockups and a final printed poster, we can see Klucis reuse existing photographic material. He has used diagonal lines to convey movement and project the forward force of the Communist state. The series represents Stalin in his ascendancy, accentuating his human and comradely characteristics. He strides along next to a phalanx of marching coal miners in an overcoat and cap, like a man of the people. In subsequent posters Stalin is enlarged to a massive scale, becoming an increasingly heroic, outsize figure.—*Gail S. Davidson*

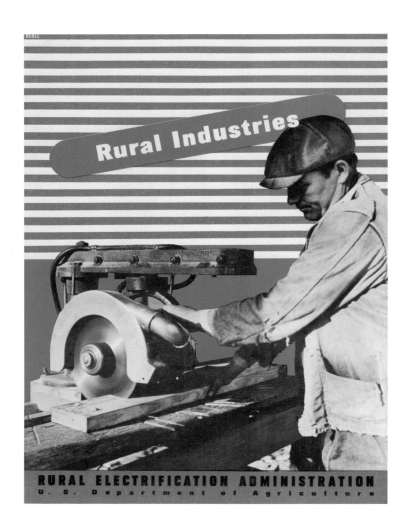

Lester Beall (American, 1903–1969) for Rural Electrification Administration (USA). *Rural Industries* and *A Better Home,* 1941. Screenprint. 101.6 × 76.2 cm (40 × 30 in.) (each). Museum purchase through gift of Mrs. Edward C. Post and from Friends of Drawings and Prints, General Acquisition Endowment Fund, Sarah Cooper Hewitt, and Smithsonian Institution Collections Acquisition Program Funds, 1995-106-1, -2.

Dada and constructivist experiments with photomontage laid the ground for the integrated use of halftone photography as a visual element of graphic design. Lester Beall isolated photographs against bold patterns and flat fields of color, transforming halftone images into tightly contained illustrations.

Paul Rand (American, 1914–1996), *H. L. Mencken (After Book Cover for* Prejudices: A Selection, *by H. L. Mencken)*, ca. 1958. Offset lithograph. 91.4 × 61 cm (36 × 24 in.). Gift of Marion S. Rand, 2002-11-29.

Paul Rand's piece *H. L. Mencken* celebrates a Dada sensibility by mismatching a roughly cut silhouette with an underlying photograph. Rand later explained that the publisher had given him a "lousy" photograph of Mencken to work with. He recounted to Steven Heller, "I cut up the photo into a silhouette of someone making a speech, which bore no relation to the shape of the [original] photo. That was funny, in part because of the ironic cropping and because Mencken was such a curmudgeon."

Ladislav Sutnar (American and Czech, 1897–1976) for A. B. Addo (Malmö, Sweden). *addo-x*, 1958. Offset lithograph. 96.8 × 60.8 cm (38 1/8 × 23 15/16 in.). Gift of Anonymous Donor, 1994-109-7.

Ladislav Sutnar created a bold new logotype for the Swedish office machine brand Addo-X in 1956; he also designed numerous posters and advertisements for the company. This poster features Swedish actress and model Kerstin Anita Marianne Ekberg, best known for her role in Federico Fellini's *La Dolce Vita* (1960).—*Rebekah Pollock*

Edward McKnight Kauffer (American, active England, 1890–1954) for Transport for London (London, England). *Motor Show, Earls Court*, 1937. Lithograph. Printed by Baynard Press (London, England). 25.4 × 31.9 cm (10 × 12 9/16 in.). Gift of Mrs. E. McKnight Kauffer, 1963-39-576.

A gradient arrow blends into a photograph to depict crowds of people flocking to a motor show.

Designers deliberately violate the seamless integrity of a photographic image in order to highlight the constructed nature of the graphic image and to depict emotional, physical, or social upheaval. Fragments of images become like words in a story, subject to rearrangement for dramatic effect. Gaps become as important as points of connection.

Andrzej Klimowski (British, active
Poland, b. 1949). Nieustajace
Wakacje [*Permanent Vacation*], 1991.
Offset lithograph. 96.2 × 67.6 cm
(37 7/8 × 26 5/8 in.). Gift of Sara and
Marc Benda, 2010-21-11.

Karl Domenic Geissbühler (Swiss,
b. 1932) for Opernhaus, Zürich
(Zürich, Switzerland). Samson et
Delila [*Samson and Delila*], 1996.
Screenprint. 128.3 × 91 cm (50 1/2
× 35 13/16 in.) Gift of Sara and Marc
Benda, 2010-21-63.

Paul Rand (American, 1914–1996).
*Dancer on Orange Ground (After
Cover for* Direction *Magazine*), 1939.
Offset lithograph. 96.5 × 65.4 cm (38
× 25 3/4 in.). Gift of Marion S. Rand,
2002-11-24.

Julia's simple method for stopping a rapist

GO FOR THE GROIN, GALS!

NOT N.E.A. FUNDED

SisterSerpents (Chicago, Illinois, USA). *Julia's Simple Method for Stopping a Rapist*, 1993. Photocopy, rubber-stamped ink, photographic reproduction. 34.1 × 21.7 cm (13 7/16 × 8 9/16 in.) Gift of SisterSerpents, 1995-114-2.

Since the Dada revolution, designers and artists have chopped up glossy magazines in their search for raw materials. The Chicago-based feminist art collective SisterSerpents, founded by Mary Ellen Croteau and Jeramy Turner, was active from 1989 to 1998. Here, they have used pictures clipped from food magazines to propose a powerful recipe for sexual self-defense.

Karel Vaca (Czech, 1919–1989). *Ro.Go.Pa.G.*, 1963. Offset lithograph. 82 × 58.4 cm (32 5/16 × 23 in.). Gift of Sara and Marc Benda, 2010-21-5.

To create this poster for a festival of contemporary avant-garde films, the designers cut away the body of Christ from a blown-up reproduction of a Renaissance painting. The blank space where the body used to be becomes a table laden with images of mass-market food products clipped from magazines. The poster celebrates the cut-and-paste process and presents a clash of visual cultures.

Claudia Schmauder (Swiss, b. 1969) for Johann Jacobs Museum (Zürich, Switzerland). Silber Reflexe: Kaffeekanne und Design [*Silver Reflexes: Coffeepots and Design*], 1996. Screenprint. 128 × 90.5 cm (50 3/8 × 35 5/8 in.). Gift of Sara and Marc Benda, 2010-21-72.

In creating this sophisticated poster for an exhibition about the history of coffeepots, Claudia Schmauder used digital techniques to combine decorative elements from different times and places, generating a fluid whole while acknowledging the disjunctions among components.

Overlap

Paul Rand (American, 1914–1996) for Wittenborn, Schultz, Inc. (New York, New York, USA). *DADA*, 1951. Screenprint. 91.5 × 61 cm (36 × 24 in.). Gift of Various Donors, 1981-29-206.

Designers use various techniques to conjure illusions of depth within the flatness of two-dimensional space. The most basic technique for simulating depth is to overlap two or more elements. By partially blocking one shape with another, the designer produces an imaginary space between figure and ground. Designers inspired by avant-garde art learned that the literal cut-and-paste actions of collage and montage could become the basis of a flexible visual language.

Paul Rand's classic 1951 poster *Dada* (based on the cover of a book) creates a rudimentary sensation of depth as the black letters float in front of white ones. Why do we accept this illusion? Similar effects occur in our perception of the physical world, where our visual system assures us that partially hidden objects exist in their entirety. The Gestalt process of *continuation* makes the white letters appear whole in Rand's poster. The brain wills the missing pieces into existence, reconnecting the interrupted letters because their visible edges align.[1]

Josef Müller-Brockmann's poster Der Film (1959–60) is considered a masterpiece of modernist design. By overlapping the word "Film" with the article "*der*" (the), Müller-Brockmann used typography to explore the principle of cinematic montage. The gray letters occupy a space behind (and a time before) the white text.

Massimo Vignelli's poster *Knoll International* (1967) uses transparency to compress overlapping letters into a common plane; none takes priority over the others. Cyan, magenta, and yellow—the basic colors of offset printing—run through one another in no particular order, creating new hues where the colors mix. The overlapping words in Michael Bierut's poster *Light/Years* (1999) also negate depth. While sketching concepts for the poster, Bierut saw that "light" and "years" are both five-letter words, so he decided to run the two words through each other. The layers of text—digitally manipulated to resemble projected light—lay equal claim to the poster's front plane.

The layers of color in Vignelli's *Knoll International* coincide with layers of ink laid down in the offset printing process. This literal correspondence of ink layers and visuals layers is an exception rather than a rule. Most of the layers we see in graphic design don't correspond with deposits of ink physically produced in separate passes of a printing press. Most layered compositions of type, image, color, and pattern are visual fictions. Software tools such as the Adobe Creative Suite are organized around a model of depthless layers that pile up one upon another within the zero space of the surface. Designers can endlessly adjust the order and transparency of digital layers, producing imaginary depth.

We perceive the surfaces of the three black squares to occupy the same depth, because their horizontal edges align. In the Gestalt process of continuation, the brain connects the three squares into a single plane.

When the horizontal edges of the black squares don't align, the illusion of depth disappears.

Transparency makes all the shapes appear to occupy the same depth.

Josef Müller-Brockmann (Swiss, 1914–1996) for Museum für Gestaltung, Zürich (Zürich, Switzerland). Der Film [*Film*], 1959–1960. Offset lithograph. 128 × 90.6 cm (50 3/8 × 35 11/16 in.). Museum purchase from General Acquisitions Endowment Fund, 1999-46-2.

Michael Bierut (American, b. 1957) for Architectural League of New York (New York, New York, USA). *LIGHT/ YEARS*, 1999. Offset lithograph. 59.7 × 97.8 cm (23 1/2 × 38 1/2 in.). Gift of Michael Bierut, 2007-12-2.

Massimo Vignelli (Italian, active USA, 1931–2014) for Knoll Textiles (East Greenville, Pennsylvania, USA). *Knoll International*, 1967. Offset lithograph. 81.3 × 120.7 cm (32 × 47 1/2 in.). Gift of Lella and Massimo Vignelli, 2009-42-1.

How Posters Work

Erik Nitsche (Swiss, 1908–1998) for
General Dynamics Corporation (USA).
Atoms for Peace, General Dynamics.
Offset lithograph. Printed by Lithos
R. Marsens (Lausanne, Switzerland).
132.5 × 96 cm (52 3/16 × 37 13/16 in.).
Gift of Arthur Cohen and Daryl Otte in
memory of Bill Moggridge, 2013-42-5.

This poster uses intersecting,
transparent bands of color to suggest
the airplanes' paths across the globe.
The poster was displayed during the
first International Conference on the
Peaceful Uses of Atomic Energy, held
in Geneva in 1955.

Hans-Rudolf Lutz (Swiss, 1939–1998) for Museum für Gestaltung, Zürich (Zürich, Switzerland). Konkrete Utopien in Kunst und Gesellschaft [*Concrete Utopias in Art and Society*], ca. 1990. Screenprint. 128.3 × 90.4 cm (50 1/2 × 35 9/16 in.). Gift of Sara and Marc Benda, 2010-21-30.

An enlarged block of handwriting runs across the giant number "68," a symbol for the student uprisings in Paris that defined a generation of artistic, political, and intellectual opposition. The handwritten text, taken from a historic poster from the May 1968 uprising, parses the French verb *participer* (to participate).

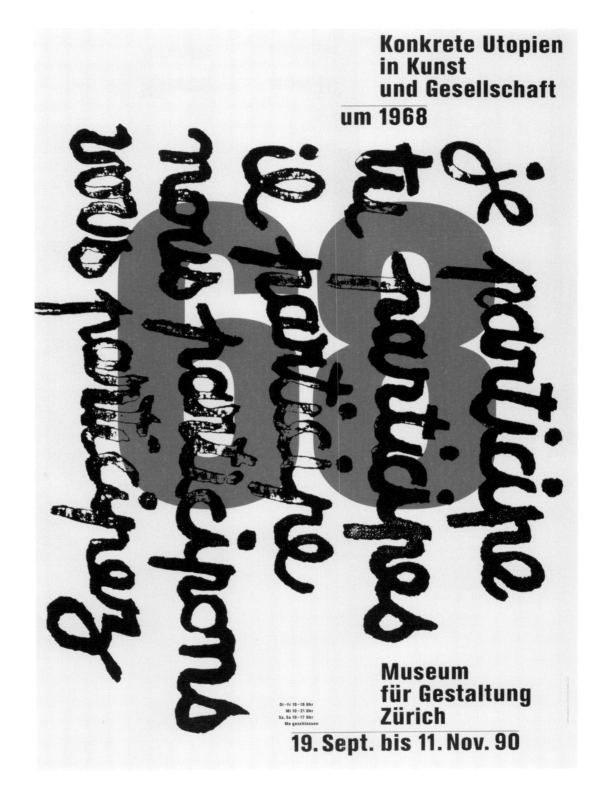

Felix Pfäffli (Swiss, b. 1986).
Salzhaus, 2014. Offset lithograph.
128 × 89.5 cm (50 3/8 × 35 1/4 in.).
Gift of Felix Pfäffli, 2014-30-1.

The music house Salzhaus in
Winterthur, Switzerland, invites
a designer each month to design
its program. Felix Pfäffli decided
to focus on the venue's name. He
employed a typeface that he had
initially designed for use in single-
day workshops that he runs for his
students. The narrow, geometric
forms of the letters allowed Pfäffli
to "distort, warp, and disassemble"
the text. Layered over one another,
the letterforms read as a vibrant
abstract composition as much as
a linear rendering of a name.
—*Caitlin Condell*

Felix Pfäffli (Swiss, b. 1986) for
Fachklasse Grafik Lucerne (Lucerne,
Switzerland). Werkschau 2012 [*Work
Show*], 2012. Offset lithograph.
128 × 89.5 cm (50 3/8 × 35 1/4 in.).
Courtesy of the designer.

Felix Pfäffli (Swiss, b. 1986) for
Weltformat Poster Festival (Lucerne,
Switzerland). Weltformat 13 [*World
Format 13*], 2013. Offset lithograph.
128 × 89.5 cm (50 3/8 × 35 1/4 in.).
Gift of Felix Pfäffli, 2014-30-2.

When Felix Pfäffli was asked to
design a poster for Lucerne's
2013 Weltformat Poster Festival,
he grappled with the "strange
duplication" involved in creating
a poster to promote a poster
show. He resolved this dilemma by
contextualizing posters as objects
made in a specific place and time,
layering multiple posters on top
of one another as if pasted onto
a wall. Each layer is a simplified,
fragmented version of an older
Pfäffli poster, visible only through
the holes and tears of other layers.
Pfäffli explains that everybody "tries
to make a clean, beautiful poster.
So I designed one that is already
destroyed." Rather than literally rip
and distress the posters by hand, he
reproduced the effect digitally. He
used metallic silver ink in sections
of the background to mimic the
steel walls where posters often hang
outdoors in Switzerland, creating
a trompe-l'oeil effect. Pfäffli, who
recalls receiving emails from
passersby who were tricked by the
illusion, enjoys confounding his
viewers and generating the déjà-
vu-like experience of a counterfeit
reality.—*Caitlin Condell*

Sulki & Min (Seoul, South Korea): Sulki Choi (South Korean, b. 1977) and Min Choi (South Korean, b. 1971) for Gyeonggi Museum of Modern Art (Ansan, South Korea). *Works in the Open Air*, 2010. Offset lithograph. 84 × 59.4 cm (33 1/16 × 23 3/8 in.). Gift of Sulki & Min, 2014-21-3.

Layers of text in two languages are rendered in patterns of dots, stripes, lines, and textures. The patterns can be seen through one another, creating an illusion of transparency. The overall composition suggests an open field or landscape with no single center point. This striking poster was designed to promote an outdoor exhibition held at the Gyeonggi Museum of Modern Art in Ansan in 2010. The English language translation of the exhibition title, "Works in the Open Air," is quite different from the literal translation of the Korean title ("Whatever happened to the theme park"). Sulki & Min were interested in incorporating the idea of porosity and transparency into their poster design, drawing on modernist references: Gerd Arntz's human figures for the Isotype system occupy the background of the poster, while the letterforms are derived from Josef Albers. The buildup of layers maintains a sense of airy space evocative of the exhibition's theme.
—*Caitlin Condell*

Alexander Gelman (Russian, active USA, b. 1967). *Walls of the City*, 1992. Screenprint. 100 × 69.9 cm (39 3/8 × 27 1/2 in.). Gift of Design Machine, 1998-32-18.

This composition references the incidental collages of torn posters that may be found layered on the street. We perceive two planes (two sheets of paper) because the lines of text that seem to be printed on each one align visually.

Assault the Surface

A large red square fills two-thirds of Fritz Fischer's 1973 poster for Die Zärtlichkeit der Wölfe (*The Tenderness of Wolves*), a film by Rainer Werner Fassbinder. The red square is more than a passive background, however. It drips into the space below, becoming an active player in the drama. From the center of the red field, a ghoulish figure locks eyes with the viewer while his victim swoons beneath him, oblivious to our gaze, her red shirt bleeding out into the surrounding square. Playing with the structures of visual perception, Fischer converts neutral ground into active figure and vice versa.

Assaulting the surface by burning, bending, or ripping an image points to the image's own artifice. Like breaking through the "fourth wall" in a theatrical production, such acts of metafictional violence crackle with mental friction as we acknowledge the image as both surface and representation.[1] Such works often call attention to edges, borders, and backgrounds in order to reveal how design focuses attention by actively framing our view.

Saul Bass played this game with bravado in his 1961 ad campaign for Otto Preminger's film *Exodus*. Set within the larger frame of the poster is a blue field consumed from below by yellow flames. Bass's poster-within-a-poster is burning away, revealing behind it the conventional components of the advertisement. Bass

had applied similar imagery to the film's title sequence, in which a yellow flame flickers along the bottom of a black screen, mingling with the stark white typography before engulfing the full frame. Bass used the flames as a symbol of Israel, connoting "the Temple" and the "eternal light."[2]

Treating an image or text as a physical object creates a narrative about the making or unmaking of the work itself. A 1981 poster by Jędrzej Stępak for Teatr Nowy features an enlarged photograph of an urban uprising. By exposing the sprocket holes of the film, the design treats the image as an artifact of history. We see the picture as a printed thing rather than as a naturalistic window onto reality. Splatters of red further flatten the photograph into an object while adding an element of action and movement, a gestural record of revolt.

Many contemporary posters tell stories about the design process. Letters are stretched and smeared. Backgrounds are torn, scratched, and crumpled. Images are processed, distorted, or enlarged to an extreme scale to expose their pixelation or halftone granularity. Such works capture—or seem to capture—the mark of time within the flat plane of print. We look *at* the surface rather than through it, perceiving it as a physical, embodied construction rather than a transparent window of representation.

The French writer and critic Denis Diderot established the idea of the fourth wall in theater in 1758: ". . . whether you are writing or acting, don't think about the audience . . . . Imagine a great wall at the edge of the stage separating you from the parterre; act as if the curtain didn't go up."

Fritz Fischer (German, 1919–1997).
Die Zärtlichkeit der Wölfe [*The Tenderness of Wolves*], 1973. Offset lithograph. 87.3 × 61.3 cm (34 3/8 × 24 1/8 in.). Gift of Sara and Marc Benda, 2010-21-15.

Fritz Fischer's studio Fischer-Nosbisch (founded with his wife Dorothea Nosbisch) designed numerous posters for the independent film distributor Atlas Filmverleigh in West Germany. Atlas commissioned original film posters and branding that broke with the standard descriptive realism of mainstream cinema promotions.
—*Rebekah Pollock*

Jędrzej Stępak (Polish, b. 1953) for Teatr Nowy (Poznań, Poland). Oskarżony: Czerwiec Pięćdziesiąt Sześć [*Accused June Fifty-Six*], 1981. Offset lithograph. 94.2 × 66.2 cm (37 1/16 × 26 1/16 in.). Gift of Sara and Marc Benda, 2009-20-24.

Saul Bass (American, 1920–1996). *Exodus*, 1961. Offset lithograph. Printed by National Screen Service Corporation (USA). 104 × 68.5 cm (40 15/16 × 26 15/16 in.). Gift of Sara and Marc Benda, 2010-21-16.

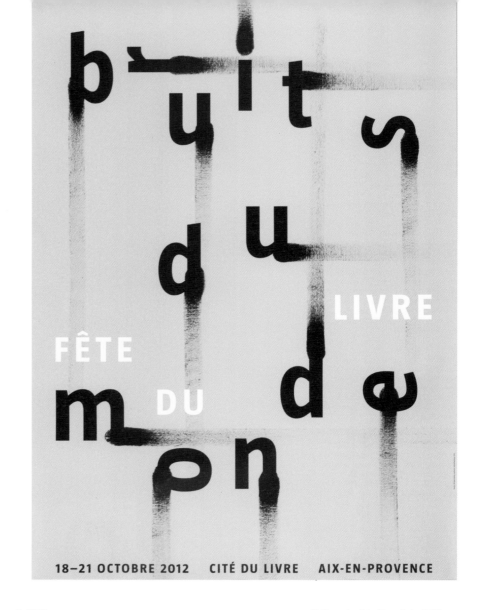

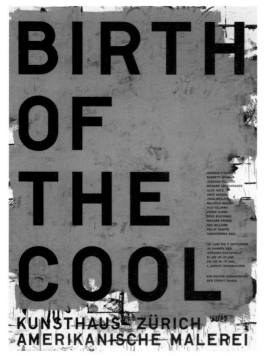

How Posters Work

Jianping He (Chinese, b. 1973) for NLB Galerija Avla (Lubljana, Slovenia). *In Between He Jianping*, 2012. Screenprint. 118.9 × 84.1 cm (46 13/16 × 33 1/8 in.). Gift of Jianping He, 2014-23-6.

Cornel Windlin (Swiss, b. 1964) for Kunsthaus Zürich (Zürich, Switzerland). *The Birth of Cool, American Painting from Georgia O'Keefe to Christopher Wood*, 1997. Offset lithograph. 127.5 × 89.5 cm (50 3/16 × 35 1/4 in.). Gift of Sara and Marc Benda, 2010-21-52.

Philippe Apeloig (French, b. 1962) for Cité du Livre (Aix-en-Provence, France). Bruits du monde [*Noises of the World*], 2012. Screenprint. 173.5 × 120.2 cm (5 ft. 8 5/16 in. × 47 5/16 in.) Gift of Philippe Apeloig, 2014-34-2.

Theseus Chan (Singaporean, b. 1961) for Ginza Graphic Gallery (Tokyo, Japan). *WERK No. 20*, 2012. Hand-distressed offset lithograph. 103 × 72.8 cm (40 9/16 × 28 11/16 in.). Gift of Theseus Chan, 2014-31-1.

Theseus Chan publishes the renowned magazine *WERK* as part of his Singapore-based studio practice WORK. The magazine is produced in small, meticulously crafted editions. Chan experiments with textures, materials, and binding techniques to explore the "extremities" of print. Each copy of this poster announcing an exhibition about the magazine has been crumpled by hand.—*Caitlin Condell*

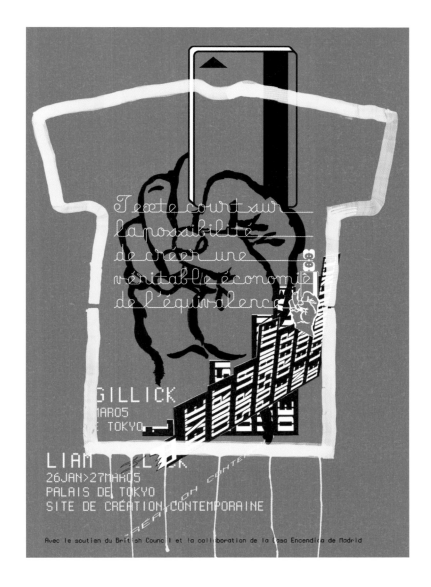

M/M (Paris): Michael Amzalag (French, b. 1967) and Mathias Augustyniak (French, b. 1967). *Texte court sur la possibilité de créer une véritable économie de l'équivalence [Short text on the possibility of creating an equivalence economy] [Liam Gillick]*, 2005. Screenprint. 176 × 120 cm (5 ft. 9 5/16 × 47 1/4 in.). Gift of M/M (Paris), 2015-4-2.

In 2005, artist Liam Gillick was disappointed by the poster originally designed and displayed by Le Palais de Tokyo in Paris on the occasion of his exhibition *Texte court sur la possibilité de créer une véritable économie de l'équivalence* [Short text on the possibility of creating an equivalence economy]. Gillick personally commissioned M/M (Paris) to create a new poster for the exhibition, just two weeks before the opening. A series of twenty-five identical "freshly redesigned" posters was displayed for the duration of the exhibition at the entrance of the museum as a sign of protest.

Takenobu Igarashi (Japanese, b. 1944). *NOH: UCLA Asian Performing Arts Institute*, 1981. Offset lithograph. 72.6 × 102.8 cm (28 9/16 × 40 1/2 in.). Gift of Takenobu Igarashi, 1981-69-2.

Activate the Diagonal

Vision is dynamic. The human eye functions by staying in constant motion. The brain's ability to process images depends on a signal that repeatedly refreshes as the eyes dart about in quick, largely involuntary movements. When we walk through a room, we collect thousands of still images, splicing them together like frames in a movie. Viewing a static image is a dynamic process as well. When we look at a poster, our eye moves across the surface, quickly focusing and refocusing on details of interest. Optical experiments have shown that if the eye is forced to become immobile for more than a few seconds, the brain perceives a blank, empty field; our vision system requires constant change, even when processing a still image.[1]

What path does the eye take? In the absence of other cues, readers of Latin-based scripts tend to process images as well as texts from left to right and top to bottom. The rectilinear frame that dominates print- and screen-based media reinforces the underlying grid of our writing system. The human brain is accustomed to vertical and horizontal lines; receptors for horizontals and verticals are the first to develop in the visual brains of infants. Some of the earliest drawings created by humans consist of gridded lines. Vertical trees and the horizontal ground plane dominate our experience of nature, and gridded structures pervade the built environment.[2]

Diagonals rebel against the regime of the grid and engage the mobility of vision, helping the eye cut across the surface and penetrate its depths. The angled text in Edward McKnight Kauffer's *Tea Drives Away the Droops* (1936) gives the poster a jolt of energy; try imagining the same design with the text set horizontally, and you will see an advertisement in dire need of caffeine. In other posters by Kauffer, converging lines create illusions of depth, guiding the eye into space rather than across it.

Diagonal lines don't always converge. Architects and engineers use axonometric projections (also called parallel projections) to create drawings whose scale remains consistent from the front of the object to its back. Unlike a traditional perspective view, an axonometric projection can be accurately measured for depth. Such drawings represent space not as we see it but as we know it.

Avant-garde architects and designers embraced axonometric projections in the 1920s because they represent space abstractly, allowing lines to stay parallel into infinity rather than imitating optical experience. Graphic designers have used this system of drawing to construct images and letterforms that convey depth yet maintain a consistent scale. Such constructions generate diagonal energy while upholding the steady empire of the grid, whose parallel vectors must never meet.

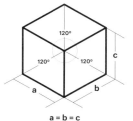

Isometric projection of a cube. In an isometric drawing, the angles between the x, y, and z axes are each 120 degrees.

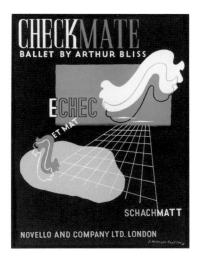

Edward McKnight Kauffer (American, active England, 1890–1954) for England's Royal Ballet Company (London, England). *Checkmate, Ballet by Arthur Bliss*, 1937. Lithograph. 32 × 23.7 cm (12 5/8 × 9 5/16 in.). Gift of Mrs. E. McKnight Kauffer, 1963-39-288.

Edward McKnight Kauffer (American, active England, 1890–1954) for New York Subway Advertising Co. (New York, New York, USA). *A Subway Poster Pulls*, 1947. Lithograph. 21.6 × 13.9 cm (8 1/2 × 5 1/2 in.). Gift of Mrs. E. McKnight Kauffer, 1963-39-166-d.

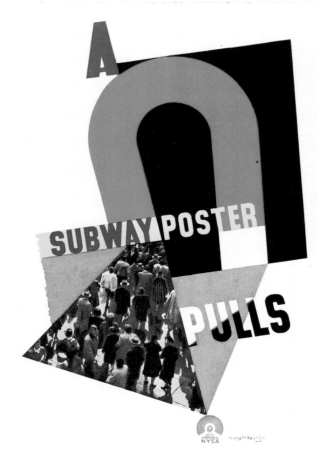

Edward McKnight Kauffer (American, active England, 1890–1954) for Empire Tea Market Expansion Board (International). *Tea Drives Away the Droops*, 1936. Lithograph. 75.7 × 50.3 cm (29 13/16 × 19 13/16 in.). Gift of Mrs. E. McKnight Kauffer, 1963-39-84.

This poster, with its cheerful Mr. T. Pott mascot, was part of a campaign to stimulate demand for tea in the United Kingdom as well as in United States and Canadian markets.
—*Rebekah Pollock*

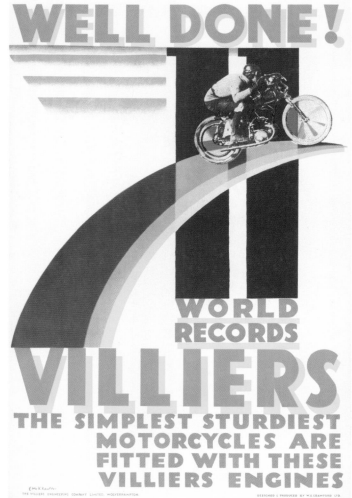

Edward McKnight Kauffer (American, active England, 1890–1954) for Underground Electric Railways Company (London, England). *Oxhey Woods*, 1915. Lithograph. 75.9 × 50.5 cm (29 7/8 × 19 7/8 in.). Gift of Mrs. E. McKnight Kauffer, 1963-39-13.

Edward McKnight Kauffer (American, active England, 1890–1954) for The Villiers Engineering Company (Wolverhampton, England). *Well Done! World Records Villiers*, ca. 1928. Lithograph. 76.1 × 50.7 cm (29 15/16 × 19 15/16 in.). Gift of Mrs. E. McKnight Kauffer, 1963-39-75.

Kauffer's early poster promoting travel in the English countryside (above left) uses a curving path to convey depth. This is a conventional technique of landscape painting. The arc in his later poster for a motorcycle company uses the same technique more abstractly to represent a modern roadway.

Edward McKnight Kauffer (American, active England, 1890–1954) for the British General Post Office (London, England). *Contact with the World / Use the Telephone*, 1934. Lithograph. 74.9 × 49.3 cm (29 1/2 × 19 7/16 in.). Gift of Mrs. E. McKnight Kauffer, 1963-39-62.

Edward McKnight Kauffer (American, active England, 1890–1954) for the British General Post Office (London, England). *Hello—the Telephone at Your Service*, 1937. Brush and gouache, graphite. 26.7 × 17.8 cm (10 1/2 × 7 in.). Gift of Mrs. E. McKnight Kauffer, 1963-39-524.

While diagonal lines often indicate depth, these posters from the 1930s use diagonal elements within a shallow, two-dimensional space to lead the eye from point to point.

Niklaus Stoecklin (Swiss, 1896–1982) for Kunsthaus Zürich (Zürich, Switzerland). Schweizerische Städtbau-Ausstellung [*Swiss Urban Planning Exhibit*], 1928. Lithograph. 128.4 × 90.3 cm (50 9/16 × 35 9/16 in.). Museum purchase through gift of Eric Kellenberger Collection, Switzerland and from General Acquisitions Endowment Fund, 2008-33-1.

This rare modernist poster promoted a Swiss city-planning exhibition held at the Zürich Art Museum in 1928. A simply constructed, three-story building in the shape of a Z—signifying the Zürich museum—creates a visual path for the lettering running over the flat roof. Niklaus Stoecklin was one of a group of early twentieth-century Swiss graphic designers—including Emile Cardinaux, Otto Morach, and Otto Baumberger—who originally trained as painters. While many of these early graphic designers celebrated the Swiss landscape, Stoecklin and fellow Swiss Burkhard Mangold, with German Ludwig Hohlwein, focused on manufactured and industrial goods and products.
—*Gail S. Davidson*

M/M (Paris): Michael Amzalag (French, b. 1967) and Mathias Augustyniak (French, b. 1967) for Centre Georges Pompidou (Paris, France). *Airs de Paris*, 2007. Screenprint. 176 × 120 cm (5 ft. 9 5/16 in. × 47 1/4 in.). Gift of M/M (Paris), 2015-4-4.

The exhibition *Airs de Paris* was curated by Christine Macel and Daniel Birnbaum at the Centre Georges Pompidou in 2007. M/M (Paris) designed a personal version of the official exhibition poster; their counter proposal was presented as an art piece displayed within the exhibition itself. The poster depicts the Centre Pompidou with a variety of small objects and museum souvenirs. The poster also announced an eight-year retrospective of M/M (Paris)'s Art Poster Series. The retrospective featured a presentation of thirty-two full-scale posters followed by an exhibition of posters reduced to one-third of their original size, accompanied by a boxed edition of the miniature reproductions (*estampes*), exhibited throughout the space.

Presenting letterforms as three-dimensional extrusions is a technique that dates to the "drop shadows" of nineteenth-century advertising typography. The posters shown here create building-like forms out of letters that have been extruded upward. Axonometric drawings represent 3D structures with a consistent scale from front to back. Treating letterforms as architectural plan views, these posters explore the spatial possibilities of projected letters.

Massimo Vignelli (Italian, active USA, 1931–2014) and Michael Bierut (American, b. 1957) for International Design Center of New York (New York, New York, USA). *The Business of Design*, 1988. Offset lithograph. 81.3 × 45.7 cm (32 × 18 in.). Gift of Lella and Massimo Vignelli, 2009-42-14.

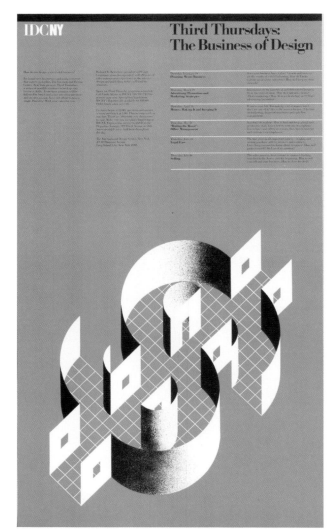

Italo Lupi (Italian, b. 1934). *World Cities and the Future of the Metropoles*, 1988. Offset lithograph. 98 × 69.6 cm (38 9/16 × 27 3/8 in.). Gift of Unknown Donor, 1989-21-14.

Takenobu Igarashi (Japanese, b. 1944) for *IDEA* magazine (Japan). *Graphic Designers on the West Coast*, 1975. Offset lithograph. 102.7 × 72.5 cm (40 7/16 × 28 9/16 in.). Gift of Takenobu Igarashi, 1981-69-1.

Mark Gowing (Australian, b. 1970)
for Sherman Contemporary Art
Foundation (Paddington, Australia).
*Jonathan Jones: untitled (the tyranny
of distance)*, 2008. Screenprint. 84
× 51.6 cm (33 1/16 × 20 5/16 in.). Gift
of Mark Gowing, 2014-32-2.

Australian designer Mark Gowing
explains that the repeating forms
of his country's minimalist
landscape are manifested in his
geometric compositions. This poster
was designed to advertise a solo
exhibition of the work of Jonathan
Jones, a Sydney-based Aboriginal
artist from the Kamilaroi/Wiradjuri
nations located in South Eastern
Australia. Jones's work in sculpture
and installation features fluorescent
tubes and incandescent bulbs, often
arranged in patterns that have their
origins in the Kamilaroi/Wiradjuri
traditions. His exhibition at Sherman
Contemporary Art Foundation,
untitled (the tyranny of distance),
showcased a piece with fluorescent
lights enclosed in a blue tarpaulin.
For the poster, Gowing adopted the
colors, light, and shade of Jones's
artwork and created a typeface
that echoes the angular lines of the
fluorescent tubes.—*Caitlin Condell*

Jonathan Jones:
untitled
(the tyranny of distance)

1 May – 26 July 2008

Sherman Contemporary
Art Foundation

New Commission of
a conceptual lighting
installation.

Sherman Contemporary Art Foundation

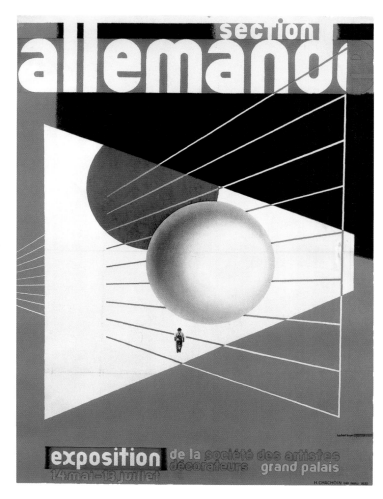

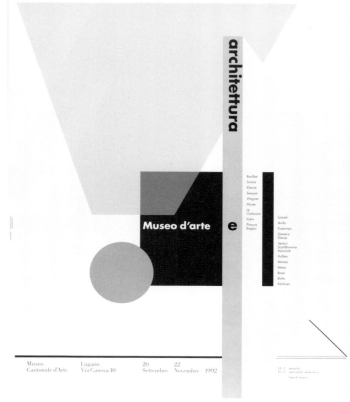

Herbert Bayer (Austrian, active Germany and USA, 1900–1985). Section Allemande [*German Section*], 1930. Lithograph. Printed by H. Chachoin (Paris, France). 158.1 × 117.2 cm (62 1/4 × 46 1/8 in.). Collection of Merrill C. Berman.

This poster promoted an influential exhibition about the Bauhaus. Two intersecting planes receding dramatically in space represent the character of modern architecture and design. The white plane is like a movie screen, reflecting the shadow of a giant white sphere. The tiny spectator below is dwarfed by this totalizing optical experience.

Bruno Monguzzi (Swiss, b. 1941) for Museo Cantonale d'Arte (Lugano, Switzerland). Museo d'Arte e Archittectura, 1992. Offset lithograph. Printed by Fratelli Roda (Taverne, Switzerland). 128.1 × 90.5 cm (50 7/16 × 35 5/8 in.). Gift of Bruno Monguzzi, 2009-14-2.

Bruno Monguzzi's 1992 poster for a museum of art and architecture pays homage to Herbert Bayer's famous poster for the Bauhaus.

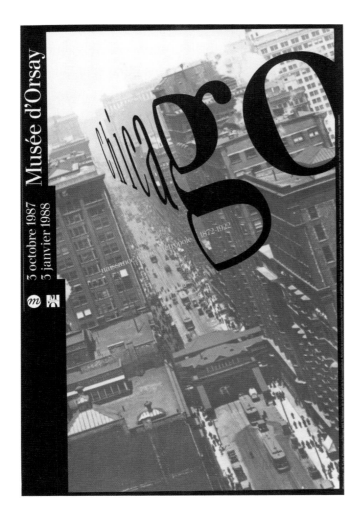

Philippe Apeloig (French, b. 1962) for Musée D'Orsay (Paris, France). *Chicago*, Naissance d'une métropole [*Birth of a metropolis*], 1872–1922, 1987. Screenprint. 150 × 100 cm (59 1/16 × 39 3/8 in.). Museum purchase from General Acquisitions Endowment Fund.

To create his *Chicago* poster in 1987, Philippe Apeloig used an early CAD-based typesetting system to produce letterforms that bend to follow the space of the photograph.

Philippe Apeloig (French, b. 1962) for Théâtre du Châtelet (Paris, France). *American in Paris*, 2014. Screenprint. 150 × 100 cm (59 1/16 × 39 3/8 in.). Courtesy of the designer in honor of Gail S. Davidson.

Apeloig continues to explore typography and architecture, using software to bend letterforms into elegant illusions. Bending the Eiffel Tower gives it a lyrical and even comic effect.

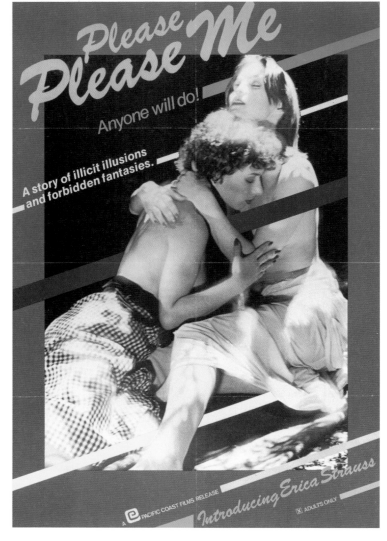

From walls and ground planes to modern street grids, vertical and horizontal elements dominate our experience of the built environment. These posters use diagonal elements to activate our view of architecture and the city.

Ladislav Sutnar (Czech and American, 1897–1976). Kutná Hora, ca. 1930. Lithograph. Printed by V. Neubert (Czechoslovakia). 94.2 × 64.6 cm (37 1/16 × 25 7/16 in.). Gift of Radoslav L. and Elaine F. Sutnar, 1998-70-1.

Tomoko Miho (American, 1931–2012) for Container Corporation of America (Chicago, Illinois, USA). 65 Bridges of New York, 1968. Offset lithograph and screenprint. 115 × 75.2 cm (45 1/4 × 29 5/8 in.). Gift of Sara and Marc Benda, 2009-20-50.

Massimo Vignelli (Italian, active USA, 1931–2014) for Designer's Saturday, Inc. (New York, New York, USA). Designer's Saturday, 1973, 1973. Offset lithograph. 59.7 × 90.2 cm (23 1/2 × 35 1/2 in.). Gift of Lella and Massimo Vignelli, 2009-42-2.

April Greiman (American, b. 1948) for Pacific Coast Films (Los Angeles, California, USA). Please Please Me, Anyone Will Do, 1977. Offset lithograph. 88.4 × 59.7 cm (34 13/16 × 23 1/2 in.). Gift of Ken Friedman, 1997-19-286.

April Greiman studied with Wolfgang Weingart in Switzerland in the late 1970s. She revolted against the hyperrational "international style" of Swiss modernism. Like Weingart, she sought looseness and complexity within modernism's abstract visual language while maintaining a strong interest in systems and structures. Diagonal elements became a hallmark of her methodology. The lines in this early work cut violently through the composition rather than lead the eye through a carefully orchestrated journey.

April Greiman (American, b. 1948) for Pacific Design Center (Los Angeles, California, USA). *Your Turn, My Turn, International Contract Furniture Design Symposium*, 1983. Offset lithograph. 91.5 × 61.1 cm (36 × 24 1/16 in.). Gift of April Greiman, 1995-167-3.

April Greiman printed her poster in two layers for viewing with 3D glasses. Any way you look at it, the poster conveys dynamism through its angled shapes and off-kilter layers.

Rebeca Méndez (Mexican and American, b. 1962). *Open House at Art Center*, 1993. Offset lithograph. 82.5 × 62.1 cm (32 1/2 × 24 7/16 in.). Gift of Rebeca Méndez, 1996-59-3.

While April Greiman's posters use diagonals in a systematic way, this poster by Rebeca Méndez combines elements at diverse angles to create a feeling of informality.

Manipulate Scale

Herbert Matter (Swiss, active USA, 1907–1984). *Engelberg, Trübsee, Switzerland*, 1935. Photogravure. Printed by A. Trüb & Cie (Aarau, Switzerland). 101.9 × 63.7 cm (40 1/8 × 25 1/16 in.). Museum purchase from General Acquisitions Endowment Fund, 2006-15-1.

Every piece of printed matter has its own scale. Armin Hofmann's 1965 poster for the Stadttheater, Basel, is over four feet tall and nearly three feet wide. Encountering this poster in person triggers a physical reaction. The enormous letter *T* makes the laughing figure seem small, and it makes us feel small, too. Bleeding beyond the frame, the *T* is too big to contain. Hofmann used black and white to resist the "trivialization of color" seen in everyday commercial advertising.[1] By narrowing his language to type, shape, and image, he sought to confront direct processes of perception.

Shifts in scale are signals of depth. Larger objects appear closer to the viewer, and smaller ones appear farther away. Designers often exaggerate scale differences in order to amplify the illusion of depth. Designers also use shifts in scale abstractly, to create visual tension among the elements of a composition.

Herbert Matter's poster *Engelberg, Trübsee, Switzerland* (1935) sets up a play between flatness and depth. The blunt frontality of the young woman's hand and face reinforces the two-dimensionality of the picture plane, but the size of her hand creates a shift in depth, pushing forward from her face. The gloved hand blocks half of her face, emphasizing her remaining eye as a point of visual focus and emotional eye contact with the viewer.

These two exemplars of Swiss modernism use formal means to engage our faculties of perception. Designers manipulate scale in symbolic and rhetorical ways as well. The size of an element can simply indicate its value within a ranked hierarchy—thus big type is often more important than little type. Scale can also become a narrative device. Many film and theater posters feature a large-scale portrait surrounded by smaller figures, objects, and scenes. This conventional technique of visual storytelling establishes a point-of-view character, using the smaller images to illustrate the hero's actions or thoughts. We instinctively accept this narrative use of scale.

René Magritte sowed absurdist discord by painting an apple the size of a small room. Claes Oldenburg constructed giant cheeseburgers and massive layer cakes to deflate the seriousness of monumental sculpture. Graphic designers see a ready-to-use language of humor and surprise in these surrealist and pop gestures, creating countless posters and advertisements that catch our attention by enlarging the scale of everyday things.[2]

Scale is relative. An object or image is only big or small in relation to what surrounds it. Designers use scale to change how things look and what they mean, activating our processes of vision as well as our ability to read and interpret pictures as a narrative medium.

Change in scale is a basic depth cue.

Stadttheater

Basel

Armin Hofmann (Swiss, b. 1920) for
Stadttheater (Basel, Switzerland.
Saison 1960/61; 1960. Offset
lithograph. 128.6 × 90.3 cm (50 5/8
× 35 9/16 in.). Gift of Ken Friedman,
1997-19-148.

Während
der Saison
1960/61
finden Sie
an dieser
Stelle
den
Spielplan

Entwurf: Armin Hofmann · Photo: Mario · Druck: Wassermann AG Basel

These posters use scale for narrative purpose rather than abstract effect. The large heads establish a point-of-view character, while the smaller elements suggest thoughts, memories, and actions.

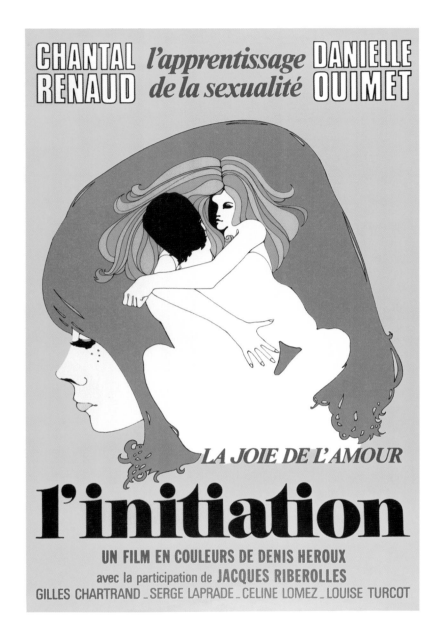

Batiste Madalena (Italian, active USA, 1902–1988) for Paramount Pictures (Los Angeles, California, USA). *Old Ironside*, 1928. Brush and gouache. 111 × 61.9 cm (43 11/16 × 24 3/8 in.). Gift of Judith and Steven Katten, 1986-118-11.

Jacques Delisle (Canadian, b. 1941) for Cinépix Propertie, Inc. (CFP) (Montreal, Canada). L'Initiation [*The Initiation*], 1970. Offset lithograph. 107 × 71.4 cm (42 1/8 × 28 1/8 in.). Gift of Sara and Marc Benda, 2010-21-97.

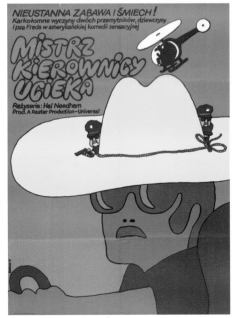

Rafael Enriquez (Cuban). *Day of the Heroic Guerrilla*, 1980. Offset lithograph. 71 × 48 cm (27 15/16 × 18 7/8 in.). Gift of Dr. and Mrs. Milton Brown, 1989-107-1.

Maciej Zbikowski (Polish, b. 1935). Mistrz kierownicy ucieka [*Smokey and the Bandit*], 1978–1979. Offset lithograph. Printed by WDA-Offset (Zam, Poland). 95.2 × 66.5 cm (37 1/2 × 26 3/16 in.). Gift of Sara and Marc Benda, 2010-21-17.

Jouineau Bourduge (France): Guy Jouineau (French) and Guy Bourduge (French). L'Enfant Sauvage [*The Wild Child*], 1970. Offset lithograph. 79.7 × 60.3 cm (31 3/8 × 23 3/4 in.). Gift of Sara and Marc Benda, 2010-21-28.

François Truffaut's film *L'Enfant Sauvage* (*The Wild Child*) is about a young boy discovered in the wilderness; the blank green field surrounding his head suggests an absence of language and structured memory.

herman miller summer picnic   august 20, 1971

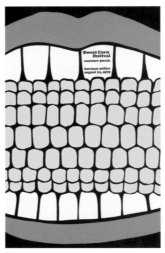

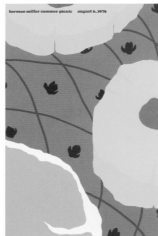

herman miller summer picnic   august 6, 1976

herman miller summer picnic   august 8, 1975

Steve Frykholm (American, b. 1942) for Herman Miller Furniture Company (Zeeland, Michigan, USA). *Summer Picnic*, 1970, 1971, 1975, 1976. Screenprints with gloss ink. 100.6 × 63.6 cm (39 5/8 × 25 1/16 in.) (each). Gift of Various Donors, 1981-29-172, -173, -165, -166.

This series of posters served to celebrate summer parties organized by the modern furniture manufacturer Herman Miller Furniture Company. Enlarged details of picnic fare become flat graphic elements, rendered in the spirit of pop.

Milton Glaser (American, b. 1929)
for Tomato Records (New York,
New York, USA). *Tomato: Something
Unusual Is Going on Here*, 1978.
Offset lithograph. 91.5 × 58.5 cm (36
× 23 1/16 in.). Gift of Milton Glaser,
1979-42-8.

Milton Glaser became one of the
most influential American designers
of his generation. His distinctive
use of illustration and humor had
a global impact beginning in the
1950s. This surrealist-inspired
poster demonstrates Glaser's strong
training in classical drawing as well
as his quirky wit.

Use Text as Image

Visual and verbal expression are inextricably linked. A poet or novelist paints images that readers conjure in their own minds.[1] Text, whether printed on a page or rendered on a screen, is itself a visual image; each letterform reflects centuries of tradition and reinvention. Yet despite the visibility of text, readers rarely stop to notice its physical form and presence. Indeed, well-designed typography often disappears, playing a supporting role to content. In poster design, however, typography often moves to the front of the stage, amplifying or obscuring a message through the size, style, and arrangement of letters.

The characters of a typeface are designed for mechanical repetition. The rise of commercial lithography in the nineteenth century encouraged poster designers to draw custom letterforms that integrated fluidly with illustrated content. Letterpress continued to be used for some poster work, however, challenging designers to defy the rigid uniformity of type.[2] The diagonal text blocks in Max Bill's 1931 poster Tanzstudio Wulff (*Dance Studio Wulff*) disrupt the mechanical grid of letterpress. Inspired by Dada typography, Bill's poster mixes various display faces with ornamental rules, employing existing components in a dynamic way. Two passes of ink overlap in Bill's poster: a black layer plus a rainbow of colors combined directly in the printing process.

Today, the limitless supply and endless malleability of digital typefaces fuel—and sometimes overwhelm—the design process. Many designers use digital tools to construct their own letterforms or customize existing typefaces. To create his poster *Ryan Francesconi* (2011), Mark Gowing built letters from primitive pixels enlarged to an extreme scale. The text in Felix Pfäffli's *Au Revoir Simone* (2013) gets thinner from left to right, telling a story of farewell (*au revoir*) through a visual transformation.

Sometimes designers make us see more than letters. Paula Scher's poster *Public* (2012) magically constructs the shape of a bicycle out of a seemingly casual jumble of characters spelling the word "public." To make sense of the poster, the viewer must toggle between reading and seeing, finding delight in discovering forms that say two things at once. The giant blue letter at the top of Ralph Schraivogel's *Paul Newman* (2001) works overtime, functioning as both a *W* and an *M* as we read the poster clockwise starting from the bottom.

Typography is the raw material of graphic design. The works shown here foreground the visual presence of text. Yet the verbal meaning of writing refuses to disappear. We can shut off the insistent referentiality of the word for a moment, but it keeps coming back, bringing with it the sound and signification of language.

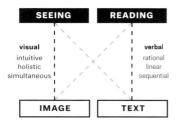

SEEING	READING
visual	**verbal**
intuitive	rational
holistic	linear
simultaneous	sequential

IMAGE	TEXT

This diagram by designer and educator Katherine McCoy (1990) shows how designers dissolve the opposition between seeing and reading.

Max Bill (Swiss, 1908–1994) for Stadttheater, Basel (Basel, Switzerland). Tanzstudio Wulff [*Dance Studio Wulff*], 1931. Letterpress. Printed by Berichthaus (Zürich, Switzerland). 64.1 × 90.8 cm (25 1/4 × 35 3/4 in.). Museum purchase through gift of Eleanor and Sarah Hewitt, 2004-1-1.

Clockwise from top left:

John Neuhart (American, 1928–2011) and Alexander Hayden Girard (American, 1907–1993) for Herman Miller Furniture Company (Zeeland, Michigan, USA). *Textiles & Objects*, 1961. Screenprint. 66.4 × 50.8 cm (26 1/8 × 20 in.). Gift of Marilyn and John Neuhart, 2004-13-1.

Paula Scher (American, b. 1948) for PUBLIC (San Francisco, California, USA). *Bicycle, Public*, 2012. Digital offset lithograph. 91.4 × 68.6 cm (36 × 27 in.). Gift of Paula Scher, 2013-25-10.

Felix Pfäffli (Swiss, b. 1986) for Südpol (Kriens, Switzerland). *Au Revoir Simone*, 2013. Risograph. 42 × 29.4 cm (16 9/16 × 11 9/16 in.). Gift of Felix Pfäffli, 2015-3-5.

Mark Gowing (Australian, b. 1970) for Preservation (Marrickville, Australia). *Ryan Francesconi*, 2011. Laser plotter print. 118.9 × 84.1 cm (46 13/16 × 33 1/8 in.). Gift of Mark Gowing, 2014-32-1.

Ralph Schraivogel (Swiss, b. 1960) for Filmpodium der Stadt Zürich (Zürich, Switzerland). *Paul Newman*, 2001. Screenprint and lithograph. Printed by FotoArt Schrofer (Lyss, Switzerland). 128 × 90.4 cm (50 3/8 × 35 9/16 in.). Gift of Anonymous Donor, 2010-8-1.

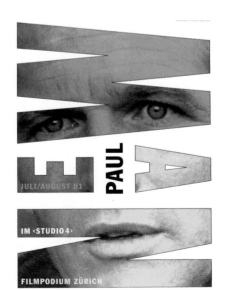

Gustav Klucis (Latvian, 1895–1938). Design for Magazine Cover, Gorn [*The Forge*], no. 1, 1923. Gouache, ink, pencil, cut paper. 22.9 × 18.4 cm (9 × 7 1/4 in.). Collection of Merrill C. Berman.

Gustav Klucis (Latvian, 1895–1938). Design for a Rostrum with Projector Screen (*Ekran*), 1923. Linocut. 23.1 × 11.3 cm (9 1/16 × 4 7/16 in.). Collection of Merrill C. Berman.

Gustav Klucis embraced constructivist typography by building geometric letterforms with the tools of the draftsman. He was interested in extending visual communication into new media, as seen in his influential designs for propaganda kiosks.

Unknown designer for Kolizey Cinema (Kirov, Russia). Niebelungen, ca. 1924. Lithograph. 62.5 × 93.3 cm (24 5/8 × 36 3/4 in.). Museum purchase through gift of Lucy Work Hewitt, 1992-167-2.

Piet Zwart (Dutch, 1885–1977). ITF Internationale tentoonstelling op filmgebied [*International Film Exhibition*], 1928. Letterpress. 85 × 61 cm (33 7/16 × 24 in.). Museum purchase through gift of Susan Hermanos, Judith and Charles Bergoffen, Cathy Nierras, and Anonymous Donors and from Drawings and Prints Council and General Acquisitions Endowment Funds, 2013-20-1.

Piet Zwart's iconic poster advertises a 1928 avant-garde film festival held in The Hague. With its carefully organized proportions and balance—of color, of positive and negative space, and of image and typography—this poster is arguably the greatest accomplishment of Dutch modernism.—*Caitlin Condell*

Philippe Apeloig (French, b. 1962).
Four designs for Vivo in Typo, 2008.
Pen and black ink. 30.1 × 22.6 cm
(11 7/8 × 8 7/8 in.) (each). Gift of
Philippe Apeloig, 2014-34-3/6.

Philippe Apeloig (French, b. 1962).
Design for Vivo in Typo, 2008. Pen
and black ink. 42.1 × 29.7 cm
(16 9/16 × 11 11/16 in.). Gift of Philippe
Apeloig, 2014-34-8.

Philippe Apeloig (French, b. 1962).
Eight designs for Vivo in Typo, 2008.
Digital prints. Various sizes. Gift of
Philippe Apeloig, 2014-34-10, -11,
-13/19.

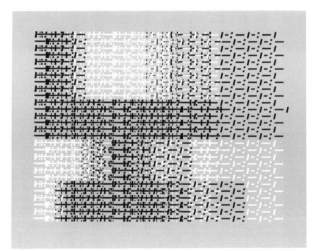

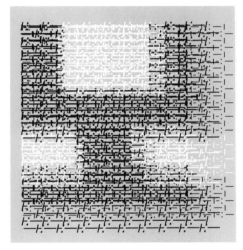

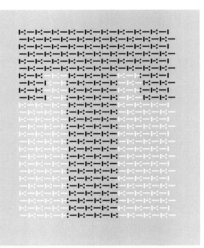

Philippe Apeloig's working method moves seamlessly between hand drawings and computer-generated graphics. For his *Vivo in Typo* poster announcing an exhibition of his own work, he began with pen-and-ink drawings to wrestle with different lettering layouts. He then turned to the computer to compose a system of punctuation marks that became the matrix from which the letters would emerge. His sketches and working prints show how he built up a richly textural surface through multiple layers of marks with varied spacing and colored inks. For Apeloig, typography is not only a tool, but also the material itself.—*Gail S. Davidson*

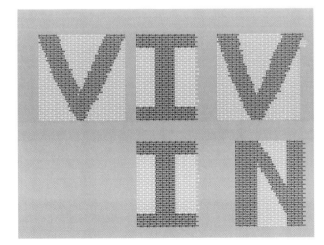

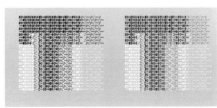

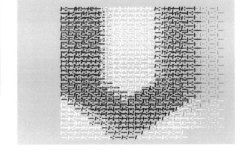

Philippe Apeloig (French, b. 1962).
Design for Vivo in Typo, 2008. Digital
print. 42.1 × 29.7 cm (16 9/16 × 11
11/16 in.). Gift of Philippe Apeloig,
2014-34-21.

Philippe Apeloig (French, b. 1962). *Vivo in Typo, Affiches et alphabets*, 2008. Screenprint. 175 × 118 cm (5 ft. 8 7/8 in. × 46 7/16 in.). Gift of Philippe Apeloig, 2013-16-2.

Philippe Apeloig
Affiches
et alphabets animés
12 avril – 25 mai
2008
Espace Topographie
de l'art
15 rue de Thorigny
Paris 3ᵉ

M/M (Paris): Michael Amzalag (French, b. 1967) and Mathias Augustyniak (French, b. 1967). *About*, 1999. Screenprint. 176 × 120 cm (5 ft. 9 5/16 in. × 47 1/4 in.). Gift of M/M (Paris), 2015-4-7.

Mathias Augustyniak and Michael Amzalag are partners in the legendary design team M/M (Paris), founded in 1992. This poster, *About* (1999), marked the beginning of their ongoing Art Posters Series. Each poster operates within the context of the art world "as a medium and not as a decorative object." The series title refers to the tradition of selling reproductions in museums as artworks affordable to the general public. A selection from the series is shown on these pages. Rather than represent a subject in a direct or subservient way, each poster develops the designers' intricate, idiosyncratic graphic language, demonstrating the poster's role as a "perfomative medium." *About* is based on a title sequence created by Amzalag and Augustyniak for three films by Pierre Huyghe, Philippe Parreno, and Dominique Gonzalez-Foerster, presented at the Venice Biennial in 1999.

M/M (Paris): Michael Amzalag (French, b. 1967) and Mathias Augustyniak (French, b. 1967). *Cosmodrome [Dominique Gonzalez-Foerster & Jay-Yay Johanson]*, 2001. Screenprint. 176 × 120 cm (5 ft. 9 5/16 in. × 47 1/4 in.). Gift of M/M (Paris), 2015-4-1.

This poster was designed to promote *Cosmodrome*, a contemplative light and sound space designed by Dominique Gonzalez-Foerster and Jay-Jay Johansson. The poster was designed to follow and announce the presence of *Cosmodrome* wherever it was on view, in art spaces throughout the world.

M/M (Paris): Michael Amzalag (French, b. 1967) and Mathias Augustyniak (French, b. 1967). Crustinien des Galapagos, *a Film by François Curlet*, 2013. Screenprint. 176 × 120 cm (5 ft. 9 5/16 in. × 47 1/4 in.). Gift of M/M (Paris), 2015-4-6.

François Curlet is a French artist whose practice encompasses sculpture, drawing, installation, painting, writing, curating, and filmmaking. *Crustinien des Galapagos* is a short film (five minutes long) about the meaning of signs in multiple formats.

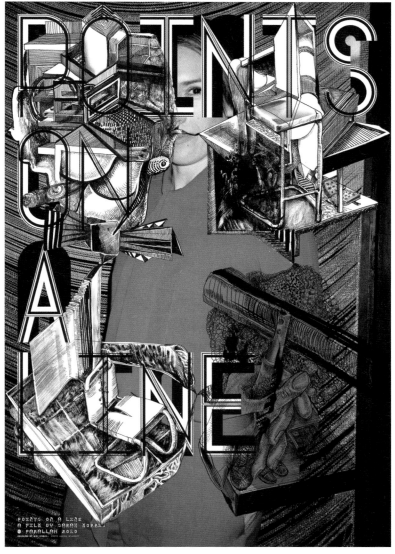

M/M (Paris): Michael Amzalag (French, b. 1967) and Mathias Augustyniak (French, b. 1967) for Parallax Film Productions (White Rock, British Columbia, Canada). *Los Angeles, a Film by Sarah Morris*, 2013. Screenprint. 176 × 120 cm (5 ft. 9 5/16 in. × 47 1/4 in.). Gift of M/M (Paris), 2015-4-3.

M/M (Paris): Michael Amzalag (French, b. 1967) and Mathias Augustyniak (French, b. 1967) for Parallax Film Productions (White Rock, British Columbia, Canada). *Points of a Line, a Film by Sarah Morris*, 2010. Screenprint. 176 × 120 cm (5 ft. 9 5/16 in. × 47 1/4 in.). Gift of M/M (Paris), 2015-4-5.

Sarah Morris creates experimental films within the context of the art world. Her films are displayed in museums and art spaces surrounded by her own related paintings, and are announced and promoted with posters designed by M/M (Paris). Each film and its accompanying poster explores a city or architectural landscape. *Los Angeles* (2005) is a study of image production within the decentered plan and complex architecture of Los Angeles; the poster uses the title of the film as a prism.

Points of a Line (2010) documents the daily maintenance of two architectural masterworks: Mies van der Rohe's Farnsworth House and Philip Johnson's Glass House. In the poster, drawings of objects and architectural elements merge with lettering to frame the photograph behind them.

Jianping He (Chinese, b. 1973) for Detour Design Show (Hong Kong, China). *Detour Design Show*, 2008. Offset lithograph. 118.9 × 84.1 cm (46 13/16 × 33 1/8 in.). Gift of Jianping He, 2014-23-3.

Jianping He designed this poster to promote a 2008 solo exhibition organized by the InnoCentre Hong Kong and the Hong Kong Polytechnic University. As He labored over packing his work to ship to Hong Kong from his studio in Berlin, he found himself caught up in thoughts over his long initial journey from China to Europe. He titled his exhibition *Detour* to reflect the "backward" journey of his graphic design pieces. He modified a typeface so that the ends of many of the letters trail off into meandering lines. Some of the lines curve inward toward the center of the poster, while other lines extend out the edges. —*Caitlin Condell*

Jianping He (Chinese, b. 1973). *China Image*, 2004. Screenprint. 118.9 × 84.1 cm (46 13/16 × 33 1/8 in.). Gift of Jianping He, 2014-23-1.

After studying graphic design at the China Academy of Art, Jianping He earned an MFA from the Berlin University of the Arts and a PhD in cultural history from the Free University of Berlin. In 2002, he founded Hesign, a Berlin studio that not only designs posters, books, and corporate identities, but also curates exhibitions and organizes cultural events. This poster features the two Chinese characters that together translate as "China." The characters were modeled in ceramic by artist Sonny Kim; the painting recalls the iconic blue-and-white floral pattern associated with the country. He staged these two ceramic models against a bough of white cherry blossoms. —*Caitlin Condell*

Jianping He (Chinese, b. 1973). *AGI—To Kyo To*, 2007. Offset lithograph. 118.9 × 84.1 cm (46 13/16 × 33 1/8 in.). Gift of Jianping He, 2014-23-2.

After the occasion of its annual conference held in Kyoto in 2006, the Alliance Graphique Internationale (AGI) published the book entitled *To Kyo To*, featuring posters designed by eighty international AGI members. Jianping He designed the book and created this delicately rendered poster to commemorate the publication. A thin, free-flowing line scribbles across the page and doubles back on itself to densely fill the space. The central textforms that make up the title consist of layers of concentric circles, as if he had repeated his motions over and over with a ballpoint pen. The forms echo the punctured holes that make up the title on the cover of the publication itself.—*Caitlin Condell*

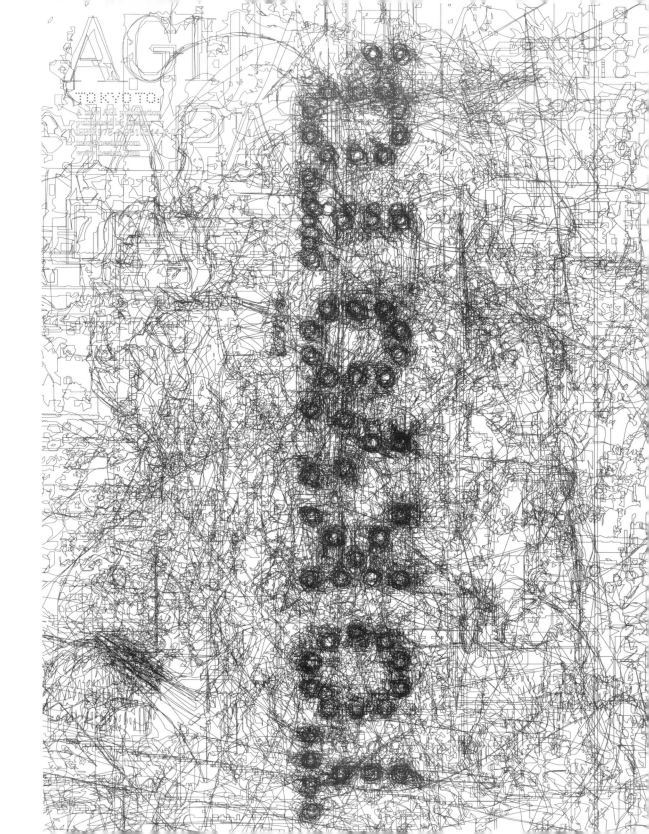

터전을
불태우라
BURNING
DOWN
THE
HOUSE

2014 광주비엔날레
GWANGJU BIENNALE 2014
9.5–11.9

장소
광주비엔날레 전시관 및
광주 중외공원문화예술벨트 일원

주최
재단법인 광주비엔날레
광주광역시

www.gwangjubiennale.org

Venues
Gwangju Biennale
Exhibition Hall
and select locations
in Joongwee Park,
Gwangju, Korea.

Hosts
Gwangju Biennale Foundation
Gwangju Metropolitan City

Sulki & Min (Seoul, South Korea):
Sulki Choi (South Korean, b. 1977)
and Min Choi (South Korean, b.
1971). *Cabbage Thoughts*, 2009.
Offset lithograph. 84 × 59.4 cm (33
1/16 × 23 3/8 in.). Gift of Sulki & Min,
2014-21-2.

This poster was designed to
promote a performance entitled
Cabbage Thoughts, given by the
Korean dancer Park Na Hoon and
his company in 2009. Sulki & Min
designed a typeface that creates
letterforms out of layered curving
bands. The resulting characters
give the illusion of depth, which is
heightened by their being printed in
shiny ink. Beneath them is a sketchily
rendered image of a cabbage, the
primary ingredient in the Korean
national dish kimchi and an
important symbolic reference point
for the dance production.
—Caitlin Condell

Sulki & Min (Seoul, South Korea):
Sulki Choi (South Korean, b. 1977)
and Min Choi (South Korean, b. 1971).
Gwangju Biennale 2014, 2014. Offset
lithograph. 93.9 × 63.6 cm (36 15/16
× 25 1/16 in.). Gift of Sulki & Min,
2014-21-5.

For the tenth Gwangju Biennale,
Sulki & Min strove to evoke the
art festival's provocative theme:
"Burning Down the House." The
designers created a typographic
system featuring three different
weights and five different line
breaks. Used together, the system
allowed the design to cover as much
surface area of the poster with as
much text as possible. The designers
also redrew the Korean characters,
modifying some of the more
traditional conventions, allowing
them to work seamlessly with the
Latin characters.—Caitlin Condell

Sulki & Min (Seoul, South Korea):
Sulki Choi (South Korean, b. 1977)
and Min Choi (South Korean, b. 1971).
Now Jump, 2008. Offset lithograph.
84 × 59.4 cm (33 1/16 × 23 3/8 in.).
Gift of Sulki & Min, 2014-21-1.

Sulki & Min designed the graphic
identity for an art festival celebrating
the legendary Korean-American
artist Nam June Paik, considered
one of the pioneers of video art. At
a planning meeting for the festival,
one of the participants noticed that
the title of the festival, Now Jump,
featured the initials of the artist.
The designers were inspired by
this coincidence and modified the
typeface Helvetica Ultra Compressed
so that the three letters, *N*, *J*, and *P*
would stand out.—*Caitlin Condell*

백남준아트센터 개관 백남준페스티벌
Nam June Paik Festival
Presented by NJP Art Center

| ?-? = ∞ |
NAM JUNE PAIK ART CENTER

2008.10.8 – 2009.2.5
백남준아트센터
신갈고등학교 체육관
지앤 아트 스페이스

8 October 2008 – 5 February 2009
NJP Art Center
Shingal High School Gymnasium
ZIEN ART SPACE

NOW JUMP

주최
경기문화재단
백남준아트센터
용인시
주관
백남준 페스티벌 조직위원회
후원

Tell a Story

Whether advertising a product, agitating for a cause, or promoting a movie or play, many posters tell stories, employing image and text within the fixed frame of a single sheet of paper to indicate an event unfolding in time. What just happened? What will happen next?

Aristotle defined a story is a whole action of a certain magnitude. A story has a beginning, middle, and end. It introduces a problem, reaches a peak, and finds resolution.[1] Whether it's an epic tale or a casual anecdote, a story provides readers or listeners with a feeling of surprise or discovery, and it satisfies them with a desired outcome or the convincing thud of completion.

Stories happen everywhere, not just in movies and books. Going to a mall or restaurant is a kind of story, and so is the act of placing a call or starting a car. Designers plan these interactions to feel like whole events. A trip to Starbucks may not be suspenseful, but it has a clear beginning, middle, and end.

A typical work of drama or fiction opens with a brief period of exposition. Where are we? Who is the protagonist? The story also establishes a point of view. Will we see events through the eyes of the protagonist, or from the overhead view of an omniscient narrator? The principle character confronts a mystery or challenge and faces off against various obstacles before reaching a high point of discovery or struggle. The tension unwinds as the final conflict plays out and loose ends are resolved.

In Massimo Vignelli's poster for *That's Entertainment: The American Musical Film* (1976), dancer Fred Astaire leaps across the surface in a series of still images. Vignelli has stopped the story arc at its peak, leaving it to the viewer to complete the action. By choosing the high point in the narrative (physically and metaphorically), Vignelli has amplified the sense of drama and movement.

When telling a story with just one image, designers must choose a single point in a narrative to suggest the whole story. During World War II, the U.S. Office of War Information used phrases such as "Loose lips sink ships" to discourage idle talk about ship movements that might expose naval forces to attack. Anton Otto Fischer's poster *A Careless Word* (1942) depicts a lifeboat loaded with distressed and wounded sailors pulling away from a burning ship. As viewers, we put ourselves in the boat with the sailors, seeing the scene of devastation from their perspective. Frederick Siebel's *Someone Talked!* (1942) pulls us even closer into the story, bringing us eye to eye with one sailor who is about to disappear forever into the deep. Eliminating expository details, Siebel focuses our attention on a single human experience—and he holds us responsible for the event we are witnessing.

Freytag's Pyramid is a famous diagram of dramatic structure, created by Gustav Freytag in 1863.

Massimo Vignelli (Italian, 1931–2014) for Fort Worth Art Museum (Fort Worth, Texas, USA). *That's Entertainment: The American Musical Film*, 1976. Offset lithograph. 61 × 91.4 cm (24 × 36 in.). Gift of Lella and Massimo Vignelli, 2009-42-5.

Frederick Siebel (American, Austrian, and Czech, 1913–1991). *Someone Talked!*, 1942. Lithograph. Printed by Devoe & Reynolds Painting Company (USA). 101.6 × 71.1 cm (40 × 28 in.). Gift of Louise Clémencon, 1949-108-10.

Anton Otto Fischer (German, active USA, 1882–1962) for the Office of War Information (Washington D.C., USA). *A Careless Word*, 1942. Lithograph. 94.5 × 72.2 cm (37 3/16 × 28 7/16 in.). Gift of Unknown Donor, 1987-24-25.

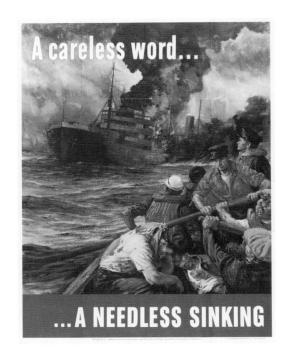

Dmitry Moor (Russian, 1883–1946). *A Red Present to the White Pan*, 1920. Lithograph. 70.1 × 53 cm (27 5/8 × 20 7/8 in.). Museum purchase through gift of Mrs. John Innes Kane, 1992-123-1.

Created during the Russian Civil War (1917–1922), this poster uses conventional illustration techniques to depict strong young soldiers in the Bolshevik Red Army battling against the White Army, represented with a caricature of a figure who is overweight and underprepared.

Georgii Augustovich Stenberg
(Russian, 1900–1933) and Vladimir
Augustovich Stenberg (Russian,
1899–1982). *Adventures of an
Abandoned Child*, 1926. Lithograph.
101.3 × 71.9 cm (39 7/8 × 28 5/16 in.).
Gift of Merrill C. Berman in honor of
Ellen Lupton, 2014-20-1.

The Stenberg brothers produced
numerous film posters at the height
of the new cinema culture in the
Soviet Union. They used techniques
similar to those employed in avant-
garde film: montage, close-ups,

and distortion. Photomontage,
the process of creating a collage
from photographic elements, had
become a popular design tool in
Russia by the early 1920s. The
Stenbergs used their own invented
projection device to aid in the
creation of dramatic juxtapositions,
which were hand-drawn but inspired
by photomontage, as seen in this
striking figure of a man with a
disembodied head between his
feet.—*Caitlin Condell*

Georgii Augustovich Stenberg
(Russian, 1900–1933) and Vladimir
Augustovich Stenberg (Russian,
1899–1982). *The Ghost That Isn't
Returning*, 1929. Lithograph. 94.9 ×
62.5 cm (37 3/8 × 24 5/8 in.). Gift of
Merrill C. Berman in honor of Ellen
Lupton, 2014-20-4.

This rhythmic poster promotes the
film *The Ghost That Isn't Returning*,
directed by Abram Room, which
tells the saga of Jose Real, a South
American oilfield worker sentenced
to life in prison for protesting his

country's totalitarian regime. Real
is granted a furlough from prison,
during which the guards plan to
assassinate him. An agent tracks
Real across the desert. Although the
chase unfolds over many scenes, the
Stenberg brothers drew inspiration
from a specific moment in the
film, when the agent walks down
a long dirt road, streaked with the
shadow of a row of fence posts. The
Stenbergs transformed the graphic
effect of the shadows to suggest the
steps of a staircase.—*Caitlin Condell*

The U.S. Office of War Information (OWI) was established by an executive order of President Franklin D. Roosevelt on June 13, 1942. The OWI sought, in the words of the president, to "formulate and carry out, through the use of press, radio, motion picture, and other facilities, information programs designed to facilitate the development of an informed and intelligent understanding, at home and abroad, of the status and progress of the war effort and of the war policies, activities, and aims of the Government." The OWI employed dramatic storytelling to stir the emotions of citizens who were wary of U.S. intervention in the war. Posters published by the OWI addressed numerous themes, from religious freedom to buying war bonds.

Edward McKnight Kauffer (American, active England, 1890–1954) for the Office of War Information (Washington, D.C., USA). Libertad de Cultos [*Freedom of Worship*], 1947. Offset lithograph. 50.6 × 36.2 cm (19 15/16 × 14 1/4 in.) Gift of Mrs. E. McKnight Kauffer, 1963-39-129.

Barbara J. Marks (American) for the Office of War Information (Washington, D.C., USA). *This Is the Enemy*, 1943. Lithograph. 71.3 × 51 cm (28 1/16 × 20 1/16 in.). Gift of Unknown Donor, 1987-24-24.

Lawrence Beall Smith (American, 1909–1989). *Don't Let That Shadow Touch Them*, 1942. Lithograph. Printed by U.S. Government Printing Office (Washington, D.C., USA). 101.4 × 72.3 cm (39 15/16 × 28 7/16 in.). Gift of Louise Clémencon, 1949-108-8.

The younger children don't know that evil hovers above them, but the older boy is on the cusp of understanding. He is the point of view character in the scene, and we are expected to identify with his situation. Like him, we must "grow up" and take responsibility for the more naive people around us. As war propaganda, the poster promoted U.S. involvement in World War II, which many citizens did not support.

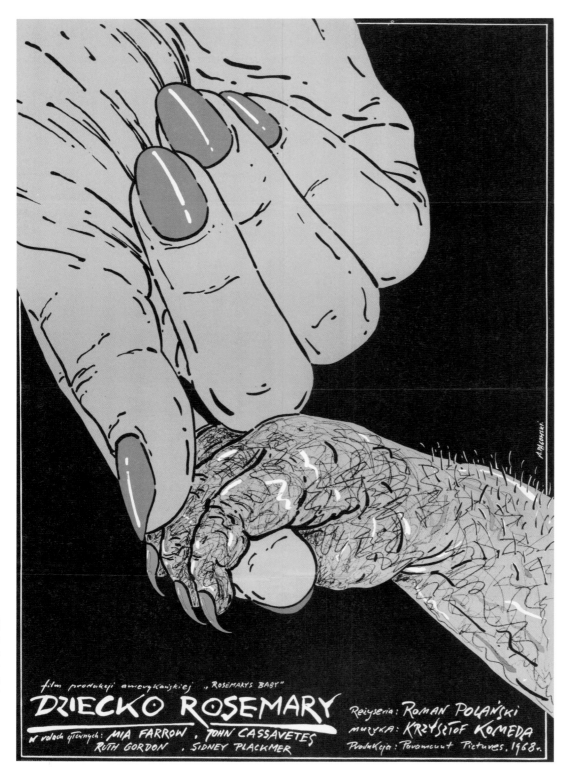

Andrzej Pagowski (Polish, b. 1953). Dziecko Rosemary [*Rosemary's Baby*], 1984. Offset lithograph. 95.3 × 67 cm (37 1/2 × 26 3/8 in.). Gift of Sara and Marc Benda, 2010-21-20.

Andrzej Pagowski is a leading member of the third generation of the Polish School of Poster Art. By actively interpreting a subject with emotionally charged images, often drawn or painted by hand, these designers tell stories through the medium of the poster. Pagowksi created this poster for the Polish distribution of Roman Polanski's legendary 1968 horror film *Rosemary's Baby* (based on the novel by Ira Levin). This moment of intimacy between Rosemary and her demon child is only implied in the film, never shown directly.

Jan Sawka (Polish, active USA, 1946–2012). *CRASH*, 1977. Offset lithograph. 96 × 66.1 cm (37 13/16 × 26 in.). Gift of Sara and Marc Benda, 2009-20-25.

Jan Sawka belonged to the Polish School of Poster Art. His poster for the film *Crash!* (directed by Marc Marais in 1977) uses the title of the movie to dramatize the action.

Unknown designer. *The Stepford Wives*, 1975–1976. Screenprint. 69.7 × 98 cm (27 7/16 × 38 9/16 in.). Gift of Sara and Marc Benda, 2010-21-24.

This image of a cracked mannequin or statue with a photographically real face sums up the banal horror of Bryan Forbes's 1975 film *The Stepford Wives*, based on a novel by Ira Levin. Rather than depict an actual scene from the film, the designer chose to represent its inner psychology.

Stefan Sagmeister (Austrian, active USA, b. 1962) for AIGA National Conference, featuring photography by Bela Borsodi (Austrian, active USA, b. 1966). *Hurry!*, 1997. Offset lithograph. 67.3 × 95.3 cm (26 1/2 × 37 1/2 in.). Gift of Sagmeister, Inc., 2000-61-5.

The phrase "chicken with its head cut off" is a commonplace description of a person swept up in a state of mindless frenzy. In this poster for a graphic design conference, Stefan Sagmeister illustrates the cliché in a literal fashion, stepping up the emotional impact with shooting drops of blood and letters made of chicken feet.

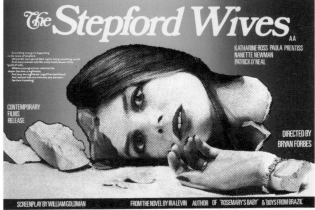

Seymour Chwast (American, b. 1931) for Amnesty International. *Human Rights Now*, 1988. Offset lithograph. 94 × 61.2 cm (37 × 24 1/8 in.). Gift of Steven Heller and Karrie Jacobs, 1993-53-55.

Seymour Chwast cofounded Push Pin Studio in 1954 with Milton Glaser and Reynolds Ruffin in New York City. Together they created an influential style that swept the international design world in the 1950s, 1960s, 1970s, and beyond. Chwast's distinctive approach to visual communication combines gently outlined illustrations with quirky humor and an eye for soft, inviting color. This poster for Amnesty International conveys the inclusiveness of the organization's message by showing different ways to shine a light.

Seymour Chwast (American, b. 1931) for the American Cancer Society (Atlanta, Georgia, USA). *Question: What's wrong with this picture?*, 1976. Lithograph. 58.5 × 34.2 cm (23 1/16 × 13 7/16 in.). Gift of Various Donors, 1981-29-85.

Misdirection is a key technique in comedy and humor. The reader or audience is expecting the narrative to resolve in a certain way when the action suddenly changes course. In this poster, the obvious answer to the question "What's wrong with this picture?" gets a surprising answer. Misdirection often functions by changing a situation's anticipated emphasis or point of focus. Here, we assume the man's problem consists of three extra mouths, but we learn instead that his real problem is a very ordinary one (smoking).

Seymour Chwast (American, b. 1931). *March for Peace and Justice*, 1982. Lithograph. 61.3 × 44.5 cm (24 1/8 × 17 1/2 in.). Gift of Steven Heller and Karrie Jacobs, 1993-53-84.

Seymour Chwast (American, b. 1931) for the Brooklyn Institute of Arts and Sciences (Brooklyn, New York, USA). *The Brooklyn Children's Museum*, 1977. Lithograph. 63.5 × 48.2 cm (25 × 19 in.). Gift of Various Donors, 1981-29-38.

Showing a person or other creature walking in a profile view is a simple way to suggest a story unfolding in time. We expect these characters to keep moving across the poster and out of the frame.

Jean Carlu (French, active USA, 1900–1997). *Give 'em Both Barrels*, 1941. Offset lithograph. Printed by U.S. Government Printing Office (Washington, D.C., USA). 76.2 × 101.6 cm (30 × 40 in.). Gift of Unknown Donor, 1980-32-1201.

Double the Meaning

Signs often point to other signs. We represent love with a heart, death with a skull, and the Nazi party with the bent blades of the swastika. Designers construct metaphors, puns, irony, and other devices to create double meanings, turning abstract ideas into vivid mental images and generating humor and surprise.

Similes, such as "blind as a bat" or "proud as a peacock," use the word "as" or "like" to compare two ideas. Jean Carlu's World War II propaganda poster *Give 'em Both Barrels* (1941) compares a machine gun to a rivet gun, telling us that factory work was crucial to the war effort. Edward McKnight Kauffer's poster *Power: The Nerve Centre of London's Underground* (1930) equates a human arm with a power station, comparing human and industrial might.

A metaphor collapses two signs into one rather than placing them side by side. Clichés such as "He held the key to her heart" and "She was a ticking time bomb" equate human emotions with mechanical objects, inviting the reader to visualize inner states of mind. Designers create compact graphic metaphors by fusing together conflicting images. Art Chantry's poster *The Adding Machine* (1981) employs a simple act of cut and paste to transform a keyboard into a row of teeth, while Peter Kuper and Seth Tobocman's *Crack House White House* (1991) converts the presidential residence into the grin of a skull.

These graphic metaphors are visual puns. Just as a verbal pun or homonym uses one sound to convey two meanings ("stare" and "stair"), a visual pun exploits arbitrary similarities in appearance (a row of columns becomes a row of teeth). While many words happen to be homonyms, puns are funny only when they carry an unexpected twist. The expression "Time flies like an arrow; fruit flies like a banana" brings an absurd image to mind (a flying banana) before the puzzle gets resolved.

Parody, functioning as a kind of extended metaphor, borrows familiar features from well-known stories, songs, or images. Spoofs of mass advertising campaigns hijack brand messages to promote wholly different products or values. Advertisers work hard to saturate the mediascape with the colors, fonts, and phrases of consumer goods. When artists and activists divert commercial speech into social commentary, they lay claim to a privately owned idiom whose relentless messaging blankets public life.

Reading a poem brings vivid pictures and multiple meanings to mind. Reading a poster can conjure a similar clash of ideas and sensations, adding flesh and bones to abstract concepts. Metaphors deliver humor and surprise in the compressed space where incompatible ideas collide and converge.

Simile:
A heart is like
a lock.

Metaphor:
A heart
is a lock.

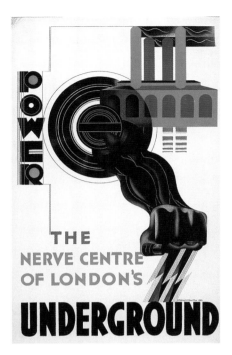

Edward McKnight Kauffer (American, active England, 1890–1954) for Transport for London (London, England). *Power—The Nerve Center of London's Underground*, 1930. Lithograph. 101.6 × 61.4 cm (40 × 24 3/16 in.). Gift of Mrs. E. McKnight Kauffer, 1963-39-45.

Peter Kuper (American, b. 1958) and Seth Tobocman (American, b. 1958). *Crack House White House*, 1991. Airbrush. 61 × 48.4 cm (24 × 19 1/16 in.). Gift of Steven Heller and Karrie Jacobs, 1993-53-83.

Art Chantry (American, b. 1954) for Bathhouse Theatre (Seattle, Washington, USA). *The Adding Machine*, 1981. Screenprint. 45.1 × 30.5 cm (17 3/4 × 12 in.). Gift of Art Chantry, 1995-69-31.

Paul

Rand

Art

Directors

Club

of

Cincinnati

Art

Museum

May

17

1994

7-8

pm

Paul Rand (American, 1914–1996)
for Consolidated Cigar Co. (Fort
Lauderdale, Florida, USA). *Santa's
Favorite Cigar*, 1953–57. Offset
lithograph. 52.9 × 49.7 cm (20 13/16
× 19 9/16 in.). Gift of Paul Rand,
1991-69-70.

Paul Rand (American, 1914–1996)
for Consolidated Cigar Co. (Fort
Lauderdale, Florida, USA). *Santa's
Favorite Cigar*, 1953–57. Offset
lithograph. 53 × 50.9 cm (20 7/8
× 20 1/16 in.). Gift of Paul Rand,
1991-69-69.

Paul Rand (American, 1914–1996)
for Consolidated Cigar Co. (Fort
Lauderdale, Florida, USA). *For Dad
. . . with Love and Kisses*, 1953–57.
Offset lithograph. 61 × 50.8 cm (24
× 20 in.). Gift of Marion S. Rand,
2002-11-12.

Paul Rand often used minimal
elements to serve more than one
purpose. With the addition of a few
playful signifiers, Rand turned a
cigar into Santa Claus or a debonair
gentleman.

Paul Rand (American, 1914–1996)
for the Cincinnati Art Museum
(Cincinnati, Ohio, USA). *Art Directors
Club*, 1994. Offset lithograph. 91.4 ×
61 cm (36 × 24 in.). Gift of Marion S.
Rand, 2002-11-13.

Here, a column of type stands in
for the body of a young boy. We
take pleasure in discovering the
seemingly effortless double function
of this typographic picture.

Paul Rand (American, 1914–1996) for
IBM (New York, New York, USA). *Eye,
Bee, M (IBM)*, 1981. Offset lithograph.
91.4 × 61 cm (36 × 24 in.). Gift of
Marion S. Rand, 2002-11-20.

This famous poster by Paul Rand
is an example of a rebus. We read
the pictures of the eye and the
bee as sounds, spelling out the
company name: IBM. Using pictures
to represent sounds is the basis of
various writing systems, including
Egyptian hieroglyphs.

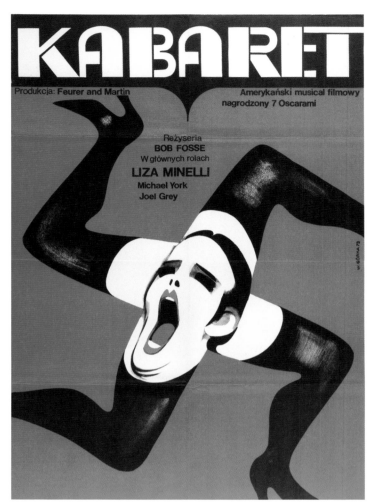

Wiktor Górka (Polish, 1922–2004). Kabaret [Cabaret], 1973. Offset lithograph. 83.7 × 58 cm (32 15/16 × 22 13/16 in.). Gift of Sara and Marc Benda, 2010-21-100.

Wiktor Górka, a leading participant in the Polish School of Poster Art, was a master of visual metaphor. Bob Fosse's film Cabaret (1972) is set in a German nightclub during Hitler's rise. In Górka's visual pun, a strange cast of body parts converges to create a single disturbing image.

Hans Hillmann (German, 1925–2014). Sein oder Nichtsein [To Be or Not to Be], 1964. Offset lithograph. 84.7 × 59 cm (33 3/8 × 23 1/4 in.). Gift of Sara and Marc Benda, 2010-21-78.

Influenced by modern art and design, Hans Hillmann designed 130 richly interpretive film posters between 1953 and 1974. His striking, metaphoric posters were commissioned by Neue Filmkunst, a leading distributor of independent films in Germany. This poster equating Hitler with Humpty Dumpty makes fun of the monstrous leader and his ultimate downfall.

POST NO BILLS ©1992

hmmm...

BUSH/QUAYLE'92

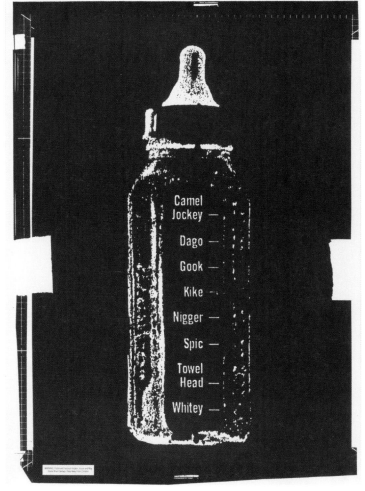

Camel
Jockey —

Dago —

Gook —

Kike —

Nigger —

Spic —

Towel
Head —

Whitey —

Post No Bills (New York, New York, USA): John Gall (American, b. 1964) with Steven Brower, Leah Lococo, Morris Taub, James Victore, Susan Walsh. *hmmm . . . Bush / Quayle '92*, 1992. Offset lithograph. 73.5 × 51 cm (28 15/16 × 20 1/16 in.). Gift of Steven Heller and Karrie Jacobs, 1993-53-46.

The line of type is also a mustache, transforming an ordinary press photo into something else. The poster draws a rather overstated comparison between Hitler and a presidential candidate.

Post No Bills (New York, New York, USA): Steven Brower (American, b. 1952) with John Gall, Leah Lococo, Morris Taub, James Victore, Susan Walsh. *Baby Bottle*, 1994. Offset lithograph. 73.6 × 51 cm (29 in. × 20 1/16 in.). Gift of Steven Brower, 1997-53-1.

Irony is the art of using one statement to mean its opposite. Here, an image associated with warmth and nurturing conveys a dark message. The markings on a baby bottle suggest that cultural stereotypes are taught early in life.

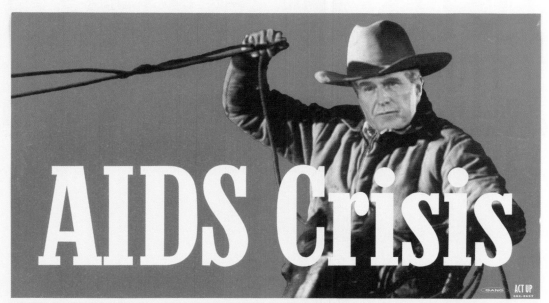

Vincent Gagliostro (American, b. 1955) and Avram Finkelstein (American, b. 1952). *Enjoy AZT*, 1989. Screenprint. 58.6 × 48.4 cm (23 1/16 × 19 1/16 in.) Gift of Steven Heller and Karrie Jacobs, 1993-53-103.

In 1987 the U.S. Food and Drug Administration approved AZT for the treatment of AIDS. Because the drug was both toxic and ineffective, many AIDS activists demanded that drug companies develop alternative treatments. This self-published poster compares AZT to Coke, condemning the drug as a consumer product that profited from the misery of AIDS patients.

Tibor Kalman (Hungarian and American, 1949–1999) for the Artis Association (Paris, France). Images pour la lutte contre le sida [*Images for the fight against AIDS*], 1993. Screenprint. Printed by Graficaza (France). 84.1 × 59.4 cm (33 1/8 × 23 3/8 in.). Museum purchase from General Exhibitions Funds, 1995-86-6.

Tibor Kalman is remembered for creating emotionally powerful responses to the AIDS crisis as art director of *COLORS* magazine in the 1990s. This poster promoting condoms takes a lighter touch.

Gang (probably American) for ACT UP (AIDS Coalition to Unleash Power) (New York, New York, USA) after Leo Burnett. *AIDS Crisis*, 1990. Lithograph. 34.4 × 52.1 cm (13 9/16 × 20 1/2 in.). Gift of Steven Heller and Karrie Jacobs, 1993-53-112.

Comparing President George H. W. Bush to the Marlboro Man, this poster critiques the administration's emphasis on military spending and its neglect of healthcare research and reform.

Doug Minkler (American, b. 1949) for Doctors Ought to Care (DOC) (Augusta, Georgia, USA). *Mr. Camel's Kids Club*, 1990. Screenprint. 66.4 × 55.2 cm (26 1/8 × 21 3/4 in.). Gift of Doug Minkler, 2000-15-1.

Studies published by the *Journal of the American Medical Association* in 1992 showed that animal characters appearing in cigarette ads appeal strongly to children, putting Old Joe the Camel on a par with Mickey Mouse. Many activists petitioned retailers to stop posting images of Old Joe. Doug Minkler's poster conflates the camel's nose with human genitalia, reflecting a popular view at the time that camel's portrait was a deliberate form of subliminal suggestion.—*Rebekah Pollock*

Founded in 1983, the Minnesota AIDS Project provides services to Minnesotans living with HIV and seeks to slow the spread of the virus through education, testing, and community outreach. In each of these approachable, humorous posters, headline and image interact to give new meaning to a familiar phrase or object. Embracing the tradition of high-concept advertising, these posters speak with cool authority and gentle humor about matters of life and death.

He Loves Me.

He Loves Me Not.

Using a condom is one of the best ways to prevent AIDS. And protect the one you love.

For more information, call the Minnesota AIDSLine. In the Twin Cities: 870-0700.

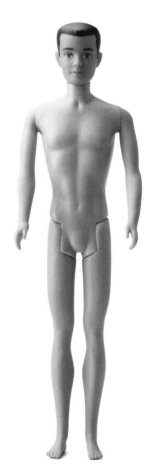

Unless You're Built Like This, You Should Be Using Condoms.

MINNESOTA AIDS PROJECT

Unknown designer for the Minnesota AIDS Project (Minneapolis, Minnesota, USA). *He Loves Me, He Loves Me Not*, ca. 1994. Lithograph. 61 × 51.3 cm (24 × 20 3/16 in.). Gift of Minnesota AIDS Project, 1995-29-1.

Unknown designer for the Minnesota AIDS Project (Minneapolis, Minnesota, USA). Photography by Tom Connors, Crofoot Photography. *Unless You're Built Like This, You Should Be Using Condoms*, ca. 1994. Lithograph. 64.2 × 42.2 cm (25 1/4 × 16 5/8 in.). Gift of Minnesota AIDS Project, 1995-29-4.

Condoms Can Protect Any Person, No Matter What Color They Are.

AIDS doesn't discriminate. But you can. And one good way to start is by learning the proper use of condoms. For more information about AIDS and how to protect yourself, call the AIDSLine.

Minnesota AIDSLine 1-800-248-AIDS

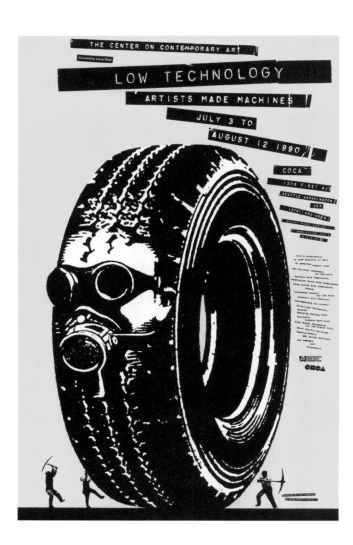

Art Chantry (American, b. 1954)
for the Center for Contemporary
Art (Bedminster Township, New
Jersey, USA). *Low Technology*, 1990.
Screenprint. Printed by Art Garcia.
77.6 × 50.1 cm (30 9/16 × 19 3/4 in.).
Gift of Art Chantry, 1995-69-89.

Art Chantry (American, b. 1954)
for the Empty Space Theatre
(Bakersfield, California, USA).
Tartuffe, 1983. Lithograph. 61.3 × 42.1
cm (24 1/8 × 16 9/16 in.). Gift of Art
Chantry, 1995-69-54.

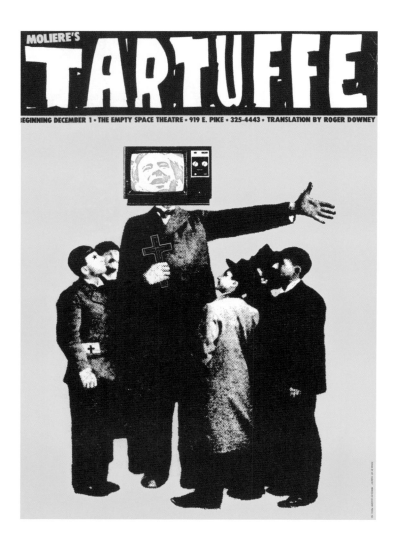

Art Chantry (American, b. 1954)
for the Empty Space Theatre
(Bakersfield, California, USA).
The Rocky Horror Show, 1986.
Screenprint. 74.7 × 43.2 cm (29
7/16 × 17 in.). Gift of Art Chantry,
1995-69-42.

Art Chantry's posters from the 1980s
combine simple collage techniques
with low-cost printing. Chantry
often cut images out of magazines
and catalogs, photocopying them
to create high-contrast images that
he could put together into arresting
illustrations. Each poster uses mass
media to comment on its own
idioms.

Amplify

Art Chantry (American, b. 1954). *Ready for War*, 1982. Screenprint. 60.9 × 45.5 cm (24 × 17 15/16 in.). Gift of Steven Heller and Karrie Jacobs, 1993-53-27.

According to designer Art Chantry, this poster became a piece of long-term political street art in Seattle. It was reprinted numerous times and wheat-pasted during the "war scare" incidents of the Reagan era.
—*Rebekah Pollock*

What does typography sound like? Lowercase letters can seem calm and conversational, while uppercase letters can project anger, agitation, or firm, unflappable authority, depending on the context. Writing an email in all caps lets you shout at your recipient (while at the same time making you, the sender, seem utterly unhinged). Flip through this book and listen to each poster's tone of voice. Some are quietly contemplative, while others clamor and clang with rage. Colors can be "loud," and so can typefaces.

Typography has an underlying auditory dimension. When we see a word, we mentally process its sound along with its shape and meaning. That is how the alphabet works—it depicts spoken sounds with graphic signs. The sounds of language, however vague and muffled they might be, pervade the experience of reading. The marks of punctuation guide intonation, the rise and fall of the voice. A question mark, an exclamation mark, or a period alters the way text sounds in our minds and affects its meaning. A rhyming verse still rhymes when you read it inside your head. Literary devices such as alliteration (*printed posters always please me*) and assonance (*Helvetica makes a mellow yell*) play with how language sounds. A writer's "voice" is a distinctive way of assembling words and describing the world; the music of the author's voice reverberates within the stillness of the page.[1]

An audio amplifier translates an electrical signal back into waves that vibrate air particles to create sound. Used more broadly, the verb amplify means to turn up, boost, or intensify any signal or message. Designers amplify texts by scrawling, stenciling, enlarging, underlining, slanting, angling, framing, or otherwise manipulating the scale, emphasis, and physical expression of letterforms.

In classical rhetoric, amplification means to expand upon a message by reiterating or exaggerating the main point. The Greek word for amplification, *auxesis*, means growth. Deploying the rhetoric of amplification, the headline in a poster by the Guerilla Girls announces the "advantages of being a woman artist"; the list that follows features such surprising and subversive points as "Working without the pressure of success."

Words make sounds inside your head, and so can pictures. We use our faces to communicate with other people and with ourselves, shaping our own facial muscles in response to what we see and feel. Smiling can make you feel happier, even when you have nothing warm or funny to smile about. Graphic designers use images of screaming mouths to trigger visceral, embodied responses in viewers, while actors practice silent screams in order to physically express anger or pain without taxing their vocal chords.[2] A scream can be loud even when you can't hear it.

NO SMOKING!
no smoking?
Smoking? No.

Case and punctuation change the intonation and meaning of a text.

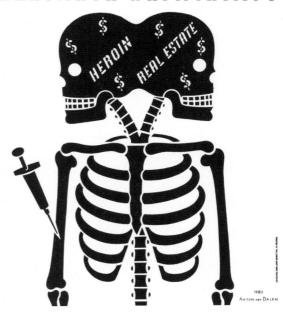

Unknown designer. *No War*, ca. 1980.
Lithograph. 84.7 × 58.7 cm (33 3/8 × 23
1/8 in.). Gift of Steven Heller and Karrie
Jacobs, 1993-53-39.

Terry Forman (American, b. 1950) of
Fireworks Graphics Collective (San
Francisco, California, USA) for Prairie
Fire Organizing Committee (Chicago,
Illinois, USA). *U.S. Out of Grenada*, 1983.
Screenprint. 61 × 45.9 cm (24 × 18 1/16
in.). Gift of Steven Heller and Karrie
Jacobs, 1993-53-31.

Anton van Dalen (Dutch and
American, b. 1938). *Two-Headed
Monster Destroys Community*, 1983.
Screenprint. Printed by Lower East
Side Print Shop, Inc. (New York, New
York, USA). 61.1 × 48.4 cm (24 1/16 ×
19 1/16 in.). Gift of Steven Heller and
Karrie Jacobs, 1993-53-117.

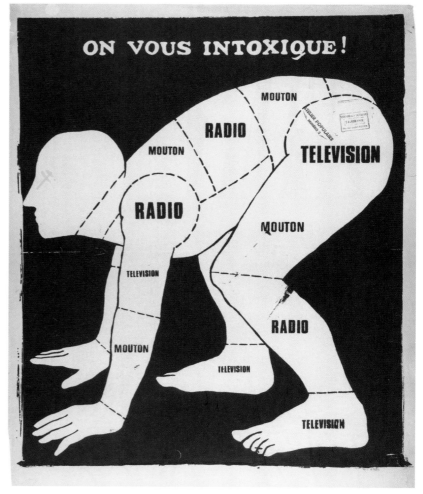

Unknown designer. Vermine Fasciste,
Action Civique [*Fascist Vermin, Civil
Action*], 1968. Screenprint. 80 × 60
cm (31 1/2 × 23 5/8 in.). Courtesy of
Georgina Gerrish Fine Art.

Unknown designer. On Vous Intoxique,
Radio, Television, Mouton! [*You Are Being
Poisoned, Radio, Television, Mutton!*],
1968. Screenprint. 82 × 66 cm (32 5/16
× 26 in.). Courtesy of Georgina Gerrish
Fine Art.

Unknown designer. *Capital*, 1968.
Screenprint. 60 × 55 cm (23 5/8 ×
21 5/8 in.). Courtesy of Georgina
Gerrish Fine Art.

These three posters document a
period of civil unrest in France that
started in March 1968 with student
protests at the University of Paris
in Nanterre and subsequently arose
at the Sorbonne. What began as
criticism over class discrimination
and the policy of university funding
turned into larger protests against
capitalism, consumerism, and
out-of-touch institutions. The
demonstrations then spread to
factory workers and trade unions,
and eventually involved 22 percent
of the entire population of France.
The protest became the largest
nationwide wildcat strike in French
history.

   The posters distributed during
the two-month demonstrations
were pasted daily over the walls,
kiosks, and barricades of Paris.
Generally screenprinted in a single
color, they are characterized by
their crude, confrontational imagery
and rough handmade text. The
recurrent themes include resistance
against the de Gaullist government;
criticism of capitalism, the media,
and the actions of the police; unity
of students, unions, and workers;
and support of strikers throughout
France.—*Gail S. Davidson*

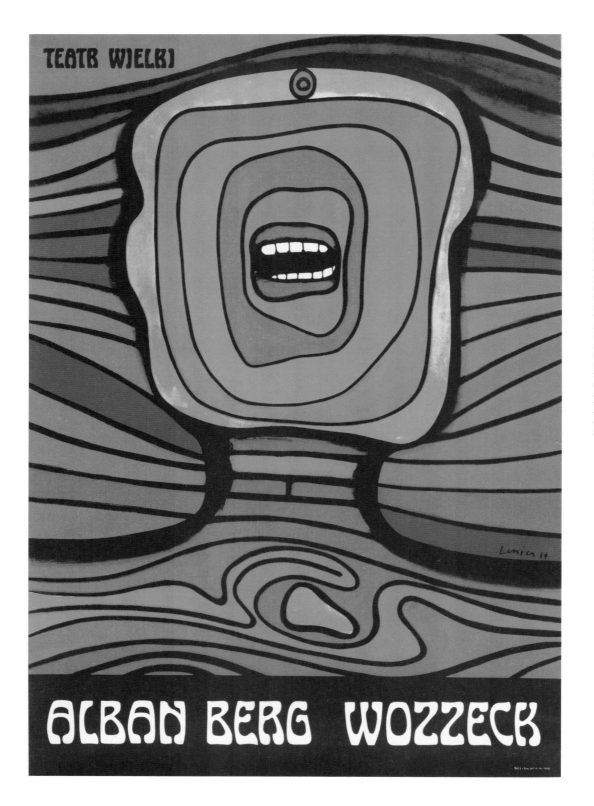

Jan Lenica (Polish, 1928–2001). *Wozzeck*, 1964. Offset ithograph. 97.3 × 67.6 cm (38 5/16 × 26 5/8 in.). Museum purchase from Friends of Drawings and Prints Fund, 2013-30-1.

Jan Lenica was a leading figure in the Polish School of Poster Art, a term he coined in 1960 in the Swiss magazine *Graphis*. This poster depicts a scene from of Alban Berg's atonal opera *Wozzeck*. The opera's title character stabs the mother of his child in a fit of jealousy and then throws the bloodied weapon into a lake. Transfixed by the moon, Wozzeck decides to retrieve the knife and cast it deeper into the water. As he wades into the lake, the water appears to turn to blood. Overtaken by the water, Wozzeck drowns. His moans—which seem to come from within the lake itself—are loud enough to startle passersby. Lenica's alarming composition unites the form of the drowning Wozzeck with the rippling currents of the bloodied water and the full, blood-red moon above.—*Caitlin Condell*

Paula Scher (American, b. 1948) for the Public Theater (New York, New York, USA). *The Diva Is Dismissed*, 1994. Screenprint. Printed by Ambassador Arts, Inc. (Long Island City, New York, USA). 117.2 × 76.8 cm (46 1/8 × 30 1/4 in.). Gift of Paula Scher, 1996-88-17.

Dynamic wedges of outlined type emanate from the mouth of actress/playwright Jenifer Lewis. The typography references posters created by Alexander Rodchenko in the Soviet Union in the 1920s.

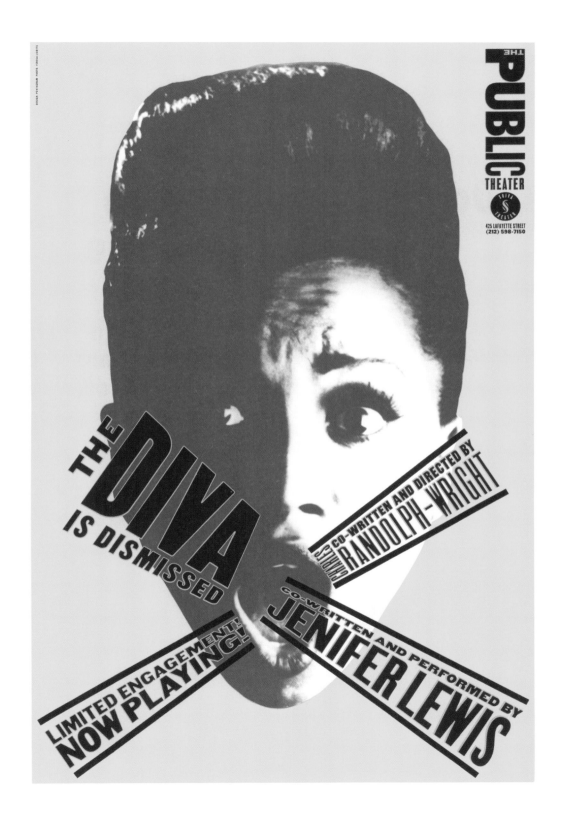

Guerrilla Girls (USA). *Do Women Have to Be Naked to Get into the Met. Museum?*, 1989. Offset lithograph. Image: 27.5 × 71.1 cm (10 13/16 in. × 28 in.) Gift of Sara and Marc Benda, 2009-20-2.

Guerrilla Girls (USA). *The Advantages of Being a Woman Artist*, 1988. Offset lithograph. 43.1 × 56 cm (16 15/16 × 22 1/16 in.). Gift of Sara and Marc Benda, 2009-20-1.

Founded in 1985, the Guerrilla Girls are an anonymous collective of woman artists who draw attention to the status of women and people of color in the art world. Fashioning themselves as "masked avengers" in the tradition of Wonder Woman and the Lone Ranger, they wear gorilla masks to shield their identities during performances and provocations. Their posters use irony and double entendre to bring crisp humor to hard-hitting statistics and commentary. Their work appropriates the rhetorical character of copy-driven advertising rather than formally rich graphic design.

THE ADVANTAGES OF BEING A WOMAN ARTIST:

Working without the pressure of success.

Not having to be in shows with men.

Having an escape from the art world in your 4 free-lance jobs.

Knowing your career might pick up after you're eighty.

Being reassured that whatever kind of art you make it will be labeled feminine.

Not being stuck in a tenured teaching position.

Seeing your ideas live on in the work of others.

Having the opportunity to choose between career and motherhood.

Not having to choke on those big cigars or paint in Italian suits.

Having more time to work after your mate dumps you for someone younger.

Being included in revised versions of art history.

Not having to undergo the embarrassment of being called a genius.

Getting your picture in the art magazines wearing a gorilla suit.

Please send $ and comments to: **GUERRILLA GIRLS** CONSCIENCE OF THE ART WORLD
Box 1056 Cooper Sta. NY, NY 10276

Make Eye Contact

Francisco Dosamantes (Mexican, 1911–1986) for Galeria de Arte de la Universidad Nacional (Mexico). Exposicion Litografías [*Exhibition of Lithographs*], 1939. Lithograph. 45.1 × 59.7 cm (17 3/4 × 23 1/2 in.). Museum purchase from General Acquisitions Endowment Fund, 2000-34-1.

The eye appears throughout modern design as a sign for graphic communication and for modernity's powerful new tools of expression. Above, Francisco Dosamantes's 1939 poster for an exhibition of lithographic prints employs an eye to symbolize modern media and visual creativity. But the eye is more than a symbol. The eye in this arresting poster is looking at you, initiating an intimate form of communication.

Human vision is drawn to faces.[1] We see eyes not only on living creatures, but also on nearly anything that follows the general pattern of a face, from the headlights of a car to a pair of x's stitched onto a rag doll. A face can emerge from minimal ingredients, and eyes, even rendered with simple forms, are powerful attractors.

Graphic designers intuitively grasp the emotional pull of eye contact. Eyes looking out challenge the viewer to look back. A palpable exchange takes place when two creatures meet each other's gaze, even though no direct physical contact has taken place. Touching someone with your eyes can be intimate or seductive, aggressive or

Eye-tracking software shows that when given a picture of a face, the viewer's attention repeatedly returns to primary facial features, especially the eyes. From Alfred L. Yarbus, *Eye Movements and Vision* (New York: Plenum Press, 1967).

disarming. In Paula Scher's theater poster for *Nude Nude Totally Nude* (1996), two startling eyes fill the width of the page. Printed in red, the eyes force the rest of the face to recede into the background. Scher has amplified the drama of the image, using scale and color to emphasize the poster's arresting gaze.

Making eye contact is a powerful form of action. Theater historian Robert Cohen has noted that the word "eyes" appears 585 times in the plays of Shakespeare, and the words "look" and "see" occur 2,403 times. Shakespeare referred less often to sound than to sight, using "hear" and "hears" only 883 times. According to Cohen, actors in Shakespeare's time used their eyes not only to express an emotional state to the audience, but also to trigger thought and action in other players on the stage. "Eye contact," writes Cohen, "is how people . . . adjust their behavior to most effectively find what they need from others, and how they can get what they want from them as well."[2] Eyes are tools for inducing change in ourselves and others. When we look into a pair of eyes onstage, on-screen, or in a poster or advertisement, we participate in an active exchange. Looking at a poster—like witnessing a theatrical production—takes place over time and invokes an embodied response, as we touch the eyes of the other with our own eyes.

For the graphic designer, eyes can be as compelling in their absence as in their presence. Blocking the eyes implies violence both physical and emotional, suggesting states of denial and desolation. In her poster for the play *Him* (1994), Paula Scher has placed text where the eyes should be, making tangible the title character's emptiness or superficiality. The magnetic attractor of eye-to-eye contact draws us in, but the poster refuses to give us what we are looking for.

WRITTEN AND PERFORMED BY ANDREA MARTIN•DIRECTED BY WALTER BOBBIE

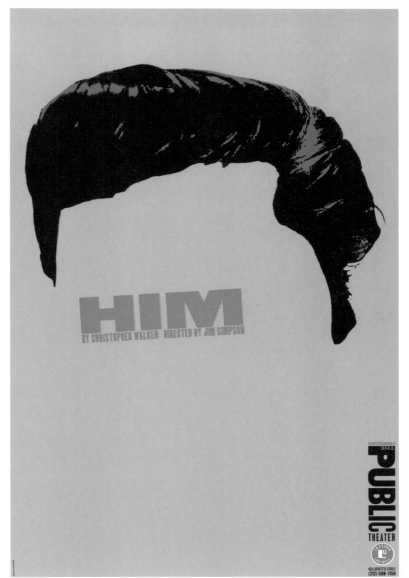

Paula Scher (American, b. 1948)
for the Public Theater (New York,
New York, USA). *Nude Nude Totally
Nude*, 1996. Offset lithograph. 119.2
× 75.9 cm (46 15/16 × 29 7/8 in.)
Gift of Pentagram, 1997-99-3.

Paula Scher (American, b. 1948) for
the Public Theater (New York, New
York, USA). *Him*, 1994. Screenprint.
117 × 76.7 cm (46 1/16 × 30 3/16 in.).
Gift of Paula Scher, 2013-25-1.

Paul Rand (American, 1914–1996) for the International Design Conference in Aspen. *The Prepared Professional*, 1982. Screenprint. Printed by Sanders Printing. 96.5 × 53.7 cm (38 × 21 1/8 in.). Gift of Marion S. Rand, 2002-11-11.

The targets in Paul Rand's poster double as a pair of eyes. This ingeniously simple poster harbors a surprisingly complex metaphor, asking the viewer to identify alternately with the shooter and the target.

Edward McKnight Kauffer (American, active England, 1890–1954) for New York Subway Advertising Co. (New York, New York, USA). *Subway Posters Perform*, 1948. Lithograph. 21.6 × 14 cm (8 1/2 × 5 1/2 in.). Gift of Mrs. E. McKnight Kauffer, 1963-39-166-c.

This advertising placard personifies the subway poster as a theatrical performer. Minimal means create a face whose gaze is hard to avoid. The text objectifies viewers as "pairs of eyes" to be attracted and seduced by advertising.

Marlene McCarty (American, b. 1957) for Women's Action Coalition (New York, New York, USA). *WAC Is Watching*, 1992. Offset lithograph. 56.9 × 56.9 cm (22 3/8 × 22 3/8 in.). Gift of Marlene McCarty, 1996-44-1.

Founded in 1992, the Women's Action Coalition (WAC) staged public demonstrations or "actions" to raise the visibility of women in art, culture, and society. The organization was founded in response to the Clarence Thomas/ Anita Hill congressional hearings, which riveted national attention on sexual harassment. The wide-open eye logo, designed by Marlene McCarty and Bethany Johns, signaled that WAC's members were paying attention. The poster was watching, and so was WAC.

April Greiman (American, b. 1948) and Tom Ingalls for the University of Southern California (Los Angeles, California, USA). *Temporal, Contemporary, Spatial, Dynamic*, 1977. Offset lithograph. 90 × 61 cm (35 7/16 × 24 in.). Gift of Ken Friedman, 1997-19-209.

April Greiman studied typography in Switzerland with Armin Hofmann and Wolfgang Weingart in the 1970s. Here, she has used a disembodied eye and ear—framed against the background of the sky and universe—as symbols of global communication.

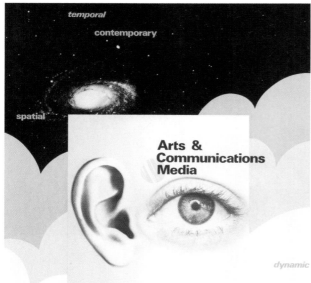

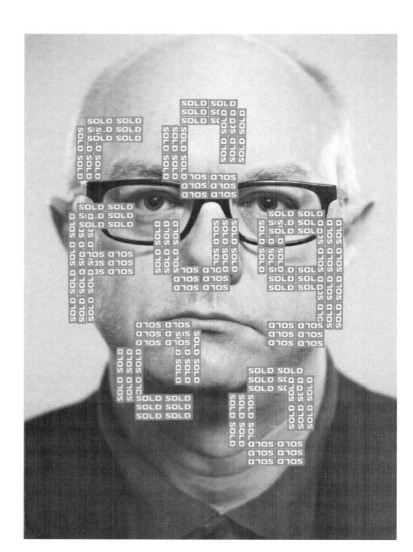

Mark Gowing (Australian, b. 1970). *Labelled 1/8 (Refugee)*, 2009. Laser plotter print with hand-applied stickers. 115.9 × 82.1 cm (45 5/8 × 32 5/16 in.). Gift of Mark Gowing, 2014-32-4.

This poster, one of a series of eight designed by Mark Gowing as a self-initiated project, was inspired by Gowing's observation that "[o]ur contemporary world seems to be in a constantly heightening state of panic over people's origins and intents. Judging individuals on face value seems to be an increasing concern at both a social and political level as the global melting pot takes a firm step backwards." Gowing created this *Refugee* series of posters to highlight the problem of labeling people based on their appearance. Gowing sourced his images from a royalty-free image bank and printed them at large scale in black and white using a laser plotter printer. He purchased off-the-shelf stickers and applied them by hand to the surface of each poster, creating "labels" such as "homeless," "religious," and "indigenous." For this poster, Gowing use red stickers printed in white with the word "SOLD" to form the word "refugee" across the face of a man in glasses.—Caitlin Condell

Richard Avedon (American, 1923–2004) for Richard Avedon Posters, Inc. (New York, New York, USA), *John Lennon*, 1967. Offset lithograph. Published by Cowles Education Corporation, Maximus Enterprises, Ltd., NEMS Enterprises, Ltd. Printed by Waterlow & Sons, Ltd. (England). 78.9 × 57.2 cm (31 1/16 × 22 1/2 in.). Gift of Various Donors, 1981-29-511.

This poster suggests an altered state of mind by filling John Lennon's glasses with a swirling optical illusion. The photograph has been converted to a high-contrast image, a technique sometimes called "posterization."

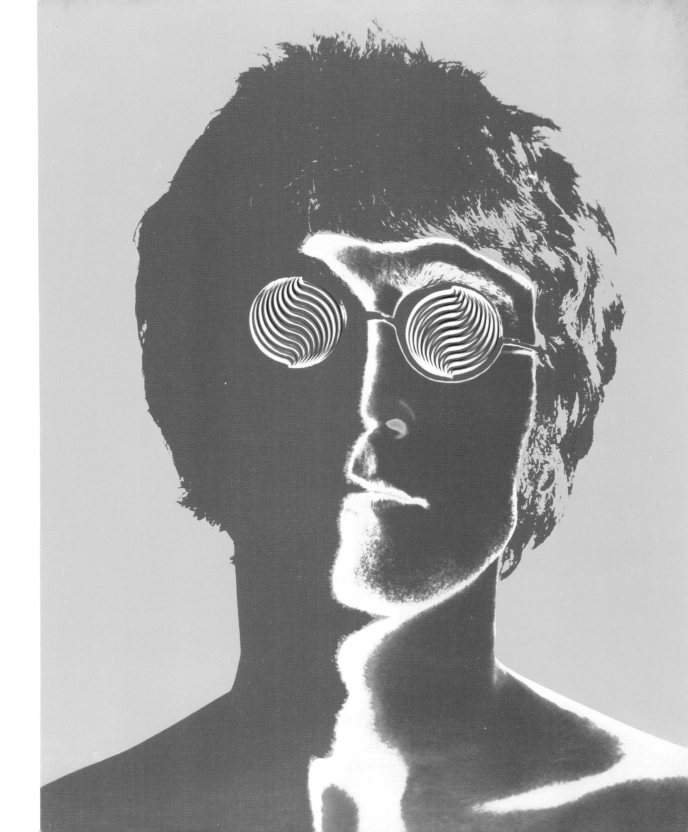

Art Chantry (American, b. 1954). *The Strange Case of Dr. Jekyll and Mr. Hyde*, 1981. Offset lithograph. Printed by Central Lithograph (Seattle, Washington, USA). 52.1 × 34.5 cm (20 1/2 × 13 9/16 in.). Gift of Art Chantry, 1995-69-84.

Robert Louis Stevenson's famous 1886 novella about a man with a split personality became the basis of several stage productions and films, entering the popular culture. To represent the concept of double identity, Art Chantry has ripped away the eyes of Dr. Jekyll to reveal the deranged and sinister stare of evil Mr. Hyde.

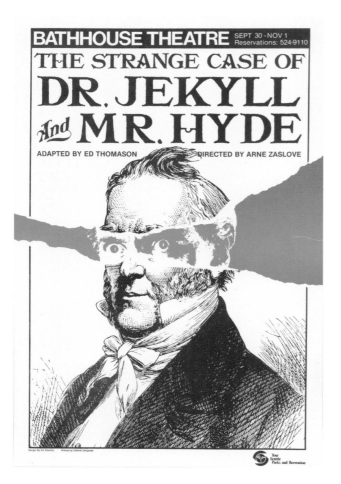

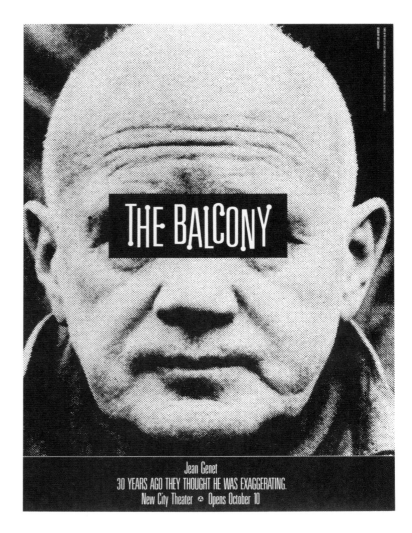

Art Chantry (American, b. 1954) for The New City Theater (Seattle, Washington, USA). *The Balcony*, 1985. Offset lithograph. 61 × 45 cm (24 × 17 11/16 in.). Gift of Art Chantry, 1995-69-45.

Jean Genet's 1957 play *The Balcony* takes place in a brothel where male patrons play roles of social power (bishop, judge, and general). Meanwhile, a revolution unfolds on the streets outside; by the play's end, these figures of power have been killed. In Art Chantry's poster, the blocked eyes suggest a mental state of self-delusion, while the blindfold represents a tool of physical dominance (one often used in brothels). The photograph depicts the playwright.

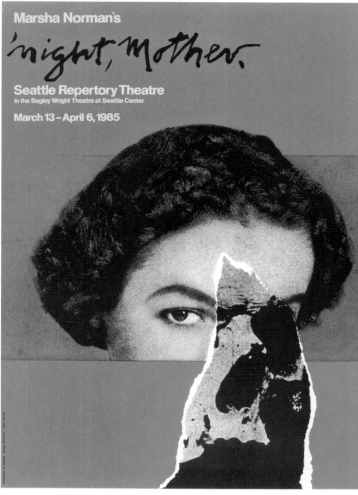

Art Chantry (American, b. 1954) for the Bathhouse Theatre (Seattle, Washington, USA). *Macbeth,* 1982. Offset lithograph. 63.3 × 50 cm (24 15/16 × 19 11/16 in.). Gift of Art Chantry, 1995-69-50.

Red ink splattered on a vintage photograph portends the violence of *Macbeth.* The ink pooling near the man's eyes implies that he is thinking about the dark deeds to come.

Art Chantry (American, b. 1954) and Rick Elber for the Seattle Repertory Theatre (Seattle, Washington, USA). *'night, Mother,* 1985. Lithograph. Printed by the Artcraft Company (North Attleboro, Massachusetts, USA). 61.1 × 45.9 cm (24 1/16 × 18 1/16 in.). Gift of Art Chantry, 1995-69-55.

In the Pulitzer-Prize–winning play *'night, Mother,* a young woman casually informs her mother that she plans to kill herself at the end of the day. The ensuing drama consists of a dialogue between mother and daughter, as the two go about their daily household routine and move toward the play's dark conclusion. Art Chantry's collage turns a banal photograph into a portrait of dark emotional resolve.

は

テレビ番組のニュースキャスターは限られた時間制限の中で情報を毎日伝えています。それは、無数にある出来事の情報の中から取り上げられる会議に通して回し合い放送時間を勝ち取って来た訳又はわ情報の相関通です。その情報は私達の興味を惹き付け、目と耳を釘付けにさせ、実像は回らずテレビに向かって感動を抱きます。しかし、その裏で小さい出来事も、そして決して小さくない出来事も起こり続けています。何故、そのニュースを伝えたのでしょうか、何故、何故、そのニュースは伝えられなかったのでしょうか。

メディアリテラシー は 想像力だ。

How Posters Work

Shiro Shita Saori (Japanese, b. 1990) for the Ad Council Japan (Nishi-ku, Osaka, Japan). *Media Literacy Is an Imagination*, 2014. Digital print. 73 × 102.9 cm (28 3/4 × 40 1/2 in.). Gift of Shiro Shita Saori, 2014-35-3.

For her poster campaign for the Ad Council of Japan on the theme "Media Literacy Is an Imagination," Shiro Shita Saori turned to the classic Japanese proverb of the three wise monkeys, who embody the maxim "See no evil, hear no evil, speak no evil." This poster plays on the first element of the maxim, "see no evil." Saori illustrated a collective of identical, stylized white figures with stark black eyes. Saori then redacted the title of the poster beneath two black bars, a clever play on the illusion that, in our media saturated age, the flood of information may make it difficult to see clearly.—*Caitlin Condell*

Benker & Steiner Werbeagentur AG (Zürich. Switzerland) for Zürcher Theater Spektakel (Zürich, Switzerland). Zürcher Theater Spektakel [*Zürich Theater Festival*], 1996. Offset lithograph. 128 × 90.5 cm (50 3/8 × 35 5/8 in.). Gift of Sara and Marc Benda, 2010-21-91.

An ordinary family dinner takes a strange turn when Mother is standing on a chair and Father is chained to a table leg like a dog. The man beneath the table stares straight at us, looking resigned to his fate. By blocking the other faces with colored dots, the poster intensifies our connection with the beleaguered patriarch.

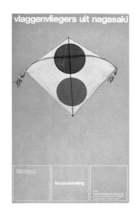

Make a System

Systems pervade graphic design. Typography is a system of interrelated characters, styles, sizes, and spaces. A grid is a system of columns, rows, and margins. A branding campaign is a system of logos, type styles, colors, and layout devices employed across multiple applications in a consistent way. Each of these systems allows for both uniformity and change, repetition and variation. Each one addresses spatial relationships among visual elements. Each establishes a set of rules for making decisions about the composition of a poster, publication, or product.

Pieter Brattinga's exhibition poster *The Man behind the Design for the Dutch Post Office* (1960) is a twentieth-century classic. The square grid that dominates the surface of the poster becomes a semitransparent scrim through which we view a man's portrait. Brattinga's poster, which celebrates the design contributions of the Netherlands' innovative postal and telephone service (PTT), belongs to a larger series of posters he designed for a Dutch printing company.[1] A grid of squares governs the composition of each poster in the series. Brattinga has visibly outlined some of the squares while leaving others unexpressed, using the grid to construct individual solutions within the constraints of the overall series.

Creating a system and revealing its rules is a key operation of modern design.[2] After World War II, progressive designers transformed avant-garde experiments into a rational methodology.[2] They used grids to organize and align elements and to generate visual forms. In the 1960s and '70s, Massimo Vignelli's influential posters and information systems employed horizontal grid lines as visual and structural elements.

Conceptual artists during the same period were challenging the cultural autonomy of art and its separation from daily life. In the late 1960s, Daniel Buren began creating uniform patterns of stripes—printed or painted on canvas or paper—and inserting them into public spaces. He installed hundreds of striped posters throughout Paris; these *affichages sauvages* (wild posters) both melded with the urban environment and stood apart from it.

Designers today create systems that allow surprising forms to emerge from a problem or situation. *The Flocking Diplomats* (2008) poster series, created by the Dutch design collective Catalogtree, visualizes data about the parking violations of international diplomats in New York City. To create a poster format for the Amsterdam concert venue Paradiso (1996–2010), Experimental Jetset cut holes into each poster that allow the surface underneath to show through; the surrounding context penetrates the designed artifact.

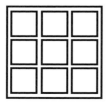

A typographic grid consists of columns, rows, margins, and gutters; it defines space for content to occupy as well as space between and around content. Typically an invisible background structure, the grid can become an active visual element.

Pieter Brattinga (Dutch, 1931–2004) for Steendrukkerij de Jong and Company (Hilversum, Netherlands). Offset lithographs. Printed by Steendrukkerij de Jong and Company. 62.9 × 38.1 cm (24 3/4 × 15 in.). Gift of Pieter Brattinga, 2000-75-7, -3, -2.

De Man achter de Vormgeving van de P.T.T. [*The Man behind the Design for the Dutch Post Office*], 1960; Zeven Creatieve Vrouwen [*Seven Creative Women*], 1968; Vlaggenvliegers uit Nagasaki [*Kites from Nagasaki*], 1970.

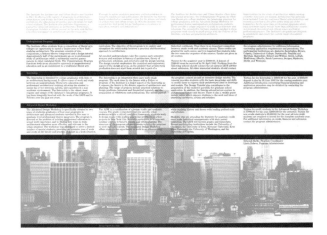
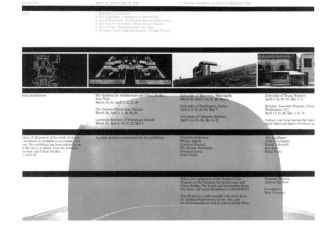

Massimo Vignelli (Italian, active USA, 1931–2014) for Institute for Architecture and Urban Studies (New York, New York, USA). Offset lithographs. approx. 57.2 × 57.2 cm (22 1/2 × 22 1/2 in.) (each).

Clockwise from upper left: *The IAUS Advanced Workshop*, 1979, and *Architectural Education: Alternatives*, 1982, Gift of Lella and Massimo Vignelli, 2009-42-6, -7; *A New Wave of Austrian Architecture*, 1980, Gift of Massimo Vignelli, 1991-69-83; *Architecture in Japan*, 1984, Gift of Lella and Massimo Vignelli, 2009-42-9.

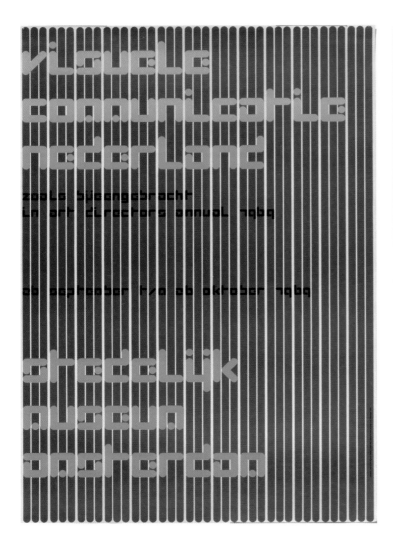

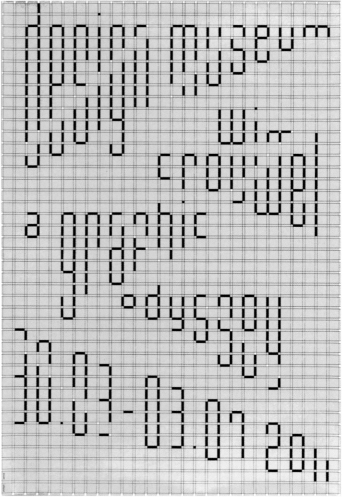

Wim Crouwel (Dutch, b. 1928) for Stedelijk Museum Amsterdam (Amsterdam, Netherlands). Visuele Communicatie Nederland [*Visual Communication in the Netherlands*], 1969. 94.6 × 64.7 cm (37 1/4 × 25 1/2 in.). Offset lithograph. Museum purchase from General Acquisitions Endowment Fund, 2009-13-1.

Wim Crouwel designed posters, publications, and exhibitions for the Stedelijk Museum in Amsterdam beginning in 1964. This poster uses a grid of vertical stripes to generate letterforms. Rounded ends make the letters distinctively soft and bulbous. Crouwel is the designer of several influential modular typefaces, including New Alphabet (1967), intended for low-resolution cathode ray screens, and Gridnik (1974), commissioned by Olivetti for use on electric typewriters.

Philippe Apeloig (French, b. 1962) for the Design Museum (London, England). *Wim Crouwel: A Graphic Odyssey*, 2011. Screenprint. 95 × 63.5 cm (37 3/8 × 25 in.). Gift of Philippe Apeloig, 2013-16-5.

This poster was designed for the 2011 exhibition *Wim Crouwel: A Graphic Odyssey*, at the Design Museum, London. Philippe Apeloig, along with six other designers and studios, was commissioned to produce a poster using the grid structure Crouwel had devised for his influential Stedelijk Museum posters. Apeloig drew from his experience as an intern in the 1980s at Crouwel's firm, Total Design. Utilizing the grid to generate the letterforms, Apeloig created characters that occupy the "gutters" of the grid (the spaces between the areas that traditionally contain content). The black letters are punctuated by white dots that create a playful diagonal pull against the strict axes of the grid.—*Caitlin Condell*

Philippe Apeloig (French, b. 1962).
Octobre fait danser la saison,
Octobre en Normandie [*October
Makes the Season Dance, October in
Normandy*], 1995. Screenprint. 175 ×
118.5 cm (5 ft 8 7/8 in. × 46 5/8 in.).
Courtesy of the designer in honor of
Gail S. Davidson.

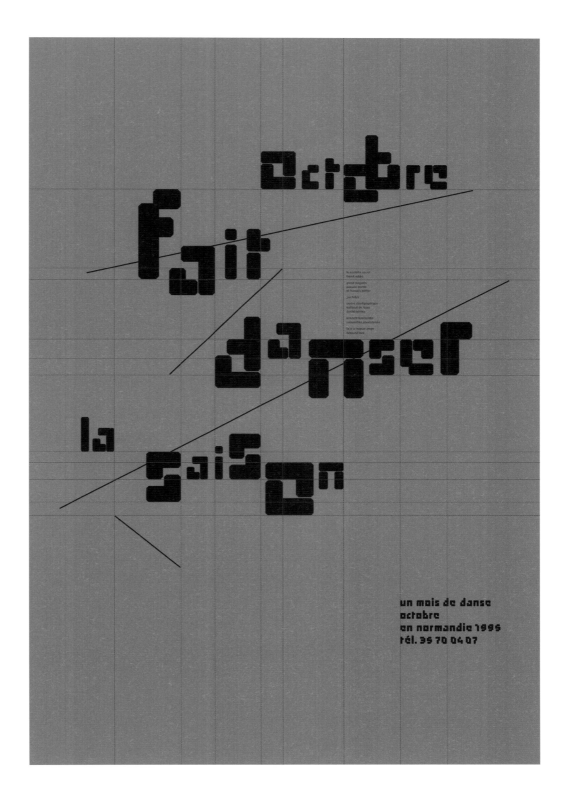

Daniel Buren (French, b. 1938) for Wide White Space Gallery (Antwerp, Belgium). *Exhibition Poster*, 1971. Offset lithographs. 52.1 × 77.5 cm (20 1/2 × 30 1/2 in.). Museum purchase from General Acquisitions Endowment and Smithsonian Institution Collections Acquisition Program Funds, 1999-45-8, -9.

Conceptual artist Daniel Buren is known for his ongoing series of works featuring alternating white and colored stripes, 8.7 cm (3 2/5 in.) wide. These printed announcements for an exhibition in Belgium feature Buren's signature stripes at full scale. Stripes like these are commonly seen on awnings and commercial signs in France. The evenly spaced stripes have an ambiguous figure/ground relationship; likewise, Buren's work challenges the separation of works of art from their environmental and institutional setting.

Ivan Chermayeff (English, active USA, b. 1932) for Chermayeff & Geismar Associates (New York, New York, USA) for the International Design Conference (Aspen, Colorado, USA). *The Invisible City*, 1972. Offset lithograph. 91.4 × 61 cm (36 × 24 in.). Gift of Chermayeff and Geismar Associates, 1981-29-59.

Ivan Chermayeff's famous poster uses a system of found typography to represent an international conference of designers. The designers have traveled from cities around the world to attend the event.

Cornel Windlin (Swiss, b. 1964) and
Laurent Benner (Swiss, b. 1975)
for Museum für Gestaltung, Zürich
(Zürich, Switzerland). Die Linke ins
Museum, Hoffnung und Widerstand
[*The Left in the Museum, Hope and
Resistance*], 1998. Screenprints,
some with stencil and black spray
paint. 127.8 × 89.7 cm (50 5/16 ×
35 5/16 in.) (each). Gift of Sara and
Marc Benda, 2010-21-50, -109/-111.

This poster for an exhibition about
the history of political posters
features a screenprinted image
of Ernesto "Che" Guevara, the
Argentine revolutionary whose face
became synonymous with leftist
oppositional movements in the
twentieth century. Variations of the
poster were produced by directly
spray-painting different messages
and marks over Guevara's portrait.

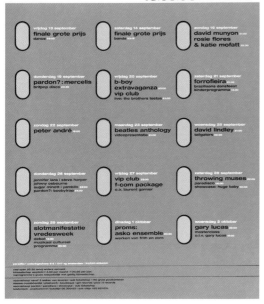

Experimental Jetset (Amsterdam, Netherlands): Erwin Brinkers (Dutch, b. 1973), Marieke Stolk (Dutch, b. 1967), and Danny van den Dungen (Dutch, b. 1971) for Paradiso (Amsterdam, Netherlands).

Paradiso 1996, 1996. Die-cut, screenprint. Printed by Zeefdrukkerij Kees Maas (Amsterdam, Netherlands). 59.4 × 42 cm (23 3/8 × 16 9/16 in.). Gift of Experimental Jetset, 2014-40-1.

Paradiso 2010, 2010. Die-cut, offset lithographs. 59.4 × 42 cm (23 3/8 × 16 9/16 in.). Gift of Experimental Jetset, 2015-2-1, 3/5.

Based in Amsterdam, Experimental Jetset was founded by Erwin Brinkers, Marieke Stolk, and Danny van den Dungen in 1997. Experimental Jetset's poster series for Paradiso, an Amsterdam concert venue, established the studio's systematic approach early in its career. The designers claim to have been "completely absorbed" as teenagers by numerous post-punk movements: psychobilly, garage punk, new wave, two-tone, and American hardcore. They were drawn to both the music and its graphic manifestations, such as record sleeves, T-shirts, patches, band logos, and posters. Today, their inspirations remain modernism and rock culture.—*Caitlin Condell*

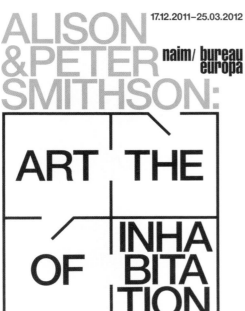

Experimental Jetset (Amsterdam, Netherlands): Erwin Brinkers (Dutch, b. 1973), Marieke Stolk (Dutch, b. 1967), and Danny van den Dungen (Dutch, b. 1971) for NAiM / Bureau Europa (Maastricht, Netherlands).

Playboy Architecture 1953–1979, 2012. Offset lithograph. 59.5 × 42 cm (23 7/16 × 16 9/16 in.). Gift of Experimental Jetset, 2014-40-3. *Out of Fashion*, 2011. Screenprint.

118.9 × 84.1 cm (46 13/16 × 33 1/8 in.). Gift of Experimental Jetset, 2014-40-4.

The Art of Inhabitation, 2011. Offset lithograph. 59.5 × 42 cm (23 7/16 × 16 9/16 in.). Gift of Experimental Jetset, 2014-40-5.

Experimental Jetset has designed numerous identities, posters, and publications for Bureau Europa, a Dutch architectural institute. Seen together, these posters demonstrate Experimental Jetset's consistent methodology, applied to subject matter ranging from architecture featured in *Playboy* magazine to the work of the New Brutalist architects Alison and Peter Smithson.
—*Caitlin Condell*

FD-1

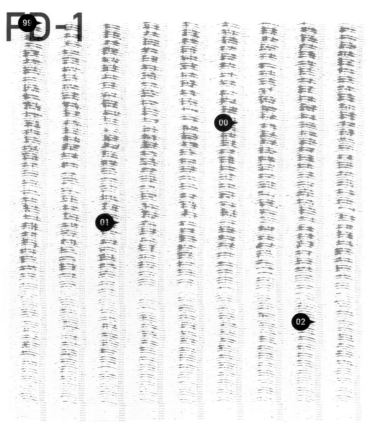

FLOCKING
DIPLOMATS NYC
1999 – 2002

// VIOLATIONS/HOUR

Parking Violations by Diplomats / Hour in 1999 to
2002 in New York City. The violations are plotted in
relation to the sun-position as seen from Central
Park (LATITUDE 40° 47' N / LONGITUDE 73° 58' W)

ANNUAL TOTALS (YEAR: TOTAL (MAX / DATE))

1999 42,542,165 / 09-24) - Security Council /
Fifty-fourth Year, 4048th Meeting, Small Arms.
Friday, 24 September 1999, 9.30 a.m.

2000 38,336,162 / 02-24) - Security Council /
Fifty-fifth Year, 4104th Meeting, The situation
concerning the Democratic Republic of the Congo.
Thursday, 24 February 2000, 11.30 a.m.

2001 25,390,156 / 02-12) - Security Council /
Fifty-sixth Year, 4276th Meeting, The situation
along the borders of Guinea, Liberia, Sierra Leone
Monday, 12 February 2001, 3 p.m.

2002 12,703 (33 / 04-23) - Security Council /
Fifty-seventh year, 4517th Meeting, The situation
in Angola. Tuesday, 23 April 2002, 10.30 a.m.

SOURCES

- Based on data from: Ray Fisman and Edward Miguel,
"Corruption, Norms and Legal Enforcement: Evidence
from Diplomatic Parking Tickets", December 2007,
Journal of Political Economy.
- Daylight Saving Time: http://sunearth.gsfc.nasa.gov/
eclipse/SEhelp/daylightsaving.html
- Sun-position (method of calculation) http://answers.
google.com/answers/threadview?id=782686 G. Floresl
- Time of sunrise and dawn: http://aa.usno.navy.mil/
data/docs/RS_OneYear.php
- New York City Department of Finance

DATA MINING / SCRIPTING / DESIGN

Catalogtree, January 2008

Printed at Plaatsmaken, Arnhem, NL

FD-2

FLOCKING
DIPLOMATS
NEW YORK

FD-3

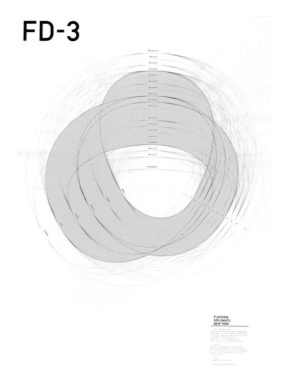

FLOCKING
DIPLOMATS
NEW YORK

Catalogtree (Arnhem, Netherlands): Joris Maltha (Dutch, b. 1974) and Daniel Gross (German, b. 1973). *Flocking Diplomats.* Offset lithographs. Printed by Plaats Maken (Arnhem, Netherlands). 100.2 × 68.9 cm (39 7/16 × 27 1/8 in.). Gift of Joris Maltha and Daniel Gross, 2009-30-1/6.

FD1: Flocking Diplomats NYC 1999–2002//Violations/Hour, 2008; *FD2: Flocking Diplomats New York: Individual Frequency Traces 1999,* 2008; *FD3: Flocking Diplomats New York: Same Time, Same Place,* 2008; *FD4: Flocking Diplomats New York: Same Place, Multiple Times,* 2008; *FD-5: Flocking Diplomats New York: Time of Violation,* 2008; *FD6: Flocking Diplomats New York: Locations 1998–2005,* 2008.

Data visualization is the art and science of creating graphic representations of numerical data. The *Flocking Diplomats* series consists of multiple visualizations of a rich body of data concerning the parking violations of international diplomats in New York City. This conceptual project employs the poster as a research tool, as "posters" are used in scientific conferences to share research outcomes as static graphics mounted to poster boards. *FD-1* tracks violations hour by hour, 1999–2002, and plots them in relation to the position of the sun as seen from Central Park. *FD-2* focuses on the twenty diplomats who perpetrated the most violations in 1999. *FD-3* is a polar graph that connects the twenty addresses with the most violations to the time and day of the week. *FD-4* depicts the twenty most violated addresses photographically; the larger the image, the more violations at that address. The photograph in *FD-5* is built from raster dots that are tiny clock faces marking the time of every violation that took place between 1998 and 2005. *FD-6* uses geocoding to mark the location of 141,369 parking violations that occurred between 1998 and 2005.

FD-4

**FLOCKING
DIPLOMATS
NEW YORK**

DAME PLACE, MULTIPLE TIMES
Parking Headquarters by Diplomats or DPMV (shown in time/date). The Top 1% of violations with most violations as used the surface of the image as related to the number of violations identifying at that level.

Top 5: 305 E 44 ST (2804 violations), 303 E 44 ST (2806 violations), 304 E 45 ST (1497 violations), 333 E 39 ST (1250 violations) and 805 UN PLAZA (835 violations).

SOURCES
Based by kind permission on data from Ray Fisman and Edward Miguel, Corruption, Norms, and Legal Enforcement: Evidence from Diplomatic Parking Tickets, December 2007, Journal of Political Economy.

DESIGN
Catalogtree, June 2008.

PHOTOGRAPHY
Nathalie Lardier, New York City.

Printed by Studiodumbar, Arnhem, NL.

FD-5

**FLOCKING
DIPLOMATS
NEW YORK**

FD-6

**FLOCKING
DIPLOMATS
NEW YORK**

Notes

Vision is a Process

1. Johanna Drucker explores the history of representing and generating knowledge through graphic tables, diagrams, maps, and other means in *Graphesis: Visual Forms of Knowledge Production* (Cambridge, MA: Harvard University Press, 2014).
2. Collector and historian Maurice Rickards decried the decline of the medium in the late 1960s in the face of the rise of television, magazines, pop art, and psychedelia; these and other social forces meant that "The poster, as it has been understood for three-quarters of a century, is unlikely to survive." See Rickards, *The Rise and Fall of the Poster* (New York: McGraw-Hill, 1971). Andrew Blauvelt chronicles the changing social role of the poster and its strange survival into the early twenty-first century in "The Persistence of the Poster," Andrew Blauvelt et al., *Graphic Design: Now in Production* (Minneapolis, MN; New York: Walker Art Center; Distributed by D.A.P., 2011), 92–110.
3. Karrie Jacobs and Steven Heller, *Angry Graphics: Protest Posters of the Reagan/Bush Era* (Salt Lake City, UT: Peregrine Smith Books, 1992).
4. Peter Bi'lak, "Graphic Design in the White Cube," Typotheque.com, 2006, https://www.typotheque.com/articles/graphic_design_in_the_white_cube. Bryn Smith documents various complaints about graphic design exhibitions in her short essay "Here and Now: The Problem with Exhibiting Graphic Design," Dcrit.sva.edu, 2013, http://dcrit.sva.edu/conference2013/here-and-now-the-problem-with-exhibiting-graphic-design/.
5. Rianne Petter et al., *Poster No. 524: Exploring the Contemporary Poster* (Amsterdam: Valiz; Lectoraat Art and Public Space; Gerrit Rietveld Academie, 2012).
6. Paul Overy, "Visions of the Future and the Immediate Past: The Werkbund Exhibition, Paris 1930," *Journal of Design History* 17, no. 4 (2004): 337–57. On Bayer's contribution, see Gwen Finkel Chanzit and Daniel Libeskind, *From Bauhaus to Aspen: Herbert Bayer and Modernist Design in America* (Boulder, CO: Johnson Books, 2005).
7. László Moholy-Nagy et al., *Painting, Photography, Film* (Cambridge, MA: MIT Press, 1969).
8. László Moholy-Nagy, *Vision in Motion* (Chicago: Paul Theobald, 1947).
9. Gyorgy Kepes, *Language of Vision* (Chicago: Paul Theobald, 1944).
10. Willis Davis Ellis, *A Source Book of Gestalt Psychology* (London: Paul, Trench, Trubner, 1938).
11. Rudolf Arnheim, *Visual Thinking* (Berkeley, CA: University of California Press, 1969). Donis A. Dondis, *A Primer of Visual Literacy* (Cambridge, MA: MIT Press, 1973).
12. David Marr, *Vision a Computational Investigation into the Human Representation and Processing of Visual Information* (Cambridge, MA: MIT Press, 2010).
13. Ferdinand de Saussure, *Course in General Linguistics* (New York: Philosophical Library, 1959).
14. Lidewij Edelkoort et al., *The Pop-up Generation: Design between Dimensions* (Amsterdam: BIS Publishers, 2012), 4.
15. Steven M. Rosen, *Topologies of the Flesh: A Multi-dimensional Exploration of the Lifeworld* (Athens, OH: Ohio University Press, 2006).
16. Ibid., 33.
17. Andy Clark, *Supersizing the Mind: Embodiment, Action, and Cognitive Extension* (Oxford; New York: Oxford University Press, 2010).

18. Claude Elwood Shannon and Warren Weaver, *The Mathematical Theory of Communication* (Urbana, IL: University of Illinois Press, 1949).
19. Wilbur Schramm and Donald F. Roberts, *The Process and Effects of Mass Communication* (Urbana, IL: University of Illinois Press, 1971).
20. Meredith Davis, *Graphic Design Theory* (London: Thames & Hudson, 2012), 19.
21. Wheatley T. et al., "Mind Perception: Real but Not Artificial Faces Sustain Neural Activity beyond the N170/VPP," *PLoS ONE* 6, no. 3 (2011).
22. On the theory of embodied cognition, see Benjamin K. Bergen, *Louder than Words: The New Science of How the Mind Makes Meaning* (New York: Basic Books, 2012); Paul Bouissac and Marcel Kinsbourne, "Gestures as Embodied Cognition: A Neurodevelopmental Interpretation," *GEST Gesture* 6, no. 2 (2006): 205–14; Lawrence A. Shapiro, *The Routledge Handbook of Embodied Cognition* (London: Routledge, 2014); and Rob Gray, "Embodied Perception in Sport," *International Review of Sport and Exercise Psychology* 7, no. 1 (January 2014): 72–86.
23. Michael Haverkamp, *Synesthetic Design: Handbook for a Multi-sensory Approach* (Basel: Birkhäuser, 2011).
24. Erving Goffman, *The Presentation of Self in Everyday Life* (Garden City, NY: Doubleday, 1959).

How Posters Are Made

1. Alois Senefelder, *A Complete Course of Lithography* (New York: Da Capo Press, 1968).
2. Ellen Lupton, "Design and Production in the Mechanical Age," in *Graphic Design in the Mechanical Age: Selections from the Merrill C. Berman Collection* (New Haven, Conn.: Yale University Press in conjunction with Williams College Museum of Art and Cooper-Hewitt National Design Museum, Smithsonian Institution, 1998).
3. Syzmon Bojko, "2 Stenberg 2: One of the Few Living Witnesses of the 20's," *Graphic Design*, no. 58 (June 1975): 54; Christopher Mount, "Stenberg Brothers: Constructing a Revolution in Soviet Design," in *Stenberg Brothers: Constructing a Revolution in Soviet Design* (New York: Museum of Modern Art: Distributed by H.N. Abrams, 1997), 16.
4. See Graham Twemlow, "Kauffer's Technique," on page 40 of this volume.
5. Reba Williams and Dave Williams, "The Early History of the Screenprint," *Print Quarterly* 3, no. 4 (December 1, 1986): 287.
6. Antony Griffiths, *Prints and Printmaking: An Introduction to the History and Techniques* (Berkeley; Los Angeles: University of California Press, 1996), 110.
7. Williams and Williams, "The Early History of the Screenprint," 288.
8. http://www.bantjes.com/project/design-ignites-change-v1

Collecting Posters

1. There were eight posters acquired earlier without documentation. One was, according to the records, "beyond repair" and eliminated.
2. The records of donations by Philip Sills in 1967-74-1/365 (movie posters of the 1920s and 1930s), 1969-160-1/574 (movie posters of the 1920s and 1930s), and 1972-29-1/2130 (movie posters of the 1950s and 1960s) are very unclear with no listed inventory in the property

files. Christopher Rohlfing wrote a letter on August 13, 1971, to Sigmund Rothschild, who had evaluated two earlier donations, ". . . we are aspiring to build up a representative survey not only of the history of poster art, but of advertising art in general." Yet it appears that the 1972 gift, which was called both movie posters and movie stills, were removed from the museum and sold.
3. The very first 1949 acquisition came as a gift from an unnamed donor and consisted of eight posters relating to the New Haven Railroad (1949-76-1/8).
4. The museum has no record revealing why Marion Dorn [Kauffer] chose the Cooper Union Museum to receive her husband's archive.
5. Kauffer said, "We live in a scientific age, an age of T-squares and compasses . . . the attention, therefore, is attracted by the geometric, held by the geometric and geometric design is retained longer in the memory than the purely pictorial." *Commercial Art*, 3, no. 13 (July 1927), quoted in Peyton Skipwith, "Design, Edward McKnight Kauffer," in Brian Webb and Peyton Skipwith, *E. McKnight Kauffer Design* (Woodbridge, England: Antique Collectors Club, 2007), 19.
6. See Leslie J. Schreyer Property File in the Registrar's Department of Cooper Hewitt, Smithsonian Design Museum.
7. Reflecting on his training in Basel under Armin Hofmann, Friedman explained his objective at the time. He said that he and his colleagues found Hofmann's reductionist agenda too limiting, "so we experimented with ways of working against those limitations by including more information, different levels of information." Responding to Hofmann's spare, mathematical, and orthogonally organized Stadttheater poster, Friedman introduced more objects and more text running diagonally. Replacing order, simplicity, and predictability, Friedman proposed disorder, complexity, and unpredictability, which he felt better reflected contemporary society.

Overwhelm the Eye

1. Josef Albers, *Interaction of Color* (New Haven, CT: Yale University Press, 1975).

Simplify

1. Armin Hofmann, *Graphic Design Manual: Principles and Practice* (New York: Van Nostrand Reinhold, 1977).
2. Jan Lenica, "The Polish School of Poster Art," *Graphis* 16, no. 88 (1960): 136–143.

Cut and Paste

1. Dawn Ades, *Photomontage* (London; New York, N.Y.: Thames and Hudson, 1986) and Maud Lavin et al., *Montage and Modern Life, 1919–1942* (Cambridge, MA: MIT Press, 1992).
2. El Lissitzky, "Our Book," 1926, in Helen Armstrong, *Graphic Design Theory: Readings from the Field* (New York: Princeton Architectural Press, 2009), 25–30.
3. Sergei Eisenstein, "A Dialectic Approach to Film Form," 1949, in *Film Form [and] The Film Sense* (New York: Meridian Books, 1957), 48.

Overlap

1. David Marr, *Vision* (Cambridge, MA: MIT Press, 2010), 287.

Assault the Surface

1. On Denis Diderot and the fourth wall in theater, see Michael Marrinan, *The Culture of the Diagram* (Stanford: Stanford University Press, 2010), 66.
2. Jennifer Bass, Pat Kirkham, and Saul Bass, *Saul Bass: A Life in Film & Design* (London: Laurence King, 2011).

Activate the Diagonal

1. A. L. Yarbus, *Eye Movements and Vision* (New York: Plenum Press, 1967).
2. Derek Hodgson, "The Visual Brain, Perception, and Depiction of Animals in Rock Art," *Journal of Archaeology* 3 (2013): 1–6.

Manipulate Scale

1. Rick Poynor, "Armin Hofmann," AIGA.org, April 19, 2012. http://www.aiga.org/medalist-arminhofmann/.
2. Rick Poynor, *Uncanny: Surrealism and Graphic Design* (Brnö: Moravian Gallery, 2010).

Use Text as Image

1. Elaine Scarry, *Dreaming by the Book* (New York: Farrar, Straus and Giroux, 1999), and Peter Mendelsund, *What We See When We Read: A Phenomenology* (New York: Vintage Books, 2014).
2. David Jury, *Graphic Design before Graphic Designers: The Printer as Designer and Craftsman 1700–1914* (New York: Thames & Hudson, 2012).

Tell a Story

1. Gustav Freytag and Elias J. MacEwen, *Freytag's Technique of the Drama: An Exposition of Dramatic Composition and Art* (Chicago: Scott, Foresman, 1900).

Make Eye Contact

1. Wheatley T. et al., "Mind Perception: Real but Not Artificial Faces Sustain Neural Activity beyond the N170/VPP," *PLoS* ONE 6, no. 3 (2011); A. Musicus, A. Tal, and B. Wansink, "Eyes in the Aisles: Why Is Cap'n Crunch Looking Down at My Child?" *Environment and Behavior*, April 2, 2014; Alfred L. Arbus, *Eye Movements and Vision* (New York: Plenum Press, 1967), 191.
2. Robert S. Cohen, *Shakespeare on Theatre: A Critical Look at His Theories and Practices* (London: Routledge, 2015).

Make a System

1. Mienke Simon Thomas, *Dutch Design: A History* (London: Reaktion Books, 2008).
2. Two classics of Swiss design theory are Karl Gerstner, *Designing Programmes; Four Essays and an Introduction* (Teufen, Switzerland: A. Niggli, 1968) and Emil Ruder and Charles Bigelow, *Typography* (New York: Visual Communication Books, 1981).

Photo credits

Unless otherwise noted, all photography is by Matt Flynn © Smithsonian Institution. © American Airlines, Inc.: 63; © Philippe Apeloig: 16, 33, 69, 126, 137, 15–53, 202; Images courtesy of the designer © Philippe Apeloig: 137, 203; © Marian Bantjes: 37, 90; © Michael Bierut/Pentagram: 117; © Pieter Brattinga: 200; © Anthony Burrill: 33; © Luis Vega De Castro: 65; © Theseus Chan: 127; © Art Chantry: 171, 180–82, 196–97; © Chermayeff & Geismar Associates: 205; © Sulki Choi and Min Choi: 92, 122, 158–59; © Seymour Chwast: 168–69; © Wim Crouwel: 202; © Sean Donahue: 37; © Lois Ehlert and Manpower International: 102–3; © Experimental Jetset: 36, 208–9; Images courtesy of the designer © Albert Exergian: 35, 104–5; © Edward Fella: 31; © Bi Xue Feng: 67; © Avram Finkelstein and Vincent Gagliostro: 59, 176; © Fireworks Graphics Collective: 57–58, 183; © Dan Friedman: 64, 75; © Steve Frykholm: 144; © Alexander Gelman: 101, 123; Use with permission of General Dynamics Corporation: 31, 76–77, 118; © M. Gerritzen: 19, 91; Images courtesy of the designer © gggrafik design: 16, 36; © Milton Glaser: 82, 145; © Mike Glier: 58; © Estate of Wiktor Górka: 174; © Mark Gowing: 135, 147, 194; © Malcolm Grear: 99; © April Greiman: 138–39, 194; © Guerrilla Girls, courtesy guerrillagirls.com: 188–89; © The Keith Haring Foundation: 83; By permission of the Hans Hillmann Estate: 68, 174; © Jianping He: 126, 156–57; © Ken White/IBM: 65, 78; © Takenobu Igarashi: 128, 134; © Sabrina Jones: 60; © Peter Kuper and Seth Tobocman: 57, 171; © Italo Lupi: 134; © Elaine Lustig Cohen: 66; © Joris Maltha & Daniel Gross (Catalogtree): 67, 210–11; © Alex Matter: 22, 140; © Marlene McCarty and WAC: 193; © Estate of Edward McKnight Kauffer: 15, 29, 38–39, 63, 106, 129, 130–31, 164, 192; © Rebeca Méndez: 139; © Fanette Mellier: 31; © Metro-Goldwyn-Mayer Media: 125; Images courtesy of the designer © M/M (Paris): 19, 127, 133, 154–55; © Bruno Monguzzi: 136; © Estate of Marek Mosinski: 97; © Museum für Gestaltung: 119, 206–7; © Christoph Niemann: 90; © Andrzej Pagowski: 166; © Antonio Pérez González: 33; © Felix Pfäffli: 17–18, 35, 79, 95, 120–21, 147; © Lady Pink: 61; © Post No Bills: 56, 175; © Marion Rand: 21, 66, 111–13, 116, 172–73, 192; © Richard Avedon Foundation: 195; © Stefan Sagmeister: 167; © Jan Sawka Estate: 167; © Paula Scher: 68, 147, 187, 191; © Claudia Schmauder: 115; © Ralph Schraivogel: 17–18, 87–89, 147; © Michiel Schuurman: 86; © Shiro Shita Saori: 18, 35, 79, 93, 198; © SisterSerpents: 35, 114; Springer and Plenum Press/Eye Movements and Vision, 1967, "Eye Movements During Perception of Complex Objects," Alfred L. Yarbus, figure 115, © Plenum Press, 1967, with kind permission from Springer Science and Business Media: 190; © Jędrzej Stępak: 125; © Estate of Ladislav Sutnar: 21, 111, 138; © El Taller de Gráfica Popular: 190; ©TfL from the London Transport Museum Collection: 63, 111, 130, 171; © Niklaus Troxler: 84–85; © Anton van Dalen: 61, 183; © Massimo Vignelli: 117, 134, 138, 160, 201; © Wolfgang Weingart: 15; © Erven H. Th. Wijdeveld: 26; © Cornel Windlin: 126; © Wolfgang's Vault: 64, 81; © Bronislaw Zelek: 97

Title sequence (details)

Rafael Enriquez (Cuban). *Day of the Heroic Guerrilla*, 1980. Offset lithograph. Gift of Dr. and Mrs. Milton Brown, 1989-107-1.
Erik Nitsche (Swiss, 1908–1998). *Atoms for Peace, General Dynamics*. Offset lithograph. Gift of Arthur Cohen and Daryl Otte in memory of Bill Moggridge, 2013-42-11.
Dan Friedman (American, 1945–1995). *Moon*, ca. 1988. Offset lithograph. Gift of Ken Friedman, 1997-19-198.
Herbert Bayer (Austrian, active Germany and USA, 1900–1985). *Divisumma*, 1953. Lithograph. Museum purchase through gift of James A. Lapides and from General Acquisitions Endowment Fund, 2009-1-1.

Closing sequence (details)

Art Chantry (American, b. 1954). *The Strange Case of Dr. Jekyll and Mr. Hyde*, 1981. Lithograph. Gift of Art Chantry, 1995-69-84.
Jan Lenica (Polish, 1928–2001). *Wozzeck*, 1964. Lithograph. Museum purchase from Friends of Drawings and Prints Fund, 2013-30-1.
Felix Pfäffli (Swiss, b. 1986). *Au Revoir Simone*, 2013. Gift of Felix Pfäffli, 2015-3-5.

Reprinted essays

Edward McKnight Kauffer, "A Note on Technique" from *Posters by E. McKnight Kauffer* © 1937 The Museum of Modern Art, New York.
Bruno Munari, "Il manifesto a imagine centrale" ("Poster with a Central Image") from Arte come Mestiere (*Design as Art*) by Bruno Munari. Copyright © 1966, Gius. Laterza & Figli, All rights reserved.
Rianne Petter and René Put, "Poster N° 524: Focal Point" reproduced from *Poster No 524*, with permission © Rianne Petter, René Put and Valiz.
Karrie Jacobs, "Night Discourse" from *Angry Graphics: Protest Posters of the Reagan/Bush Era* by Steven Heller and Karrie Jacobs. Reprinted with permission © Karrie Jacobs.

Selected Bibliography

Rebekah Pollack

Ades, Dawn. *Photomontage.* London: Thames & Hudson, 1986.

———. *The 20th-Century Poster: Design of the Avant-Garde.* New York: Abbeville, 1984.

Albers, Josef. *Interaction of Color: Text of the Original Edition with Revised Plate Section.* New Haven: Yale University Press, 1975.

Anikst, Mikhail, Elena Chernevich, and Catherine Cooke. *Soviet Commercial Design of the Twenties.* New York: Abbeville, 1987.

Aulich, James. *War Posters: Weapons of Mass Communication.* London: Thames & Hudson, 2007.

Baburina, Nina. *The Soviet Political Poster, 1917–1980.* Translated by Boris Rubalsky. Harmondsworth, UK: Penguin, 1985.

Barnicoat, John. *A Concise History of Posters: 1870–1970.* New York: Abrams, 1973.

Basilio, Miriam M. *Visual Propaganda, Exhibitions, and the Spanish Civil War.* Burlington, VT: Ashgate, 2014.

Bass, Jennifer, and Pat Kirkham. *Saul Bass: A Life in Film & Design.* London: Laurence King, 2011.

Becker, Lutz, Richard Hollis, and National Touring Exhibitions. *Avant-Garde Graphics 1918–1934: From the Merrill C. Berman Collection.* London: Hayward Gallery, 2004.

Bernstein, David. *Advertising Outdoors: Watch This Space!* London: Phaidon, 1997.

Bierut, Michael, William Drenttel, Steven Heller, and DK Holland, eds. *Looking Closer 2: Critical Writings on Graphic Design.* New York: Allworth Press and American Institute of Graphic Arts, 1997.

Bil'ak, Peter. "Graphic Design in the White Cube." Typotheque.com, 2006. https://www.typotheque.com/articles/graphic_design_in_the_white_cube.

Bill, Max, Eduard Hüttinger, and Albright-Knox Art Gallery. *Max Bill.* New York: Rizzoli, 1978.

Bird, William L., and Harry R. Rubenstein. *Design for Victory: World War II Posters on the American Home Front.* New York: Princeton Architectural Press, 1998.

Blauvelt, Andrew, Ellen Lupton, Rob Giampietro, Åbäke (Design studio), and Walker Art Center. *Graphic Design: Now in Production.* Minneapolis: Walker Art Center, 2011.

Boczar, Danuta A. "The Polish Poster." *Art Journal* 44, no. 1 (1984): 16–27.

Bogart, Michele H. *Artists, Advertising, and the Borders of Art.* Chicago: University of Chicago Press, 1995.

Chanzit, Gwen Finkel. *Herbert Bayer and Modernist Design in America.* Ann Arbor: UMI Research Press, 1987.

———. *Herbert Bayer: Collection and Archive at the Denver Art Museum.* Seattle: University of Washington Press, 1988.

Chanzit, Gwen Finkel, and Daniel Libeskind. *From Bauhaus to Aspen: Herbert Bayer and Modernist Design in America.* Boulder: Johnson Books, 2005.

Chwast, Seymour, Paula Scher, and Steven Heller. *Seymour: The Obsessive Images of Seymour Chwast.* San Francisco: Chronicle, 2009.

Cushing, Lincoln. *All of Us or None: Social Justice Posters of the San Francisco Bay Area.* Berkeley: Heyday, 2012.

———. *Revolución!: Cuban Poster Art.* San Francisco: Chronicle, 2003.

de Jong, Cees W., Alston W. Purvis, and Martijn F. LeCoultre. *The Poster: 1,000 Posters from Toulouse-Lautrec to Sagmeister.* New York: Abrams, 2010.

Drucker, Johanna, and Emily McVarish. *Graphic Design History: A Critical Guide.* Upper Saddle River, NJ: Pearson Prentice Hall, 2008.

Duffey, Elizabeth. *Posters: A Global History.* London: Reaktion Books, 2015.

Edelkoort, Lidewij, Lotte van Gelder, Paola Antonelli, and Museum of the Image, Breda, Netherlands. *The Pop-Up Generation: Design Between Dimensions.* Amsterdam: BIS Publishers, 2012.

Eisenstein, Sergei. *Film Form [and] The Film Sense: Two Complete and Unabridged Works.* New York: Meridian, 1957.

Gastaut, Amélie, and Jean-Pierre Criqui. *Off the Wall: Psychedelic Rock Posters from San Francisco.* London: Thames & Hudson, 2005.

Gerstner, Karl. *Designing Programmes: Four Essays and an Introduction.* Teufen: Arthur Niggli, 1968.

Ginkō, Nagoya. *Posters Japan: 1800's–1980's = Nihon No Posutā-Shi.* Aichi-ken Nagoya-shi, Japan: Nagoya Ginkō, 1989.

Girard, Alexander, and Cooper-Hewitt Museum. *The Opulent Eye of Alexander Girard.* New York: Smithsonian Cooper-Hewitt, National Design Museum, 2000.

Glaser, Milton. *Art Is Work.* Woodstock, NY: Overlook, 2000.

———. *Milton Glaser: Graphic Design.* Woodstock, NY: Overlook, 1973.

Glaser, Milton, and Mirko Ilić. *Design of Dissent: Socially and Politically Driven Graphics.* Gloucester, MA: Rockport, 2005.

Goldstein, Darra, Gail H. Roman, Williams College Museum of Art, and Davison Art Center. *Art for the Masses: Russian Revolutionary Art from the Merrill C. Berman Collection.* Williamstown, MA: Williams College, 1985.

Grass, Tino, Alice Morgaine, Ellen Lupton. *Typorama: The Graphic Work of Philippe Apeloig.* London: Thames & Hudson, 2014.

Grear, Malcolm. *Inside/Outside: From the Basics to the Practice of Design.* New York: Van Nostrand Reinhold, 1993.

Griffiths, Antony. *Prints and Printmaking: An Introduction to the History and Techniques.* Berkeley: University of California Press, 1996.

Grunberg, Christoph, ed. *Summer of Love: Art of the Psychedelic Era.* London: Tate, 2005.

Haworth-Booth, Mark. *E. McKnight Kauffer: A Designer and His Public.* New York: Abrams, 2005.

Helfand, Jessica. *Paul Rand: American Modernist.* New York: William Drenttel, 1998.

Heller, Steven, and Carol A. Wells. *The Graphic Imperative: International Posters for Peace, Social Justice & the Environment, 1965–2005.* Boston: Massachusetts College of Art, 2005.

Heller, Steven, and Véronique Vienne. *100 Ideas That Changed Graphic Design.* London: Laurence King, 2012.

Heller, Steven, Armin Hofmann, George Lois, and Jessica Helfand. *Paul Rand.* London: Phaidon, 1999.

Hofmann, Armin. *Graphic Design Manual: Principles and Practice.* New York: Van Nostrand Reinhold, 1977.

Hollis, Richard. *About Graphic Design.* London: Occasional Papers, 2012.

———. *Graphic Design: A Concise History.* London: Thames & Hudson, 1994.

———. *Swiss Graphic Design: The Origins and Growth of an International Style, 1920–1965.* New Haven: Yale University Press, 2006.

Jacobs, Karrie, and Steven Heller. *Angry Graphics: Protest Posters of the Reagan/Bush Era.* Layton, UT: Peregrine Smith, 1992.

Jury, David. *Graphic Design before Graphic Designers: The Printer as Designer and Craftsman 1700–1914.* London: Thames & Hudson, 2012.

Kamekura, Yūsaku, Masataka Ogawa, Ikkō Tanaka, and Kazumasa Nagai. *Kamekura Yūsaku No Dezain = The Works of Yusaku Kamekura.* Tokyo: Rikuyōsha, 1983.

Kepes, Gyorgy. *Language of Vision: Painting, Photography, Advertising-Design.* Chicago: Paul Theobald, 1944.

Klingelfuss, Jessica. "In the frame: graphic designer Hans Hillmann's film posters go on show at Kemistry Gallery, London." Wallpaper.com, August 21, 2014. http://www.wallpaper.com/art/in-the-frame-graphic-designer-hans-hillmanns-film-posters-go-on-show-at-kemistry-gallery-london/7858.

Lasky, Julie. *Some People Can't Surf: The Graphic Design of Art Chantry.* San Francisco: Chronicle, 2001.

Laver, James. *Art for All: London Transport Posters 1908–49.* London: London, Transport Executive, 1949.

Lavin, Maud, Annette Michelson, Christopher Phillips, Sally Stein, Matthew Teitelbaum, and Margarita Tupitsyn. *Montage and Modern Life, 1919–1942.* Cambridge: MIT Press, 1992.

Lengwiler, Guido. *A History of Screen Printing: How an Art Evolved into an Industry.* Cincinnati: ST Media Group International, 2013.

Lenica, Jan. "The Polish School of Poster Art." *Graphis* 88 (1960): 136.

Lewis, John. *Anatomy of Printing: The Influences of Art and History on Its Design.* London: Faber & Faber, 1970.

———. *Printed Ephemera: The Changing Uses of Type and Letterforms in English and American Printing.* London: Faber & Faber, 1962.

Lupton, Ellen. *Mixing Messages: Graphic Design in Contemporary Culture.* New York: Cooper-Hewitt, National Design Museum, and Princeton Architectural Press, 1996.

McCoy, Katherine. "American Graphic Design Expression." *Design Quarterly* 148 (1990): 3–22.

———. *Paula Scher.* Paris: Pyramyd, 2008.

Meggs, Philip B., and Alston W. Purvis. *Meggs' History of Graphic Design.* Hoboken: John Wiley & Sons, 2006.

Moholy-Nagy, László. *Painting, Photography, Film.* Cambridge: MIT Press, 1969.

———. *Vision in Motion.* Chicago: Paul Theobald, 1947.

Moore, Colin. *Propaganda Prints: A History of Art in the Service of Social and Political Change.* London: Herbert, 2011.

Mount, Christopher, and Peter Kenez. *Stenberg Brothers: Constructing a Revolution in Soviet Design.* New York: Museum of Modern Art, 1997.

Müller, Lars. *Josef Müller-Brockmann: Pioneer of Swiss Graphic Design.* Zurich: Lars Müller, 1994.

Munari, Bruno. *Design as Art.* Translated by Patrick Creagh. London: Penguin, 2008.

———. *Il quadrato.* Milan: All'insegna del pesce d'oro, 1960.

Museum of Modern Art, New York, and Mildred Constantine. *Word and Image: Posters and Typography from the Graphic Design Collection of the Museum of Modern Art, 1879–1967.* New York: Museum of Modern Art, 1968.

Museum of Modern Art, New York. *Posters by E. McKnight*

Kauffer. New York: Museum of Modern Art, 1937.

Nunoo-Quarcoo, Franc, ed. *Bruno Monguzzi: A Designer's Perspective*. Baltimore: The Center for Art, Design and Visual Culture, 1999.

———. *Paul Rand: Modernist Designer*. Baltimore: The Center for Art, Design and Visual Culture, 2003.

Oldham, Todd, and Kiera Coffee. *Alexander Girard*. Los Angeles: AMMO, 2011.

Poynor, Rick. "Armin Hofmann." Aiga.org, 2012. http://www.aiga.org/medalist-arminhofmann/.

———. *Uncanny: Surrealism and Graphic Design = Cosi Tísnivého: Surrealismus a Grafický Design*. Brnö: Moravian Gallery, 2010.

Rand, Paul. *Thoughts on Design*. San Francisco: Chronicle, 2014.

Resnick, Elizabeth, and Javier Cortés. *Graphic Intervention: 25 Years of International AIDS Awareness Posters, 1985–2010*. Boston: Massachusetts College of Art and Design, 2010.

Rickards, Maurice. *The Rise and Fall of the Poster*. New York: McGraw-Hill, 1971.

Rivadulla, Jr., Eladio. "The Film Poster in Cuba (1940–1959)." Translated by Jessica Gibbs. *Design Issues* 16, no. 2 (July 1, 2000): 36–44.

Rothschild, Deborah Menaker, Ellen Lupton, and Darra Goldstein. *Graphic Design in the Mechanical Age: Selections from the Merrill C. Berman Collection*. New Haven: Yale University Press / Williamstown, Massachusetts, in conjunction with Williams College Museum of Art and Cooper-Hewitt, National Design Museum, Smithsonian Institution, 1998.

Rothschild, Joan, ed. *Design and Feminism: Re-Visioning Spaces, Places, and Everyday Things*. With the assistance of Alethea Cheng. New Brunswick, NJ: Rutgers University Press, 1999.

Ruder, Emil, and Charles Bigelow. *Typography*. New York: Visual Communication Books, 1981.

Sagmeister, Stefan, Steven Heller, Daniel Nettle, and Nancy Spector. *Things I Have Learned in My Life So Far*. New York: Abrams, 2008.

Scher, Paula. *Make It Bigger*. New York: Princeton Architectural Press, 2005.

Schraivogel, Ralph, and Robert Massin. *Poster Collection 09: Ralph Schraivogel*. Edited by Museum für Gestaltung, Zürich. Zurich: Lars Müller, 2003.

Senefelder, Alois. *A Complete Course of Lithography*. New York: Da Capo, 1968.

Smith, Bryn. "Here and Now: The Problem with Exhibiting Graphic Design." Dcrit.sva.edu, 2013. http://dcrit.sva.edu/conference2013/here-and-now-the-problem-with-exhibiting-graphic-design/.

Sutnar, Ladislav, Iva Janáková, Šimon Pellar, and Museum of Decorative Arts. *Ladislav Sutnar—Prague—New York—Design in Action*. Prague: Museum of Decorative Arts: Argo, 2003.

Szczuka, Stanisław. *Polish Poster*. Powidz: AGPOL, 1976.

Tomlinson, Sally, Walter P. Medeiros, and D. Scott Atkinson. *High Societies: Psychedelic Rock Posters of Haight-Ashbury*. San Diego: San Diego Museum of Art, 2001.

He, Jianping, ed. *The Master of Design: Niklaus Troxler*. Kaki Bukit Techpark II, Singapore: Page One, 2006.

Ubu Gallery. *Aspects of Russian Art, 1915–1935: Selections from the Merrill C. Berman Collection.* New York: Ubu Gallery, 2005.

Vignelli, Massimo. *Grids: Their Meaning and Use for Federal Designers*. Based on a presentation to the Second Studio Seminar for Federal Graphic Designers, November 10, 1976. Washington, D.C.: National Endowment for the Arts, 1978.

———. *The Vignelli Canon*. Zürich: Lars Müller, 2010.

———. *Vignelli from A to Z*. Mulgrave: Images Publishing Group, 2007.

Vignelli, Massimo, and Lella Vignelli. *Design Is One*. Mulgrave: Images Publishing Group, 2004.

Webb, Brian, and Peyton Skipwith. *Design: E. McKnight Kauffer*. Woodbridge: Antique Collector's Club, 2007.

Weill, Alain. *The Poster: A Worldwide Survey and History*. Boston: G. K. Hall, 1985.

White, Stephen. *The Bolshevik Poster*. New Haven: Yale University Press, 1988.

Wichmann, Hans, ed. *Armin Hofmann: His Work, Quest, and Philosophy = Werk, Erkundung, Lehre*. Basel: Birkhäuser, 1989.

Williams, Reba, and Dave Williams. "The Early History of the Screenprint." *Print Quarterly* 3, no. 4 (December 1, 1986): 286–321.

Yelavich, Susan. *Design for Life*. New York: Cooper-Hewitt, National Design Museum, Smithsonian Institution, 1997.

Index

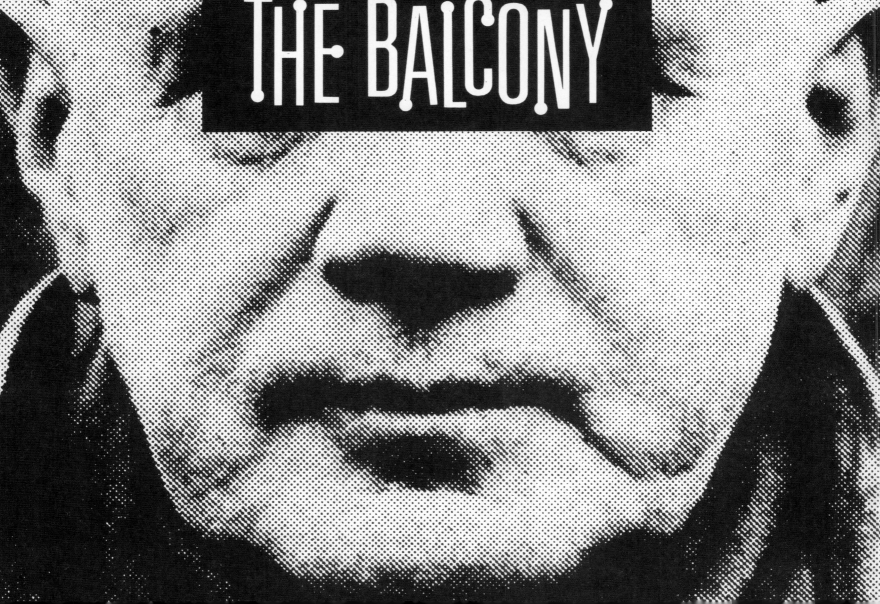

TEATR WIELKI

AUREVOIR

SÜDPOL

Au Revoir Simone US | Konzert: Pop
Eintritt: Fr. 25.– / 18.– | Tür 20h | Beginn 21h